A Portrait in Inter-Views

Selected Writings 9

Spanning a period of fifteen years, these five 'inter-views' explore the writings of a poet of our time, his methods, motives, and patterns of thought. This book adds to the previous eight volumes in Richard Berengarten's *Selected Writings* already published by Shearsman, as well as to the *Companion* to his oeuvre, edited by Norman Jope, Paul Scott Derrick and Catherine E. Byfield.

RICHARD BERENGARTEN was born in London in 1943, into a family of musicians. He has lived in Italy, Greece, the USA and former Yugoslavia. His writing integrates multiple strands, including English, French, Mediterranean, Jewish, Slavic, American and Asian influences. Under the name RICHARD BURNS, he has published more than 25 books. In the 1970s, he founded and ran the international Cambridge Poetry Festival. In the UK he has received the Eric Gregory Award, the Wingate-Jewish Quarterly Award for Poetry, the Keats Poetry Prize, and the Yeats Club Prize. In Serbia, he has received the international Morava Charter Poetry Prize and the Great Lesson Award, and in Macedonia (FYR), the Manada Prize. He has been Writer-in-Residence at the international Eliot-Dante Colloquium in Florence, Arts Council Writer-in-Residence at the Victoria Centre in Gravesend, Royal Literary Fund Fellow at Newnham College, Cambridge, and a Royal Literary Fund Project Fellow. He has been Visiting Associate Professor at the University of Notre Dame and British Council Lecturer in Belgrade. He is currently a Fellow of the English Association, a Bye-Fellow at Downing College, Cambridge, an Academic Associate at Pembroke College, Cambridge, and poetry editor of *Jewish Quarterly*. His poems have been translated into more than 90 languages.

PASCHALIS NIKOLAOU and Richard Berengarten have collaborated in editing *The Perfect Order: Selected Poems 1974-2010* by Nasos Vayenas (Anvil Press Poetry, 2010) and in translating *12 Greek Poems after Cavafy* (Shearsman Books, 2015).

Also by Richard Berengarten

Selected Writings, Shearsman edition
    Vol. 1   *For the Living : Selected Longer Poems, 1965–2000*
    Vol. 2   *The Manager*
    Vol. 3   *The Blue Butterfly*   (*The Balkan Trilogy, Part 1*)
    Vol. 4   *In a Time of Drought* (*The Balkan Trilogy, Part 2*)
    Vol. 5   *Under Balkan Light*   (*The Balkan Trilogy, Part 3*)
    Vol. 6   *Manual, the first hundred*
    Vol. 7   *Notness, metaphysical sonnets*
    Vol. 8   *Changing*

Other Poetry
    Double Flute
    Learning to Talk
    Half of Nowhere
    Against Perfection
    Book With No Back Cover

Prose
    Keys to Transformation : Ceri Richards and Dylan Thomas
    Imagems (1)

As Editor
    An Octave for Octavio Paz
    Ceri Richards : Drawings to Poems by Dylan Thomas
    Rivers of Life
    In Visible Ink : Selected Poems, Roberto Sanesi, 1955–1979
    Homage to Mandelstam
    Out of Yugoslavia
    For Angus
    The Perfect Order : Selected Poems, Nasos Vayenas, 1974–2010

Richard Berengarten

A PORTRAIT IN INTER-VIEWS

edited by

Paschalis Nikolaou and John Z. Dillon

Shearsman Books

This edition published in the United Kingdom in 2017 by
Shearsman Books
50 Westons Hill Drive
Emersons Green
BRISTOL
BS16 7DF

Shearsman Books Ltd Registered Office
30–31 St. James Place, Mangotsfield, Bristol BS16 9JB
(this address not for correspondence)

ISBN 978-1-84861-512-0

Introduction © Paschalis Nikolaou and John Z. Dillon, 2017.
Interviews © individual interlocutors and Richard Berengarten, 2017.
Cover design © Will Hill, 2017.
All rights reserved.

The rights of Paschalis Nikolaou and John Z. Dillon to be identified as the editors of this work have been asserted by them in accordance with the Copyrights, Designs and Patents Act of 1988.
All rights reserved.

Contents

The Interviewers	6
Editors' Introduction Paschalis Nikolaou and John Z. Dillon	9

Richard Berengarten: The Interviews

Under Greek Light with Paschalis Nikolaou	15
Managing the Art with Joanne Limburg	46
Aspects of the Work with Ruth Halkon	81
I Must Try This Telling with Sean Rys	110
The Interview as Text and Performance with John Z. Dillon	147
Acknowledgements	175
References	
Writings by RB	175
Some Critical Texts on RB, and Previous Interviews	178
References: General	179
Index	192

The Interviewers

JOHN Z. DILLON has recently completed his PhD in English at the University of Notre Dame. His dissertation, 'The Servants of Modernism: Aesthetics and Tradition in Yeats, Lorca, and Woolf', considers the key role domestic servants played in the burgeoning of European Modernism. He is currently the Postdoctoral Fellow in Learning Analytics and Text Mining at Notre Dame, and Assistant Director at the Writing Center. His areas of research and teaching are European Modernism, Digital Humanities, and Writing and Rhetoric. He is the co-founder and director of *Breac: A Digital Journal of Irish Studies*. In addition to literary research, he works with IBM Research on data mining and text analysis for learning assessment and development.

RUTH HALKON is a journalist. Born in Hull in 1989, she read English at Corpus Christi College, Cambridge, where she began writing theatre and book reviews and edited the Arts and Culture section of *The Cambridge Student*. Since then she has worked as a reporter for *The North London Times* and *Independent Series*, covering local news from five London boroughs, and for National News, a press agency dealing mainly with London's courts and crime scenes. She has also freelanced for *The Metro* and the Press Association and published in *The Independent on Sunday* and *The Telegraph*. She currently lives on a quiet street between a graveyard and a wood in one of London's leafy suburbs.

JOANNE LIMBURG writes both poetry and prose. She read philosophy at King's College, Cambridge, and published her first poetry collection, *Femenismo*, with Bloodaxe Books in 2000. *Paraphernalia*, her second collection, appeared in 2007 and was a Poetry Book Society Recommendation. Five Leaves Press brought out a pamphlet, *The Oxygen Man*, in 2012; and her collection for children, *Bookside Down*, was published by Salt Publishing in 2013. *The Woman Who Thought Too Much* (Atlantic Books, 2010), a prose memoir, was shortlisted for the Mind Book of Year. Atlantic Books published her first novel, *A Want of Kindness*, in 2015. She is currently working towards a PhD in Creative Writing at the University of Kingston.

PASCHALIS NIKOLAOU completed an MA and a PhD in literary translation at the University of East Anglia. His writings on translation studies have appeared in such publications as *Translating and Interpreting Conflict* (Rodopi, 2007), and his reviews and translations have been widely published in both English and Greek journals. With Maria-Venetia Kyritsi he co-edited *Translating Selves: Experience and Identity between Languages and Literatures* (Continuum, 2008); and with Richard Berengarten, he co-edited *The Perfect Order: Selected Poems 1974-2010* by Nasos Vayenas (Anvil Press Poetry, 2010; shortlisted for the Criticos Prize), and co-translated *12 Greek Poems after Cavafy* (Shearsman Books, 2015). He is currently Lecturer in Literary Translation at the Ionian University, Corfu and reviews editor of the academic journal *mTm*.

SEAN RYS was born in Santa Barbara, California, in 1986. He studied Literature at the University of California, Santa Barbara, and later received his MFA in Creative Writing (Poetry) from the University of Arizona. He is a former editor for *Sonora Review* and a recipient of the Academy of American Poets Prize for 'The Waning Years'. His poems have appeared in literary journals such as *Elimae, DIAGRAM, Indiana Review, Cutbank, Devil's Lake, Hobart Press, Salt Hill Journal, Verse Daily* and the *Seattle Review*. With Paul Scott Derrick, he is currently co-editing a book of critical essays on Richard Berengarten's *The Manager*. His own work includes a manuscript-in-progress with American poet Chris Nelson and a chapbook entitled *Parallax*. He lives in Tucson, Arizona, where he works as a Lecturer with the Writing Program at the University of Arizona.

Editors' Introduction

PASCHALIS NIKOLAOU AND JOHN Z. DILLON

A book of interviews is, in some respects, an assisted autobiography of the creative mind. When it comes to the writings of Richard Berengarten, the following pages offer rich and varied perspectives of both artefact and process, especially into such key works as *The Blue Butterfly*, *Black Light: Poems in Memory of George Seferis* and *The Manager*. Yet conversations of any kind always have an unpredictable element. In the environment of the interview, participants move towards realisations that might have remained inaccessible via, say, review or memoir. When elaborated conscientiously, such dialogues cannot help but remind us of the intensity of human attempts at meaning-making. Through the active co-operation of interlocutors who might otherwise have remained passive and silent, they become an integral part of the oeuvre itself, rather than mere chattering echoes on or around its fuzzy margins. Interviews are rightly embedded in the fabric of culture and literary tradition.

The interviews included in this book, which span a period of fifteen years, take their time, hospitably and expansively, to describe their settings and modes as they acquire shape, and not just in the sense of imparting atmosphere or 'setting a scene'. In the final interview, Berengarten reflects on their different modes of communication and transmission:

> Two of the interviews began as recorded conversations: Ruth Halkon's, at my house in Cambridge, and Sean Rys's, in front of a live audience in Santa Barbara. The others, including this one, have been conducted entirely via email, and in some cases with many interruptions, over a period lasting months. Whether the interviews began as spoken or email exchanges, their development has been a fascinating process. Each interviewer and I have together extensively expanded, developed and co-edited the transcripts via ensuing emails. In each case, we've found ourselves working on the texts not only by progressive extension, but also by recursive and iterative procedures, that is, deletions and accretions. We've found these reworkings occurring at any point, just as in the making of any text. So these procedures treat the text spatially, as a 'field'.

> And by saying that, I don't intend only the basic spatial metaphor. I mean as if we were digging it, and cultivating it.

This statement offers considerably more than an outline of the ways in which this book has been compiled and its parts have been shaped, since one of the articulate aims underlying the entire project has been to explore and examine the scope of the literary interview itself. Both Richard Berengarten and his five interlocutors – who include us, as co-editors – have aimed to reflect on the interview's possible formats and practices and, by encountering and re-encountering the ways in which the interview may be considered a genre in its own right, they suggest ways in which its boundaries can be tested. The resulting process – of combing, combining and recombining the angles and corners of a poet's work, in-turning and re-turning its views, perspectives and resonances, and reflecting and refracting its surfaces – is encapsulated in this book's title: *Inter-Views*. Interpretatively, in its suggestion of a multifaceted complexity, and of the interdependence of parts both to one another and to a cohering overall vision, this title tallies particularly well with the introductory text to the *Companion to Richard Berengarten* (2011, 2016). There, Norman Jope suggests that the *Companion* – a book containing thirty-three essays by writers from more than a dozen nationalities – is "a testimony to the recognition of his work by fellow writers and critics across cultural, linguistic and geographical boundaries and frontiers." And he continues: "The sheer range of poetic canons to which Berengarten's oeuvre responds … has enabled him to put down 'multiple roots' in a number of literary traditions."

Through the literary interview, the exploration of 'why and how I write' means sharing one's experience with other readers and creators. Here, discussions of literary craft and technique, together with recollections and reconstructions of creative climate, context and work methods, variously meet mechanisms and patterns of influence. Poets are readers first. And just as interesting and valuable as coming into contact with their poetry, perhaps, is the act of listening to them as they query and explore the makings of poems, and as they reflect on their own agonising, for hours and years, with pen or pencil in hand or in front of a computer screen.

This kind of writing and self-reading inspires both writing and further reading in us too.

The five interviews comprising this volume re-collect a voice and a mind over several decades, geographies and cultural habitations. The book starts in Greece in the late nineteen-sixties. The memory of these years, along with that of later returns to this country, confirms lasting bonds of poetry and place. Berengarten transmits and recombines linguistic and socio-political events through the 'slight angle' that often unmistakably belongs to foreign, fresh eyes. Greek rhythms, gestures and wordings enter poetic space and metabolise, as the young poet searches for and develops a voice. Pieces like 'The Easter Rising 1967' arise out of a matrix of everyday observations set down in radical, violent times. The transliterated Greek words and phrases that punctuate this interview echo embeddings in poems of this period, and a little later, in major works like *Black Light*. Their use intensifies both literal and metaphorical meanings as they come into contact with English. This is no surface effect: the study of Greek literature and music, past and present, goes deep, enabling Berengarten to re-position himself vis-à-vis the Anglophone tradition.

A wealth of lasting relationships with modern Greek poets has consistently led to explorations of poetic form. *The Manager*, the subject of the second interview, was published at the dawn of the millennium. But we learn that its starting point was in translating Nasos Vayenas's 1974 sequence *Biography*. In 'Managing the Art', Joanne Limburg probes the proximities between writer and narrator, the autobiographical demarcations of a long poem with often unclear lines between protagonist and persona. A quote from Northrop Frye ("To dissolve art back into the artist's experience is like scraping the past off a canvas in order to see what the 'real' canvas looked like before it assumed its painted disguise") is part of Berengarten's response; but there were times, too

> when Bruno seemed to me an alter-ego, even a doppelgänger. He haunted me for many years. In general, I find it quite hard to say where autobiography as *fact* ends and fantasy, imagination, and fictional construction or reconstruction begins. Maybe this is a common experience for fiction writers. And querying whether stories, histories, and life-stories and life-histories – and roles, masks, and personae – are fictive, factive or factitious is a component in the poem itself.

The element of time, so strongly influencing the manner of composition – "a long poem needs sustained periods of concentrated work. It has to be worked on, then left, then worked on, then left." – inevitably and necessarily reflects back onto the work itself. "Constant interruptions," the poet tells Limburg, "themselves constitute … a kind of patterning, even a patterning principle"; so that "lack or absence of continuity is both what patterns [*The Manager*] and what it's about." This helps to explain why the protagonist, Jordan Charles Bruno, is seen only in episodic 'frames'. The overall effect is of "a serial configuration designated by disjunctions, alternatives, lapses, hiatuses, hints – and contradictions. Above all, contradictions".

The interview with Ruth Halkon took place after the publication of the *Companion* and parallels its concern to evaluate an entire poetic career. Taking its cue from the poet's involvement in and response to the pieces featured in that book, 'Aspects of the Work' naturally surveys the contact points of poet and critic(s), examining the literary as well as psychological connotations and subtleties of this relationship. The discussion returns to matters of tradition, canon, influence and recognition, and to factors that intensify, validate or readjust the poet's voice, such as Berengarten's lifelong interest in numerological patterning in poems. Through stops at key works like *Avebury*, *Tree* and *Against Perfection*, poet and interviewer think carefully about primacies and roles of identity – particularly with regard to the often tricky negotiations of working with and within English, while the poet not only identifies himself as "European" but systematically pursues a stance of universalism when it comes to themes chosen and the deployments and mingling of poetic forms. Halkon's question about the poet being an "active creator, a maker, consciously and skilfully shaping the material rather than following it" elicits a response that is particularly telling. Berengarten replies that

> the artistic process *does* consist in 'following': I've used the title 'Following' for a group of poems in [*Book With No Back Cover*] with precisely that idea in mind, and it's one that's central to my poetics. One is not imposing one's self *on* the material; one is actually working *with* the material, through it, in fellowship and harmony with it, coaxing it, blending with it, asking it what it wants to do and how and where it wants to go.

The penultimate interview extends a conversation held before an audience at the University of California at Santa Barbara in 2012. Here focus on *The Balkan Trilogy* opens discussion on the poet's responsibility: in this case, when the souls of the dead "call" the poet in the form of a butterfly that silently lands on his hand. This event outside the memorial museum in Kragujevac, site of a Nazi atrocity, eventually led to Berengarten's three-year residence in Serbia from 1987 to 1990. Once again, living in another culture prompts linguistic and mythological research, intensifications of imagery and symbol in the poet's mind. Agreeing with Sean Rys's mention of Paul Celan on the poem as a "making-toward", or a conversation encountered along the way, Berengarten describes his process of writing *The Blue Butterfly* as one that again involved

> convergences and divergences. It meant layerings at intuitive and visceral levels – simultaneously intuitive and visceral – when the poetry was pouring out of me. So the conscious mind had to try to catch up later on. I also think the welling up of deep material could be construed as a continuation or a working-through of the patterns of synchronicity. … The *materia* appeared both inside me and outside, around me. I had many experiences involving those kinds of recognitions and connections during this period, gestated by the writing of the poem and by the research I was putting into it.

Concluding a book in which questions and self-analysis arrive at realisations like those above, 'The Interview as Text and Performance' departs into a new zone. Here the poet discusses with John Dillon the history of the interview as a form – or genre – that began in the twentieth century. This leads to exploration of the manifold ways in which the literary interview indeed turns out to be "part of the work". Early on, Berengarten announces that

> by encouraging, challenging, querying and testing the writer, a sensitive and attuned interviewer may elicit the expression of new ideas from the writer, not to mention buried or dormant memories. This kind of probing and extension of edges, this articulation of unexpected depths and heights, itself constitutes discovery, however small or subtle. The process is necessarily heuristic. It involves the interviewee in recursive or iterative mental processes, which themselves are key components of all original composition. I remember experiencing being pleasantly and unexpectedly drawn into reflection, in the very first interview I ever gave, for a Belgian student magazine, in 1981. The theme was translation.

The ensuing exchanges are fascinating in their detailed exploration of the interview's roles in cultural transmission, the shapes it may adopt, and its evolutions within and through different media.

Moving back from this ending, these introductory notes must now give way to the dialogues themselves.

Under Greek Light

RICHARD BERENGARTEN
AND PASCHALIS NIKOLAOU

Most of this interview was conducted over a period of two months, through emails exchanged between Cambridge, UK, and Alexandroupolis, Greece, between November 2012 and January 2013. Some final reshaping, cutting, and polishing carried on into the following months.

PN

1

Paschalis Nikolaou: Some of your first poetic sequences drew on events unfolding in Greece in the late 1960s, notably 'The Easter Rising 1967', written soon after the *coup d'état*.[1] Could you talk about the genesis of that poem? And could you reflect on the formal decisions you made in it, and whether you had any specific models in mind when composing it?

Richard Berengarten: 'The Easter Rising 1967' was triggered by the *coup d'état* on April 21st of that year. The poem's first inklings came hurtling at me in the days immediately following the *coup*, and the sequence was composed, or rather, composed itself, very rapidly. Much of the poem was an immediate response to what was going on all around, like the repeated official radio announcements about what was suddenly, arbitrarily and absurdly being 'forbidden' by the self-appointed military authorities. That Greek word, *apagorevete*, which kept reappearing in these radio announcements, pronounced in a heavily nasalised *Katharevousa*,[2] turned in my mind into the fantasy-image of a besuited minor bureaucrat spouting repressive Kafkaesque nonsense, and out of this emerged the parody in section VIII.[3] Incidentally, this response wasn't just my own: it was based on the often hilarious send-ups my Greek friends were doing, in the jokey, punning spirit of *kalambouri*,[4] as we sprawled around our portable radio, listening to the official announcements on the day of the *coup*, and those following it.

PN: It seems to me that in an extraordinary situation such as this, the violence done and the trauma inflicted immediately find their way into the twists and turns of language. The response seems paradoxical: it involves an immediate turning to, towards, and into language – and, simultaneously, away from it – perhaps because everything said and heard appears to take on an additional or dual meaning.

RB: That's right. Whatever was previously construed as 'normal' is immediately turned upside down and inside out. Nothing is any longer what it seems. The trivial becomes significant and suddenly banal again. The literal is ironised and what would previously have seemed absurd becomes standard. Meaningfulness and absurdity oscillate and blur into each other.

More broadly, however, 'The Easter Rising' arose out of the life I was leading in early 1967 and the place I was living in: Thebes. In those days, this was a working town with a dusty main street, shops for basic provisions, a small vegetable, fruit and meat market, and a few salubrious restaurants. I was twenty-four years old. My first wife, Kim, and I had met as students at Cambridge, and we had lived together in Venice before marrying in London in November 1966, after which we came straight out to Greece. Thanks to introductions given to us by our Cambridge friend Peter Mansfield, who had lived and worked firstly in Crete and then Athens from 1963 to 1965, Kim and I had a joint contract to teach at the local *frontistirio*,[5] a branch outfit with headquarters in Athens, called the 'British Institute for English Language and Literature' – which was misleading, because *all* the teaching was language, mostly at beginner and intermediate level.

PN: What was life like in Thebes at that time?

RB: Everything about Thebes involved novelty, and much of it, culture shock. Even the smallest details of life were different, puzzling, exciting. To me at least, in this setting the Greek myths seemed somehow alive, close to life's surface. Whenever I tried to hold up a mirror to myself, I found myself chortling: an Anglo-Jewish London boy walking along Oedipus Street each day, to work in Antigone Street.

We lived on a sloping track called Daglaridou Street. Higher up, there was a cave which in springtime was suddenly full of huge butterflies with long antennae. They flittered out elegantly and looked as if they were flying backwards, swallow-tailed. I was convinced that Antigone had been buried in that hill-cave. From our veranda we had a panoramic view across the plain of Plataea, site of the ancient battle between the Greeks and the Persians, to Mount Kithaeron, oval-backed in the distance and blue-grey, purplish or mauvish, depending on the light. I also worked in the village of Erythrai, tucked under the mountain. Several days a week, while Kim taught in the Thebes school, I took the rattly little blue bus across the plain. The Erythrai school was a single-roomed building with a flat roof. Once, standing on that roof, I saw a stork flying off into the distance. I had already seen nesting storks in Romania and would see more, later in Serbia, near Novi Sad. But that particular picture of a flying stork stayed in my mind and gave rise to a poem more than thirty-five years later.[6] On one Sunday at the turn of spring, Kim and I took the bus to Erythrai and walked across the plain, picking little shards of ancient pottery out of the ploughed soil. We climbed Kithaeron past clumps of anemones as far as the snow line, where crocuses peeped out. But the peak turned out to be fenced off with barbed wire. We were shocked to discover that it was a military base. The fact that the site of Zeus' and Hera's nuptial rites was now occupied by NATO became a subliminal trigger for 'The Easter Rising'.

Erythrai was then mainly an *Arvanitika*-speaking village, whose name in this Albanian dialect was *Kriekouki*, meaning 'Redheads'. The stop where I had to wait for my bus from Athens back to Thebes in the late afternoons on schooldays was directly outside the village *kafeneion*,[7] and I received cheerful challenges to chess games from the men sitting there, several of whom became friends. The games were quick, not only because they would get interrupted by the bus arriving but because, much to their delight, I always lost. I wasn't much of a backgammon player either, but did learn to twirl *komboloi* ('worry beads') as confidently as any native born.

PN: What was your house like?

RB: We occupied part of the ground floor of a small house with outside steps and two separate entrances. Upstairs lived our landlord, Yorgos Liadis, with his wife, Eleftheria, and their children Anna and Antonis. Our small kitchen had a hob with two rings fed by a calor gas cylinder, and our loo was a crouch-and-squat affair in a cubby at the back of the yard. The family owned olive trees and beehives on a local hillside. They supplied us with the richest, smoothest olive oil I had ever tasted, even in Italy, as well as jars of thick honey. Once Yorgos drove us out with the family to gather olives and collect full honeycomb trays from his hives. On that day, under one of his olive trees, we ate bread, salt and hard cheese – and of course olives. On the same small plot along Daglaridou Street lived Eleftheria's sister, Fro-Fro (*aka* Euphrosyne) and her husband, and, in a smaller house between Fro-Fro's and ours, the two sisters' ageing mother and father. To us they were simply *Yiayia* and *Papous* ('Granny' and 'Grandad').

My most vivid memory of Yiayia was soon after our arrival in Thebes. When we first moved from the local hotel to Yorgos's and Eleftheria's place, there was no mattress on our wire-mesh bed. So several men designated themselves to accompany me to buy one on the main street. I wasn't allowed to do this alone, because 'bad people might cheat you.' We often found ourselves being taken care of in this way, and by many different individuals, each one of them hospitable and solicitous towards us. We carried the mattress back, tied in string, a huge blue-and-white-striped, fibre-packed Swiss roll. When the strings were untied and it was spread out on the bed, suddenly all the women in the family appeared at once, and proceeded to take over the job of rummaging through our trunk to find our new sheets and pillowcases – the dowry, our trousseau. So the bed was made before our eyes in a jiffy. Yiayia's contribution was to disappear into her house next door and return with a handful of sugar-coated almonds, egg-shaped, which she threw gleefully onto the counterpane. She winked and cackled, nudging Kim and me in cheery blessings for fertility.[8]

PN: I can imagine all this – sounds like typically Greek behaviour …

RB: … And we used to sit out on the veranda chatting with the family, Kim more often than me; she reported back to me the frankness of the women's talk, especially about contraceptive methods, which astonished me – young and naïve as I was. I often heard the teasing complaint "Richard, what d'you think you're doing in there, all the time reading reading reading, studying studying studying. Come outside a bit, eh, sit around a bit and spend some time with us. Come on out, have a chat and a glass of wine."[9]

One good neighbour was Themistocles Valtinos, who lived on a large plot of land below, inside a sweeping, elongated curve of the main road from Athens. We marvelled to have a neighbour with such a distinguished name. He often popped in for a visit, bringing wine and attempting to engage us in philosophical discussion, despite our rudimentary Greek. When Christie Trist, an American friend of ours, arrived earlier that spring, he brought us a live duck for her. He led it up Daglaridou on a length of string like a pet. I don't remember who beheaded or cleaned it for us. We took it to the local *fournos* (bakery) to get it roasted. When we collected it, it was frazzled and inedible.

Our friends were all working people. The first person we met, on our first evening in one of the *estiatoria* (restaurants) on the main street, was Antonio, a Sardinian peasant who had been an unwilling conscript in the Italian occupation army during World War II. Now, more than twenty years later, he had returned to Greece after experiencing family difficulties and losing land at home. His job was to sweep restaurant floors and mop and wash up. Our Greek friends treated him sardonically, but kindly. His local nickname was *Makaronas* – 'Macaroni-man'. In England this might have been something like *Spaggy* or *Spaggers*. We got on well with him because we spoke Italian. His stories about the war's end and his misadventures getting back home across Italy from Greece were hair-raising. Antonio was the only other local foreigner we knew, except for the poet Dick Davis and his wife. Dick had also studied at Cambridge. They were living in Chalkida (ancient Chalcis), a small city around seventy kilometres north of Athens, working at another branch of the same *frontistirio*.

Some of our friends had an air of being faintly risqué and disreputable, like the brothers Kostas and Angelos, who ran a garage. Perhaps the reason they decided to take us under their wing was that, being foreign, we were a bit of a diversion for them. Kostas was enormously strong, with a torso shaped like an isosceles triangle, perched on powerful arms and legs. When he shook your hand in his huge paw, he would squeeze so hard till it hurt, and then mutter *sotto voce* in his minimal English, "Dead Fish," an expression that seemed to give him huge satisfaction. His muscles brimmed through whatever snazzy suit he donned after voiding his mechanic's overalls. He boasted that he could lift a car that had fallen on its side and hoist it back upright with his bare hands. Mitsos, their friend, who attested Kostas's claim, had a real (Captain-Hook-style) metal hook instead of a hand. I forget if he had lost his left or right hand, and it was taboo to ask him how this unfortunate accident had happened. This trio of friends used to take us to various village feast days for patron saints, or *panygiria*,[10] so at weekends we did a good deal of retsina drinking and dancing. We imbibed all kinds of music too, mainly *laika*, but with a good dose of *dimotika* too.[11] With much encouragement from our friends, Kim and I began, stumblingly, to pick up the steps of some of the simpler round dances, as well as the *zeibekiko* and *hasapiko*.[12]

PN: Did you miss England at all?

RB: Social life aside, I had a solid teaching timetable, so time was full. The pattern of life was totally absorbing, and unlike anything I'd ever experienced, a middle-class London boy who had studied at Cambridge and then lived in Venice. Life in Thebes couldn't have been more different from whatever was happening in England at that time – the era of Harold Wilson, Swinging London, Carnaby Street. I never felt I was missing anything at all.

We had no phone or TV, only a portable wireless. The *coup* arrived the day after two good friends of ours from Cambridge had turned up on our doorstep, unannounced and drunk. They were the unlikeliest of harbingers. One was Peter Mansfield, whom I've already mentioned. Peter was a classicist, linguist, polymath, *bon viveur*, and fluent speaker of Modern Greek. It was largely his influence that had first taken Kim and me to Greece in the first place. Most of his contemporaries, myself included, regarded him as a genius, both intellectually and for the huge and infectious gusto he brought to everything he did.[13] The other was the poet Mike Duffett,[14] who now lives in Valley Springs, California. After arriving back in England loaded with money from a teaching stint in Saudi Arabia, Mike had gone to visit Peter, who was living in Cambridge. They had decided on the spur of a sozzled moment to splash Mike's funds, fly out to Thebes, and surprise us. So they took a taxi from Cambridge to Heathrow, jumped on the first available Olympic Airways to Athens, and then transferred to a taxi to Thebes, pausing only to collect two of Peter's old (or, rather, young) *mangas* friends from his Monastiraki days[15] – Dimitrios Printzos (another Mitsos), and Babis, who was a Vlach. Later that year, when we moved to Athens, Babis taught Kim some *Vlachika*.[16]

That evening, we were all out drinking at a Theban taverna, together with Kostas, Angelos and Mitso-the-Hook. Peter had fallen asleep on – though luckily not *quite in* – the hole-in-the-ground loo, and seemed reluctant to wake up. He was a very large man, tall and overweight, and it took several of us to pull him out. Over the next couple of days, we sat drinking and cracking jokes as we fiddled with the knobs of our portable radio to get the BBC news reports. When we did manage to tune in, the bulletins bore no relation to what we were experiencing on the ground. I've entertained a healthy mistrust of the BBC ever since. A dapper army officer, who spoke quite good English, came round to check on us, icily polite. As foreigners, we weren't at risk provided we kept our heads low. Each evening we just about managed to obey the curfew. Meanwhile, as if by some automatic signal, all our Greek friends suddenly remembered – and revamped – chains of jokes, veering between the gently ironic to the bitterly sardonic, from the previous dictatorship of Metaxas in 1939, to fit what was currently going on …

PN: … showing exactly the same immediate transmission into the sort of verbal responses that we noticed earlier …

RB: Exactly. And by this point, our sense of 'normal reality' was beginning – subtly and surreptitiously – to dislocate in many small ways. A kind of skewed, semi-ironic, semi-wistful set of perspectives filtered through and leaked into everything. The situation we found ourselves in was never quite nasty enough for us to be threatened personally, but as well as crass stupidity, which we had quickly recognised, it soon became clear that underlying the increasing arbitrariness of the new official rules and laws lurked a cold, sinister ruthlessness. It spelt repression and vindictiveness. When the school term restarted, I quietly asked my students if they and their families were all right. Fifteen-year-old Christos, one of the brightest boys in my Kriekouki classes, announced with deadpan face that his father wasn't at home, but taking "a holiday, paid by the government" on one of the islands. There was a sense of surreal absurdity, anger and let-down, all weirdly juxtaposed and strongly contrasted against the setting of that balmy springtime, and the spring festivals.

PN: There was rich irony arising from the situation then – something that comes through in poems such as 'The Easter Rising 1967'. Changing the subject away from politics, how about Greek festivities, and customs? These often make an impression on people coming to Greece for the first time. For example, *Kathara Deftera*?[17] And what about Easter?

RB: Yes, on *Kathara Deftera*, the first day of Lent, the big annual festival in Thebes draws visitors from all around: the *Vlachikos Gamos* ('Peasants' Wedding', or 'Vlachs' Wedding'). To us this was the Orthodox equivalent of the Latin Carnevale. It had obviously evolved from some ancient spring fertility rite. This festival involves a pageant in which a young man from Thebes is 'married' to a young woman from the neighbouring small town of Livadia. The whole town turned out to dance in the streets, and the young men, including some of my students, wore *foustaneles* (pleated kilts), with ornate blouses, embroidered tunics, little hats with tassels, and pom-poms on curly-toed shoes. The end of the ceremony was marked with the cry, "*Einai gamimeni!*" ("She's [been] wedded!" – or rather –"She's [been] fucked, deflowered!")

Then there were the astonishing 'pagan-like' rituals of a Greek Easter, which Kim and I experienced for the first time, even to the extent of going down to the market to buy our own live lamb, which I carried home over my shoulders like some latter-day ephebe. On Good Friday, I watched the quiet, tethered creature being swiftly, expertly slaughtered and skinned by the local butcher on his rounds. I couldn't help wondering if this blameless creature could possibly entertain some premonition of its own death. Eleftheria and Yorgos helped us put the carcass on the spit, and Eleftheria used the innards to make *mageiritsa*, a special Easter soup. The meaning of sacrifice as "making a sacred gift-offering" became suddenly, graphically clear to me. At half past eleven on Easter Saturday, everyone in town trooped to the church bearing unlit candles. And at midnight, the long procession was rapidly bathed in a sweeping wave of candlelight, as each person in front turned to pass on his or her own little flame to whoever stood behind, and so on swiftly down the line, calling out the greeting and blessing, "*Christos Anesti!*" (Christ is Risen!), which elicited the obligatory response "*Alithos Anesti!*" (Truly He is Risen!). The spreading of these small lights through the darkness was extraordinarily beautiful: a radiant, transformative epiphany, which pierced right through me and made the hairs on my arms stand on end. I was deeply moved, despite my distrust of all organised religion, and in ways that I had never previously experienced from any Protestant, Catholic or Jewish ritual. In Greece, the gods come alive, including the Christian one. To anyone who hasn't experienced anything like this, it's difficult to explain this physically immediate sense of the numinous, its sheer *palpability*.

We woke early on Easter Sunday. At dawn the air above the whole town was smoky with fumes from charcoal braziers. Eleftheria and her children taught us to play a game similar to 'conkers', with eggs stained brilliant red from hard-boiling in cochineal-saturated water. You tapped your own egg over another that your partner in the game held in his or her fist, again following the formula *Christos Anesti, Alithos Anesti*, as the shells of one or other egg – or both – cracked. Eleftheria served up her delicious *mageiritsa* soup, and our lamb was roasted on the spit in front of the house, along with three others, one for each of the couples in her extended family. Gypsy musicians toured all the houses along the road with drums and clarinets, playing *klarino* music. We feasted, drank and danced on the veranda under the budding vine.

In the middle of these festivities another friend from Cambridge turned up, the novelist Alexis Lykiard, also unannounced, with English and Greek friends from Athens. As it was our vacation from teaching, Kim and I decided on the spur of the moment to go off with him to Mykonos, where for the first time in many months we found ourselves among posh, plausible westerners, British and Americans tourists – including at least one self-consciously successful writer – all of them terribly *nice*, sparkling with fashionable, inconsequential chit-chat and trivial received opinions, expressed as clichés which they weren't even aware *were* clichés.

PN: It's interesting to register how a realisation that your *position had already altered* comes about. And your comment on how *these people sounded*, now far more foreign than you to this land, again brings to mind certain lines in 'The Easter Rising 1967'. The whole of section two, if I'm not mistaken.

RB: Yes, Mykonos was a shock. It was already a tourist paradise. It belonged in another frame of space-time, and hardly at all to the Greece we knew. We were glad to get back to Thebes, *coup* or no *coup*. Then in June, I listened anxiously to news of the Six Day War on our portable wireless.

So I didn't need to impose myself stylistically on the material of 'The Easter Rising 1967'. All I needed to do was soak up what was going on, allow myself to be a kind of sponge, perhaps a filter, for this welter of contrasting and sometimes markedly contradictory impressions. There's a strong satirical vein running through the poem, and satire in any case depends on closely juxtaposed oppositions, as in the couplets of John Dryden and Alexander Pope. I can't say there were any 'direct' literary models other than a Greek folk song about swallows that I had learned: "the twittering of swallows' voices" occurs in the first line.[18] As for my reading, at the time I was deep into Malcolm Lowry's letters and Gareth Knight's two books on the practical Kabbalah (Qabalah). Kim and I were both studying Kabbalah on a correspondence course with the Society of Inner Light; and she drew and coloured a tree of life, six feet tall, to hang on our wall. Lowry was a great hero of mine: I had received my parcel containing his *Selected Letters* fresh from Bernard Stone's poetry bookshop in Kensington in February, and the first letter I received after the *coup* was from Lowry's widow Margerie, in reply to the fan-letter I had sent her.

PN: So Thebes was your first encounter with the landscape and people of Greece. Apart from your trip to Mykonos, did you also travel around during that time? To any of the other islands, for example?

RB: We spent Christmas 1966 on Paros, visiting Mike Duffett, who had rented a house there. We took the boat from Piraeus, following our first visit to Tsoumali's dive on Areos Street in Monastiraki, which had been recommended to us by Peter Mansfield. I call it a *dive* here, though the words *boite* and even *tavernaki* might do just as well. This had been one of Peter's old haunts in Athens a year or two before our arrival. A small, straggly, run-down place, it had nothing but a few tables along a sort of corridor, a meagre kitchen out back, a juke box, and an open floor space in front of it just wide enough for dancing. The decor was shabby and the food rudimentary, but the retsina was as good as anywhere and the quality of spontaneous *rebetika* dancing by the clientele, stupendous.[19] As we discovered later, most of the regulars were young working men or unemployed *mangas* types. Soon after Kim and I sat down at a table, we were approached by one of the young regulars. "You-English?" "Ye-es…" "You-friend-Peter-Mansfield?" Our astonished "Yes" produced the response "So-you-friend-ours!" We spent the night drinking and dancing with these new friends, and ended up somehow at a hotel in Piraeus. Later, when we moved to Athens, Tsoumali's became a kind of club for us.

In spring 1967, Kim was pregnant with our first child, probably conceived on Mykonos. We decided that she would give birth in Greece, and an Athenian doctor, the first educated Greek we had ever met, befriended and promised to help us. Dimitrios Rouseas and his wife Roula both had exquisite, old-fashioned manners. Kim and I agreed that I would apply for a teaching job at the British Council. I wrote a letter to sound them out, travelled to Athens on the bus for an interview, and as a result was offered a part-time teaching job at their elegant institute in Kolonaki Square, by the then English Language Officer, the kindly Jim Kerr. This multi-storeyed building was a huge contrast to the modest little *frontistirio* in Thebes. I was to start in the autumn. The move to Athens gave us a sense of huge excitement and possibility.

Thanks to an introduction from Mike Duffett, we spent summer 1967 renting a house on Paros for a few hundred drachmas (around five pounds) a month. It was an old house on a slope two hundred yards from a more or less deserted beach and about a mile from the main town – or rather, village – Parikia. The place had thick walls and no electricity. Water was supposed to be drawn from a well, but this had run dry. So I hauled our supplies up to the house each day in big plastic flasks from a tap at the end of the path, about a hundred yards away. Our landlord was Aristides and our landlady Aphrodite. She was as plump as he was skinny. Old and toothless, she rode a mule, which Aristides led, walking. She cackled when she laughed. The whole patch of dry stony land around their house was improbably full of the sweetest little melons, of various stripy colours, and whenever Aristides and Aphrodite came to visit us, they would pick and offer us several, which they would break open and we would suck and nibble together. Other friends of ours later came to live on the island, including Alan Trist, Graham Hardwick and Alexis Lykiard, though we saw little of them, except once when another Cambridge friend, David Moore arrived with his new Danish wife, and hired a boat so that we could all go to Antiparos, the neighbouring, smaller island, for a swim.

PN: So you had a wealth of images going past your eyes in just a few months. Could we talk now in a little more detail about the presence of the Greek landscape in your writing? It's all there, from mountain range to seaside village – the surprising vistas, the hidden corners.

RB: In those early days, the most stunning place of all to me was Delphi on the south side of Parnassus. From Thebes, early in 1967, we took a bus trip. The road winds up via Livadia, and then, suddenly, you're there, as if on a huge balcony, stunned by the breathtaking view down to Itea and the Corinthian Gulf. The moment you arrive, you know why the Pythoness made her home there, why Apollo's temple was built there, why it was – and still is – a womb or navel for the world. You can't help this knowing. The whole of it, the entire *locus*, is numinous. You can't *not* feel it. That view from the Delphi 'balcony' down over the valley to the sea was transmuted, more than forty years later, into these lines: "snake-guarded / Delphi brooding on waves over / its gulf of wind-tossed oliviers" and "summer-silvered / slopes to bee-haunted honeyed / Apollonian Delphi, set / in its green and ochre bowl / against Parnassian blue". Curiously, this didn't surface until 2008, in a sequence of seven poems I was working on, based on Herodotus' account of Croesus and the Delphic Oracle.[20]

PN: Then there is Greek art: especially the artefacts, votive representations and items of daily life in antiquity. Many of these speak to us millennia later. They hold meanings commonly accepted. For poets and artists, some pieces hold a more personal, 'talismanic' significance. Interest in sculpture has a prominent place in your work, particularly in your early books, *Double Flute* and *Avebury*. There appear to be recurring motifs. Can you comment on some of these significances, especially those that are more personal to you?

RB: In the museum at Delphi, I saw the bronze Charioteer (c. 470 BCE) and many other ancient pieces. When I visited the National Archaeological Museum in Athens in autumn 1967, my expectation was high. Even though I was already familiar with some of its masterpieces – from replicas in London and Cambridge, and from illustrations – it was a powerful experience to stand in front of the originals. To me the most stupendous was the naked bronze Poseidon. But the pieces that struck me in the most marked and inward way, producing an unexpected recognition tantamount to astonishment, were the two white Cycladic marble figurines of the flute player and harpist. I sensed a kind of personal connection, even a familiarity, with these pieces, because I had lived on Paros for several months. As an immediate and direct response to these Cycladic pieces, I wrote 'Male figure playing a double flute'. This poem, in rhymed quatrains, emerged surprisingly quickly and effortlessly. It also turned out to be the first of my poems to be translated and published in Greek.[21] And the same poem provided the title and cover design of my first book, *Double Flute*, five years later. The figure resurfaced once again, paired with the Cycladic harpist, in *Avebury*, in strong association with a beautiful feminised image of the sea, which I recaptured from Nikos Gatsos's poem 'Amorgos': "great dark sea with so many pebbles round your neck, so many coloured jewels in your hair".[22] Another image that re-surfaced in *Avebury* was that of the two votive phalloi on Delos.[23] From Mykonos, I had taken the short boat ride to the smaller island. A viper reared its head, spitting at the group of visitors, two yards away, on the dusty ground beside the statues of the two phalloi.

PN: I think you moved to Athens later on. When was that? And what was Athens like?

RB: In late August 1967, the time came to move from Paros to Athens. We stayed at the *Ideal* on Ermou (Hermes) Street, our favourite cheap hotel. Theodoros, the kindly, world-weary manager, was an institution to himself. Whenever we came across him at his desk in the narrow lobby, at the top of a long flight of stairs, he was ready to conduct conversations with us on the entire sad state of the world. He reminds me now of characters out of 1940s' black-and-white films or Olivia Manning's *Balkan Trilogy*.

Roaming the streets of Plaka on foot, I saw many notices stuck up on walls announcing "ENOIKIAZETAI" ("TO RENT"). We were in luck: early September was the right season to take on a flat. A sign engraved above the door of a building in Periandrou Street read: "In this house died our National Poet Kostis Palamas, 27 February 1943." I knocked to enquire on the off-chance, not really believing we could really rent such a place. The current tenant, a young seamstress, Tzeni (Jenny) was about to vacate the apartment to get married. She was happy to show me round. There were two high-ceilinged rooms, a tiny kitchen with an old-fashioned icebox, a bathroom with loo, and a corridor with a view up to the Acropolis from the little terrace inside the courtyard. It was perfect. I rushed back to the hotel and told Kim, who then came straight back with me to see for herself. Tzeni explained that a general owned the building, a supporter of Pattakos and Papadopoulos, we assumed. So I put on my only suit and best manners to be interviewed by this plump little officer. Fortunately, the British Council vouched for me, and in this way, we got to rent this wonderful first floor apartment in Plaka, in a building which itself had a poetic heritage. All this seemed a fine omen.

We were blissfully happy. We bought all our cooking and eating utensils in Monastiraki market, and some of our new (and Peter Mansfield's old) friends helped us to buy larger things we needed and carry them home. One of these friends, Babis-the-Vlach, began to give Kim language lessons, while she began to build up a small clientele for private English lessons. Our bookshelves were planks placed on bricks. We planned to build up our furniture and belongings bit by bit, including things we would soon need for our expected baby. We sometimes ate at Barba Stavrou's taverna, and went regularly to Tsoumali's bar. It was pure pleasure to watch the young Greek men dancing there and, albeit clumsily, to learn some of the basic steps from them.

From the musical point of view, we knew even then that we were living in Athens at an exciting time, although it was probably not until later that we fully realised how important this period was, and how lucky we had been to stumble in on it. It would be truer to say that we sensed rather than understood that we were in the hub of things. The early to mid-1960s was a great period in Greek music, when you could hear songs by composers like Hadjidakis, Theodorakis and Xarhakos on the jukeboxes, as well as a constant stream of fine *rebetika* and *laika*. Some of the pop songs had a haunting beauty, an unadorned raw edge, almost a breathtaking focalised *sting* to them: undraped, sharp and clear, like the Greek light itself: 'Eínai yia ména, to karávi' ('The boat is for me'), 'Ta deiliná' ('The Evenings') and the witty 'Éiha gó kai mía gáta / pou éihe galaná ta mátia' ('I too had a cat, which had blue eyes'). We twice went to hear Sotiria Bellou, one of the greatest *rebetika* exponents, at the taverna where she sang, somewhere in or near Monastiraki. We had arrived in Athens just after the peak of the wave of 1960s music. This first full experience of *rebetika* music and culture had a strong and continuing influence on my life, thinking and writing ever since. Once back in England, I wrote a short poem for Sotiria Bellou entitled 'Zeimbekiko'.[24]

Monastiraki and Plaka had few tourists at this time. The area was run down, unglossed, Balkan. The neglected ruins of temples scattered around the area seemed only to add to the overall shabbiness. Hardly anyone was around out of season except locals and a few expatriates, mainly young people like Kim and myself. Tsoumali's would routinely get raided by police, and if any of our young *mangas* friends there had left their identity cards at home, they would get carted off down to the police station, usually to be let out next morning, perhaps with a ticking off or a small fine. This never seemed like more than an inconvenience to them, which they shrugged off with typical bravado, at least in our hearing.

PN: Could you say more about friends in Athens at this time? Did you meet any other writers and artists?

RB: We met some fine people, mainly Americans, British, and Dutch expatriates, and of course many young Greeks. Our friends included Vito Orlando, a New Yorker and ex-G.I., of Albanian-speaking Sicilian descent, and Loukas, a brilliant dancer with a piercing, sardonic wit. As for intellectuals, Kim and I hadn't met any at all in Thebes, and these kinds of acquaintance began for us only in Athens. Through Peter Mansfield, I met the poet Katerina Anghelaki-Rooke, goddaughter of Nikos Kazantzakis, and through her, Kimon Friar, translator of Kazantzakis's epic *Odyssey, A Modern Sequel*. Aged twenty-four, I was deeply impressed when I first visited him. His study was full of mementoes of writers, with framed paintings, photos and texts covering every space of every wall, including portraits of his one-time lover, the poet James Merrill, who in 1977 would win the Pulitzer Prize. Kimon became a good friend. Once we took him to Tsoumali's, to see our handsome young *mangas* friends dancing. His eyes popped with an old man's nostalgic pleasure.

One morning the gentle Philip Sherrard turned up, unannounced, on our doorstep. He was very British, extremely quiet and polite. He had been recommended to make contact with us by Kathleen Raine, whom I had met in London the previous year through Peter Russell, and with whom I was corresponding. On that particular morning, however, I had been up drinking all night with a very conversational and expansive American painter, Dick somebody, whose surname I now can't remember. It was around 10 o'clock when Sherrard arrived. I had just got home and was still hazily, pleasantly drunk. To compound matters, I made the (to me) guileless and blameless mistake of mentioning that I had recently met Kimon Friar, and let it slip that he was a friend. Sherrard fled and I never heard from him again. Obviously I had blundered, making a disastrous impression, not realising how strongly he disliked Friar. ... This was a huge pity, a missed opportunity, to get to know Seferis's co-translator (with Edmund Keeley), a fine writer in his own right, and an authority on Greece. His book *The Marble Threshing Floor* was one I later relished. If I had been soberer, less tactless and less naïve, perhaps I might have gone on to meet Seferis too, who would in any case become a major influence on my writing. I was sorry but, well, too bad, I thought. It was just one of those things.

Once, when Kim and I were browsing in the flea market in Monastiraki, in a second-hand bookshop occupying a large semi-basement, I came across a copy of a paperback in English by Ezra Pound, published in Bergamo in

1942, at the time when he was ranting about Fascism and Jews. I bought it for ten drachmas and sent it by registered post to Peter Russell in Venice. He asked Pound to sign it. Astonishingly, Pound obliged and Peter returned the autographed copy to me. For one thing, this suggested to me that Pound couldn't have entirely renounced his Fascist past. For another, I sold the book on to Alan Clodd for £40, a lot of money in those days.[25] So, I thought sardonically and with no small degree of satisfaction: the young Jew profits from the old Fascist. I have an unpublished essay entitled 'Ten Drachmas for A Pound', about my strong ambivalence towards Pound and Russell and Modernist poetics.

Every day was full and huge and wonderful possibilities seemed to be opening up. Athens was exactly where Kim and I wanted to be. Even the political situation had its compensations, adding an edge, a sharpness, to daily life. As foreigners, we knew we were safe provided we kept our heads low. Anyway, I told myself, to try to get involved in politics with such a scant hold on the language and without understanding enough of what was going on would have been crassly stupid.

PN: How long did you stay in Athens overall?

RB: Very suddenly, in November 1967, after only two months of living in the city, I received a phone call in the middle of teaching my friendliest and most likeable evening class at the British Council. My cousin Brian Taylor, my mother's employer, was on the line from London. He came straight to the point. My mother was dying of cancer but didn't know it. She had secondaries, was riddled with the disease, and had only months to live. She was 56 years old.

In that instant every sense of hope and happiness drained from me. Apart from the blow of the news itself, I knew that our time in Greece was to be rudely and miserably interrupted. I cancelled the rest of my class, and walked back to our flat across Syntagma Square in a daze, stunned, not knowing how I should break the news to Kim. She was as devastated as I was. Athens was over for us: suddenly unreal, past tense, third type conditional, an idyll. I was sad, bitter and angry at once – now having had my second attempt to build a life in the Mediterranean dashed, quashed, destroyed. Kim and I had already had to give up our lives in Venice two years earlier, and return to England, owing to the illness of another close relative of mine in London. I don't remember much of that time. There was a farewell party in Sotiria Bellou's taverna, with all our friends from Tsoumali's coming along to see us off. Amid the breaking of plates scattered around the drunken dancers, the thick haze of smoke descending from the ceiling, and the intensity of Bellou's plangent voice against the background of *bouzouki* and *baglama*,[26] at one point I burst into bitter tears. Loukas saved the day by standing up and getting everyone to dance. He pointed at each person present, ordering sardonically in his broken English: "Now *you* cry, and *you* cry, and *you* cry – *everybody cry*" – which of course made us all laugh, including even me, despite myself. I careered out to the loo and found myself in the Ladies' by mistake, where I discovered two young women weeping. One, I remember, we knew to be Bellou's lover. The first line of one of Bellou's songs seemed particularly apt. "I'll send a letter to God, / with bitter words. / I'll ask him to think a bit / about me too".[27]

The American poet and translator Philip Ramp and his wife Sarah were glad to take over our lease. I can't remember a thing now about how we made it back to England. Kim reminded me later that I had returned as soon as possible, and she had followed some weeks afterwards, with our luggage, travelling by train. We didn't tell my mother that we knew she had cancer but invented the excuse for our return that we had decided that it would be better for the baby to be born in England. A very difficult year followed in London. I find it hard to speak about this.

PN: So you had to leave Greece, and there was a long hiatus before you returned.

RB: That's right. I didn't return to Greece for another fifteen years, until summer 1981.

2

PN: But am I right in thinking you were still 'involved' with Greek matters? What form did that involvement take? How, for example, did your co-translation of Antonis Samarakis' *The Flaw* come about?

RB: Apart from finding a job in London, the first thing I needed to do was to publish 'The Easter Rising'. So I let it be known among friends that I had translated a poem by a young Greek poet whose pseudonym was *Agnostos Nomolos* – i. e. *A. Nomolos* – i. e. 'Anomalous'. And *Nomolos* was, of course, also *Solomon* spelt backwards. Although several sophisticated Athenians in the London literary world seemed highly suspicious of my pseudonym, for example Nikos Stangos, editor of the *Penguin Modern*

Poets series – various London literati almost started tumbling over one another in their anxiety to get their hands on the text. 'The Easter Rising 1967' came out as a poster poem tucked into the back of the January 1968 issue of *The London Magazine*, edited by Alan Ross. It also appeared as a chapbook in 1969 from the Restif Press in Brighton, whose editors were friends of Alexis Lykiard. This was my first 'book', for which I successfully managed to evade getting credit because of its pseudonym. And for various reasons, that suited me.

Kim gave birth to our daughter Lara Sophia in London on 7 February 1968 in Queen Charlotte's Hospital, West London. We decided on her first name after *Doctor Zhivago*, having seen the film, with Julie Christie in the part months earlier. We chose her second name carefully and caringly, because of its meanings and associations in Greek ('wisdom') and because she was conceived in Greece. Meanwhile, I managed to get my old part-time teaching job back at the East London College at Toynbee Hall in Whitechapel, which I began to supplement with literary hackwork. This included writing articles about Greece and book reviewing for *Tribune*, thanks to the literary editor Elizabeth Thomas, who became a friend, and later chaired the Cambridge Poetry Festival Society. And thanks to another fine editor, the novelist and literary critic Valerie Grosvenor-Myer,[28] who was married to my cousin Michael, I began to review poetry regularly for *The Times Educational Supplement* and *The Teacher*. I also became a fiction reader for the publisher Hutchinson and several literary agents in London, earning between three and five guineas for writing reports on more or less unpublishable manuscripts, usually British, but sometimes from the Caribbean, and some written in Italian too.

Then Kimon Friar wrote from Athens asking if I could help find a publisher for Antonis Samarakis's novel *To Lathos* (*The Flaw*). I managed to interest Michael Dempsey, a young editor at Hutchinson. Peter Mansfield agreed to translate the book with me, and the Arts Council of Great Britain supported us with a grant. We each took alternate chapters as individual first drafts and then revised them together to iron out inconsistencies. It was good to do this kind of work because it would have been impossible to get on with any writing of my own in that family situation. We were cheered when Arthur Koestler listed *The Flaw* as one of his choice 'books of the year' for 1969 in *The Observer Review*.

PN: Translation remains possible, then, a sort of consolation, when the ability to do original writing is paralysed?

RB: More like a substitute, I'd say, than a consolation. For me at this time translation also fulfilled the need to keep my hand in, by engaging with, shaping written words, making a text. A commissioned translation also meant earning a bit of money.

PN: When did you move from London to Cambridge? And in what ways did your move affect your involvement with Greek matters? How did this continue there?

RB: My mother died in August 1968 in Barnet General Hospital. Then my job at the East London College turned into a full-time post. We spent around 20 months in London, from November 1967 to July 1969. Starting in September that year, I was interviewed for a lectureship at the Cambridgeshire College of Arts and Technology (CCAT), and got the job.[29] So Kim and I plus baby moved to a small semi-detached family house in Great Shelford, a village several miles south of Cambridge. The Greek 'presence' in our lives continued fully throughout the next ten years, even though neither of us had the chance to go back. And this presence took on many forms and aspects.

Until 1974, so long as the Junta was still in power, there was a distinct political flavour to most of my involvement, which often combined or overlapped with literary activities. Following publication of 'The Easter Rising 1967', I was writing more political poems, and was active in the campaign to restore democracy in Greece. I took part in protests in Cambridge[30] and in London, one of them led by Melina Mercouri, and was present at the demonstration at the Garden House Hotel, Cambridge, in February 1970, at which several protesters were arrested and later put on trial.[31] One of the student organisers of this protest was Stefanos Pesmazoglou, a Cambridge undergraduate who had been my student in Athens two years previously. Informal meetings often took place in the Gardenia Restaurant in Rose Crescent, which became a kind of late-night club for some of us. This club-like atmosphere continued well into the early 1980s, when the Cypriot painter Renos Loizou and his family ran the restaurant.[32] Renos became a close friend: an etching of his became the cover of the first edition of *Black Light*, and he later made several paintings based on my poems, especially two for 'The blue butterfly'. I also appeared in Elizabeth Thomas's *Tribune* poetry reading series at the Regent's Park Library in London, reading parts of 'The Easter Rising 1967' and my other Greek poems, along with Nikos Stangos, who read some of his Ritsos translations, and Alexis Lykiard who read from his *Paros Poems*, a chapbook he had written with Alan Trist. I published poems critical of the regime in various journals on both sides of the Atlantic, including the *Journal of the Hellenic Diaspora*, edited by the Greek-American writer Dan Georgakas, a friend since Venice days – as well as in *Tribune*, *Greek Report* and *Hellenic Review*. These last two journals were designed to look like *The New Statesman*. *Hellenic Review* was edited in London by the courteous Helen Vlachos, a newspaper magnate and publisher-in-exile.[33] Meanwhile, I reviewed Kimon Friar's translations of Miltos Sahtouris in *The Southern Review*.[34]

At around this time I got to know Stavros Papastavrou, a Fellow of Peterhouse and friend of George Seferis.[35] I was particularly excited and encouraged when Stavros told me that he had shown Seferis some of my poems, and that Seferis had praised them. Even though that information seemed remote from the way I was living and working at that time, I stored it carefully. Stavros's favourite jacket was tweed. His personality meshed gentlemanly English understatement with cutting Greek irony in filigree combination. He once remarked that one of the reasons he became an infantry officer at the outbreak of war in 1940 was that he had been trained in the cavalry. In March 1971, he chaired a fundraising event for Greek political prisoners at the Friends' Meeting House, next door to the ADC Theatre in Jesus Lane.[36] He asked me to appear on the platform with Raymond Williams, who was to give a lecture on Byron. We agreed that I should read part of 'The Isles of Greece': for me, a huge honour. Williams spoke in a quiet, authoritative manner for at least forty minutes, entirely extempore, except for a few notes scribbled on a postcard. I had regularly attended Raymond Williams's lectures as a student, and I admired him and his writings enormously. In the same year, I put my Greek poems together into a mimeographed selection of poems entitled *The Return of Lazarus*, which I published myself.

PN: Apart from your mainly political involvement, were there other Greek contacts and contexts for you, at this time?

RB: In Cambridge, in the early days, it's no exaggeration to say that through the first half of the 1970s I was sustained by Greek friendships, Greek contexts, Greek music, and Greek poetry, all of which were woven intimately into the pattern of my life.

On April 16, 1970, Kim gave birth to our son Alexander Peter Carey (Gully) at Cambridge Maternity Hospital in Mill Road. For several years after our arrival, Peter Mansfield lived in Cambridge until he moved to Stratford-upon-Avon in 1973. He had married Dimitra (née

Proestopoulou), who was born in Thessaloniki. The Mansfields had two daughters, Francesca and Angela, born in the same years as our children. With infants of the same age, we spent a good deal of time together. The Mansfields were rich sources of material and information on Greek music and poetry. Dimitra had a large Theodorakis collection. She *lived* his music. Among his many songs and song-cycles they introduced to me was *Mauthausen*.[37] I was deeply moved, and translated two of the songs; many years later I included these versions in *The Blue Butterfly*.[38] My friend James Gordon sang them to his guitar when I gave poetry readings, including one performance on a BBC radio poetry programme.[39]

In this period I also explored more *rebetika*, partly through Ilias Petropoulos's ground-breaking book, *Rebetika Tragoudia* (Rebetika Songs), which Kimon Friar sent me soon after its publication, with the author's signature – and partly through listening to recordings, especially of Sotiria Bellou, Markos Vamvakaris, Vassilis Tsitsanis and Yorgos Zampetas. Around this time, I also began listening to Grigoris Bithikotsis and, later, to Nikos Xylouris. Then there was the heartrendingly beautiful recorded version of Kornaros's *Erotokritos*, arranged by Nikos Mamangakis.[40] This had a deep effect on me. *Erotokritos* epitomised the kind of tradition I felt 'I belonged to', which I also felt 'belonged to me'. At that time – as at many others – I was regularly experiencing a sense of dislocation from a good deal of English and American twentieth century poetry. It was as if much of this corpus no longer connected at the simplest, most visceral level, either with me personally or with my aspirations as a poet. This unease, particularly towards modern English poetry, is one that I often experience. It manifests as a kind of irritation. It includes an unease with my own unease, which in turn concatenates and intensifies the original irritation. At any rate, in their place, at this time, perhaps in compensation, I don't think it's surprising that I sensed a corresponding affinity with Greek poets, a wished-for (though impossible) 'belonging'.

As for Greek poetry, during the 1970s, I deepened and widened my knowledge of contemporary Greek authors, reading Cavafy, Nikos Gatsos's 'Amorgos' and Odysseus Elytis's *Axion Esti*, Yannis Ritsos, Miltos Sahtouris, and others. And most important and formative of all for me was the bilingual edition of Seferis's *Collected Poems*, which I bought in 1971, two years after its first publication in 1969.

PN: I know of Seferis's importance to you, above all from *Black Light*. How did you respond to the *Collected Poems*?

RB: I devoured the book, and ever since then, have found myself repeatedly coming back to it. The Keeley-Sherrard translations are authoritative and as transparent as they possibly could be. They work well in English and I'm happy with them, even if here and there I might have come up with slightly different solutions. Most of all, with my imperfect fluency in literary Greek, the side-by-side placement of translations and originals on facing pages has helped me enormously in understanding the originals. They hugely extended my knowledge of Seferis, which until then had been confined to Rex Warner's earlier translations and the Keeley-Sherrard selection in the Penguin *Four Greek Poets*.

PN: Other than these poets you were reading, could you say more about your literary contacts and contexts vis-à-vis Greece during the 1970s?

RB: Seferis's poems formed one of the main undercurrents for my reading and consciousness throughout that decade. And it's curious to recognise in retrospect how other quite diverse people I knew at this time belonged, in one way or another, to that current. Stavros Papastavrou enjoyed introducing people to one another in his modest and self-effacing way. I'm glad to acknowledge my gratitude now for his gentle magnanimity of spirit. And thanks to him, I met several other people who were interested or involved in Seferis. In this way, Seferis's writing became a common thread in several friendships.

For example, Roderick Beaton often visited our house in Great Shelford, when we would drink retsina and listen to Greek music. Roddy was then an undergraduate reading English at Peterhouse. Now he's a distinguished scholar, Professor of Modern Greek and Director of the Centre of Hellenic Studies at King's College London, and author of a string of books on Greek themes, including a classic biography of Seferis. Kimon Friar was another catalyst. In September 1974, Nasos Vayenas arrived in Cambridge, where he was doing his PhD on Seferis at King's. Kimon had told him to get in touch and we quickly became friends. That meeting nearly forty years ago has had many outcomes. Nasos's supervisor for his thesis was Stavros.

In 1974, I also met the novelist, short story writer and critic, Alexandros Kodzias, who was Cultural Attaché at the Greek Embassy.[41] We had coffee together in Bayswater. I don't remember the exact context but it was probably in connection with Embassy sponsorship for the Greek poets I wanted to invite to the first Cambridge Poetry Festival. Most of our conversation was about practical matters and not especially memorable, except for one point, which eventually turned out to be crucial for me. We were talking about Seferis, when Kodzias told me that he believed that the theme of the *mavro fos* (black light) in Seferis's poem 'The Thrush',[42] as well as in his post-war journal *Meres* was the key-of-keys to an understanding of the poet's work. This certainly triggered something in me. It would lie dormant for a long while, nearly ten years – connecting with and transmuting into other motifs too – before surfacing as a major theme in my own writing, in *Black Light*.

PN: Could you say something about the first Cambridge Poetry Festival in 1975, which you founded? And about the Greek presence there?

RB: In 1973, I conceived the idea of organising an international poetry festival in Cambridge. I've written about that story elsewhere,[43] so won't repeat it here, except to say that the first Festival grew out of increasingly internationalist perspectives. It was a huge event that included nearly a hundred poets, from many different countries. I naturally made sure that we invited a Greek contingent. This included Kimon Friar, delivering a lecture in the debating chamber of the Cambridge Union, entitled 'The Use of Classical Myth by Modern Greek Poets', on April 21, 1975, months after the fall of the Junta and, coincidentally, on the eighth anniversary of the *coup d'état*. A forum on contemporary Greek poetry took place on Saturday April 19, with five participants: Kimon Friar, Katerina Anghelaki-Rooke, Nikos Stangos, Takis Sinopoulos and Nasos Vayenas. The Greek presence at the Cambridge Poetry Festival developed in successive years, culminating in the conference on Seferis in 1983.

PN: To return to your own writing, in what ways and to what extent did Greek themes recur in other poems of yours in the late 1960s and 1970s?

RB: Greek themes were never far from my mind. Some of the poems I had written in Greece and Italy surfaced in *Double Flute* (1972), *Avebury* (1972), and *Learning to Talk* (1980). I had written 'Actaeon' in Venice in 1965.[44] Apart from 'Male figure playing a double flute' itself, the title poem to the first book,[45] there were several other pieces directly connected with the figure of Orpheus ('Orpheus Singing' and 'Noon'), which emerged out of an unsuccessful attempt to write a long poem based on the myth when I was living in Thebes.[46] These pieces were influenced by Rilke's *Sonnets to Orpheus* and Elizabeth Sewell's book *The Orphic Voice*. There was also a poem entitled 'The Guest', dedicated to my friend the astronomer Michael Rowan-Robinson, who had been a fellow student at Pembroke College. Michael had been lucky enough to meet Seferis in Athens, and the poem's epigraph was taken from one of my favourite of Seferis's poems,

'Memory II': "Einai pantou to poiema" ("The poem is everywhere"). Then there was 'Ode on the End of the Third Exile', a narrative experiment in writing fourteeners, which conflated the Biblical story of Jonah being swallowed by a whale, and the Greek story of Arion, rescued by a dolphin.[47] Mediterranean landscapes and seascapes entered this poem too:

> Bearer of the double flute among those hill walled cities,
> through villages hive crowned, smelling of resin and thyme
> and the swallows going barmy in their ivy hung eaves …

The English fourteener, with its marked caesura, isn't so far from the fifteen-syllable line, the *dekapendasyllavos* of *Erotokritos* and a good deal of Greek narrative poetry.

PN: Talking of long-line poems, you've mentioned Nasos Vayenas, and you've said elsewhere that your method in *The Manager*, which deploys the long line of the *verset*, was influenced in part by him, after you had translated his early, nineteen-part sequence, *Biography*. You say you met in 1974. And of course I know that your friendship continues today, since you and I have worked together on editing Nasos's *The Perfect Order*. My understanding is that complex and subtle interchanges have gone on between you for many years. How did your relationship and collaboration as poets evolve? And could you say more about some of its literary outcomes, on both sides, including translation?

RB: Seferis was the preliminary bond between us. I don't think you can respond to Seferis only on a thin, cerebral level. If two poets meet who both like Seferis, and if they explore this, there's likely to be more than just an intellectual conversation going on, more than mere acknowledgement of superficial affinities of taste. I think Nasos's and my separate engagements with Seferis's work meant a quick sense of mutual recognition between us, combined with an initial trust – signalling that even though we were writing in different languages, there were shared grounds and directions. Perhaps these commonalities were all the more interesting and surprising because we wrote in different languages. At any rate, we soon became friends and began translating each other's poems. We've been doing this on and off ever since, not in any programmatic way but simply whenever we have felt like it.

The beginning was modest enough. Nasos's version of a poem I had dedicated to Kimon Friar appeared in the Greek literary journal *Nea Estia* in 1975,[48] and I translated two of his short poems, 'Eden' and 'Empty', for a poemcard in Anthony Rudolf's *Mencard* series.[49] Then in 1978, I translated Nasos's *Biography*, with his help. And later, after the publication of *Black Light* in 1983, Nasos included his translation of one of its poems in his book *Flyer's Fall*, which interspersed his own poems with translations from other poets – an interesting experiment in itself, and typical of Nasos's flare for poised and understated originality.[50] After that, he translated the whole of *Black Light* with Ilias Layios. *Black Light* was the last project Layios worked on before his tragic death in 2005.[51] Nasos's tribute to him and description of how the two of them worked on the book is fascinating in itself and this essay of his is included in the *Critical Companion* to my writing.[52] Then, not long after you and I met, Paschali, at that *London Magazine* party in January 2004, we started discussing the idea of making a selection of Nasos Vayenas's poems in English, which eventually appeared in late 2010.

On the surface, translating each other's work might look as if an occasional unhurried game of poetic ping-pong were in progress. While that may be true at some level, there is more to it than that. For one thing, at the micro level, Nasos and I have often borrowed phrases from each other's work, surreptitiously sneaking them in here and there. This game of intertextuality began early on, not in a particularly self-conscious way, but playfully, as sort of effervescence, *kalambouri, jeu d'esprit, sprezzatura*. We took phrases and images from each other, across languages, as if doing this were entirely natural. To give you one example in each direction: Nasos's image "keeps putting on cassettes of old songs", which I found in *Biography* III, reappears in my poem 'Salt' in *Black Light*.[53]

Conversely, my line "and so go forward into the last quarter of this century" in 'For the New Year 1976' transmutes into Nasos's "With my collar up I cross over into the last quarter of the century" in *Biography* XVI.[54] While intertextuality across generations in the same language tradition is common enough, I don't believe that either Nasos or I would ever have felt quite so free to take these kinds of liberties with each other's lines if we had been working as contemporaries in the same language.

PN: So this is translation as part of the poet's *equipage*: translation as *enabler*. Self-censorship may be part of the picture, intra-lingually, yes, but here it becomes a mechanism that fosters association. So couldn't this process, which happens internally, almost be said to be one of 'constant translation', perhaps even more so than these intertextual traces above already suggest? And aren't there influences, movements, and patterns at work here on a larger scale too? For example, in terms of structure, models, and the overall shape of a work?

RB: Precisely. And what happens at micro levels turns out to be a very good indicator of what goes on at 'higher' levels of complexity. This is certainly what happened in the direction of Nasos's key influence on my own work. Translating poems by Nasos has triggered ideas for me at periods very wide apart, first in 1979 and then in 2011.

I've commented elsewhere on the effect of co-translating *Biography* in 1978,[55] so I won't repeat that account here, except to say that the experience led directly, and in a curious way, to the writing of *The Manager*. Translating *Biography* was the key to opening up the entire process of composition.

Then more than thirty years later, after working with you, Paschali, on editing *The Perfect Order*, the challenging but enjoyable experience of translating four of Nasos's sonnets on writers and thinkers ('Einstein', 'Cavafy', 'T. S. Eliot' and 'Borges') from his book *Sti Niso ton Makaron* (On the Isle of the Blest) also influenced me in a quite similar way.[56] I often write sonnets as five-finger exercises, and have a number of drafts in my notebooks, most of which I haven't bothered (or rather, haven't had time) to polish, let alone publish. I realised that among these, accumulated over the years, there were several sonnets on painters, for example, on Goya, Rembrandt and El Greco. So the idea of producing a book of sonnets devoted to writers, artists and thinkers who have been important to me, on the model of Nasos's book in Greek, suddenly became attractive. So far, I've written sonnets on Sappho, Sir Thomas Wyatt, Sir Walter Raleigh, Jane Austen, Rimbaud, Gerard Manley Hopkins and the Galician poet Rosalía de Castro. This is a quite recent series that I've been working on sporadically, and there may be a book in the making here. It involves the pleasurable task of rereading poets I love, as well as their biographies, usually for the first time. Biography is a genre I was never especially interested in until this project emerged. I've sent some of these sonnets to Nasos and, recently, when we've talked on the phone, he has told me that he's trying to translate some of them.[57]

So this exchange goes on, in unexpected and surprising ways. What we're talking about here, I think, is literary influence that works both ways between two friends and contemporaries, across two languages. There's a recursive quality to it. This perhaps slightly unusual friendship has lasted for over forty years. Despite differences in poetic temperament, we share a great deal, and I've more of a sense of commonality with Nasos than with any contemporary poet writing in English. One of the main keys to the structure of this friendship is the practice of translation. Paschali, does any of this information suggests points that could be taken further, vis-à-vis translation theory – which I know is one of your interests?

PN: Not exactly 'theory'. But an established practice among poets is writing about other poets. Only recently an anthology of such poems was published in Greece, edited by Antonis Fostieris and Thanasis Niarchos. Poets seem to be constantly inspired by the lives and creative moments of other poets, including translations, for example Keats's 'On First Looking into Chapman's Homer'.[58] And Nasos was doing this kind of thing, albeit in freer forms, from early on in his career (e.g. 'Lord Byron in Rethymno').[59] It's interesting, actually, how certain figures invite this sort of address more intensely. Cavafy is a case in point. Whether they know each other personally or not, poets do relate to each other in curious and passionate, manifold ways. And so many relationships are imagined, not actual, based on biography and reception, and reading experiences and 'elective affinities'; but still, they come across as no less than real. Isn't this one of the ways in which poems are imbued with life? In a way, poetry can't work otherwise. Do you agree? And, even if this is perhaps going off in a different tangent, how does one explain Cavafy's continued resonance, his *increasing* popularity?

RB: Poets writing about poets is clearly one of the ways in which a living 'tradition' gets transmitted. It often starts with personal friendships and joint projects. In my own case, as a further example, I never met Seferis. But along with Octavio Paz, whom I *was* lucky enough to meet and get to know as a friend, I gladly acknowledge Seferis as one of the key influences on my writing. I've written poems dedicated to and inspired by both Paz (*Avebury*) and Seferis (*Black Light*). Goethe's notion of 'elective affinities' is right too, though it could perhaps equally be said, functionally at least, that – insofar as these 'affinities' themselves may be construed as idea-threads, energy currents, meaning-bearing-strains, phylogenetic patterns, etc. – it is they that choose their individual bearers, as conduit channels, even as 'hosts'.

As for Cavafy, Nasos explores this poet's easy translatability and his extraordinary resonance across a wide range of languages in his anthology *Conversing with Cavafy*.[60] His idea itself of assembling what he calls 'Cavafy-inspired'[61] poems, along with his elegant introduction, leaves little to be added. Following Nasos, I think the keys to Cavafy's universality are to do with a bundle of qualities: above all, his exquisitely modulated ironies (or rather, his layerings of irony within irony within irony); the apparently (deceptively?) transparent surface of his language, which seems to flow through translation across many languages; and his precise registration of particularity, combined with his sweeping historical sense. To these I think must be added his quiet celebration of homoerotic experience, a motif that has been repressed in many cultures. I think this aspect increasingly garners empathetic reading as we move towards what I have called elsewhere a 'universalist' poetics.⁶²

PN: Yet, Seferis, I believe, has influenced you more strongly than Cavafy. His presence is closer ...

RB: ... I admire them both equally. But Seferis connects with me in more personal ways and at multiple levels.

PN: Thank you for this account of some of your pathways into Greece, Richard. I remember the day in 2004 when I received a copy of the bilingual Greek edition of *Black Light* from you, with your dedication mentioning how happy you were at the 'homecoming' embodied in the translation. That book served as a further entry point into Greek poetry for me too, at a time when I was a doctoral student at UEA. It was a poignant experience, under Norwich skies, to be reminded yet again of the power of that 'Greek light' through the work of an English poet influenced by Seferis.

November 5, 2012 – March 5, 2013
Alexandroupolis and Cambridge

Notes

1. The *coup d'état* of April 21st 1967 was led by a group of mainly mid-ranking officers, who came to be known as 'the Colonels'. Its leaders were Stylianos Pattakos, who was actually a Brigadier General, and Colonels Giorgios Papadopoulos and Nikolaos Makarezos. In a confused political situation, a weak interim government had been appointed by King Constantine II in preparation for a forthcoming election. The *coup* was planned to intervene before the election could take place. The military dictatorship lasted seven years.

2. *Katharevousa* or 'Purist Greek' was an artificial, highly formalised language variety, based on the ancient language. Developed by scholars in the nineteenth century and deployed in formal writing and speech, it eschewed foreign influences, especially Turkisms, and came to be strongly associated with obscurantist, jargon-riddled officialdom. It differed from the more absorptive and organically evolving *dimotiki*, 'Demotic' or spoken Greek. Language riots sparked by controversies between supporters of the two variants occurred in Athens during the first years of the 20th century. Most major writers since the mid-nineteenth century have written in Demotic.

3. RB 2011 [1], *For the Living*: 13.

4. *Note from RB*: *kalambouri* is a culture-specific term. Stavropoulos's dictionary (404) gives "joke, pun, waggery, gag, crack, pleasantry." Add all these terms together and you get something close: a style of fast, punning, ironic repartee.

5. private language school.

6. See RB 2011 [5], *Under Balkan Light*: 77.

7. café, coffee shop.

8. *Note from RB*: We later learned that throwing sugared almonds on the bridal bed is a traditional wedding custom, the *Nifostoli*.

9. "Rihárde, tí théleis ekéi ekeí mésa, ólo diavázeis diavázeis, ólo spoudázeis spoudázeis, éla ékso ligáki moré, na kathísoume kai na kánoume paréa. Éla ékso na kouvendiásoume mazí kai na pioúme ena krasáki."

10. "[T]his 'gathering of everyone from all around' takes place when a village or neighborhood church celebrates its saint or feast day. ...The celebration consists of religious services and the two-day party (glenti) of food, music, and dancing in the church plateia (square). Itinerant vendors line the square and surrounding streets with their goods." Leontis: 231.

11. *laika*, popular songs; *dimotika*, lit. demotic songs, i. e. folk songs.

12. *zeibekiko*, a dramatically whirling, pirouetting solo dance, in the *rebetika* genre (see also notes 15 and 19 below); *hasapiko*, an elegant dance, prototype of the *sirtaki* or 'Zorba's dance'.

¹³ Among RB's tributes and acknowledgements to Peter Mansfield (1942–2008), see RB 2011 [4], *In a Time of Drought*: 100; and: 'Song, for Petro' in 'Black Light', RB 2011 [1], *For the Living*: 168–169. See also 78 in this book, note 28.

¹⁴ In 1962, as second year undergraduates, Michael Duffett and RB were among the co-founders of the Oxbridge literary magazine *Carcanet*. They brought Peter Mansfield into the Cambridge team to co-edit the second issue in 1963.

¹⁵ *Note from RB*: *mangas*: a word with so much flavour that it is impossible to translate into English. Expressions like 'layabout', 'cool guy', 'streetwise guy' come close, but not close enough. Pring's dictionary gives: "one who has learned the seamy side of life; street-urchin; sharper, spiv; clever fellow" (114). Stavropoulos gives: "1. street urchin, Street Arab, young tough. 2. smart/cunning/crafty/tricky guy" (515). There are strong association with *rebetika* music and with smoking hashish. Monastiraki: a district of central Athens, near Plaka, below the Acropolis.

¹⁶ *Vlachika*, the Vlach language. The Vlachs, also known as Arumonians or Arumanians, are a distinct Balkan linguistic and ethnic group. Their language is closely related to Romanian. Various dialects are spoken in most Balkan countries, though few if any monolingual speakers remain. For a classic study of transhumant Vlach shepherds in Greece in the early years of the twentieth century, see Wace and Thompson.

¹⁷ *Kathara Deftera*: 'Clean Monday', 'Pure Monday', the first day of Lent.

¹⁸ RB 2011 [1], *For the Living*: 3.

¹⁹ *rebetika*: a genre of urban music, singing and dancing, and a so-called 'subculture'. See also *mangas*, note 15 above.

²⁰ Poems later included in *Changing*, a sequence dedicated to the *Yijing* (hexagram 50).

²¹ RB 1969 [3].

²² RB 2011 [1], *For the Living*, 'Avebury' X: 34. For the quotation from Gatsos, see Keeley and Sherrard 1966: 99.

²³ RB 2011 [1], *For the Living*, 'Avebury' IX: 33.

²⁴ RB 1971, *The Return of Lazarus*: 9.

²⁵ Alan Clodd (1918–2002), book collector and founder of Enitharmon Press, who published four books by RB.

²⁶ *baglama*: a long necked bowl-lute, a small and higher-pitched version of the bouzouki.

²⁷ "Grámma tha steílo sto Theó, / me lógia pikraména, / tha tou zitíso na skefteí / ligáki kai yia ména."

²⁸ Valerie Grosvenor-Myer (1935–2007), probably best known for her biography of Jane Austen, 1997.

29 Now Anglia Ruskin University. RB taught there from 1969 to 1979.
30 See the photo of the march accompanying the article 'It's all-quiet as 1,000 march to Greek rally', *Cambridge Evening News*, May 11, 1970, with RB in the front row of marchers. For RB's letter in the same newspaper, see RB 1970 [2].
31 For a moderately reliable account, see 'Garden House riot'; and see also Bevan.
32 Renos Loizou (1946–2013).
33 For example RB 1968 [2], 'The Exile', *Hellenic Review* 1(1), June 1968: 6; and RB 1970 [1], 'Euripides never slept here', *Greek Report* 12, January 1970: 26.
34 RB 1969 [2], 'With Face to the Wall'.
35 Stavros Papastavrou (1916–1979), was Lecturer in Medieval and Modern Greek Language and Literature at Cambridge from 1947 until his death.
36 ADC: 'Amateur Dramatic Club', Cambridge student theatre. Many professional actors first performed there.
37 Theodorakis's song-cycle was based on poems by Iakovos Kampanellis (1922–2011). See Theodorakis and also Kampanellis. See also: http://www.mikis-theodorakis.net/mauthe-e.htm. Consulted June 15, 2013.
38 'O drapetis' and 'Otan teleiosei o polemos'. For RB's English versions, 'Man on the run' and 'When this war is over', see 2011 [3], *The Blue Butterfly*: 45-46.
39 *Poetry Now*, November 2006. For James Gordon's recording of one of the songs, 'Man on the Run', see http://www.berengarten.com/assets/rbu01/img/01%20Man%20On%20The%20Run.mp3. Consulted Dec 26, 2015.
40 *Note from RB*: *Erotokritos* is a rare example of a written narrative poem which later entered oral tradition. It was composed in the Cretan variant of Greek, according to a Venetian model, by Vitsentzos Kornaros (1553–1613). See also Mamangakis.
41 Alexandros Kodzias (1926–1992). He died in a tragic accident from falling into an empty swimming pool in the darkness during an excursion to the island of Kea.
42 Seferis 1969: 311–333.
43 See RB 2011 [6], 'The Cambridge Poetry Festival: 35 years after'.
44 RB 1972 [1], *Double Flute*: 28–32; and RB 2011 [1], *For the Living*: 17–20.
45 RB 1972 [1], *Double Flute*: 43.
46 'Orpheus Singing', RB 1980 [1], *Learning to Talk*: 26-27; and 'Noon (The Birth of Orpheus)': 38–41.
47 'Ode on the End of the Third Exile', RB 2011 [1], *For the Living*: 57–63.
48 'In his Ancestral Garden', RB 1972 [1], *Double Flute*; and in Greek translation, RB 1975.

49 Vayenas 1979.
50 'Only the Common Miracle': in RB 2011 [1], *For the Living*: 160–161; and in Greek translation in Vayenas 1987: 20–21; and in RB 2006 [2], *Mavro Fos*: 29 and 31.
51 Ilias Layios (b. 1958) committed suicide in 2005.
52 Vayenas 2011: 175–180.
53 See Vayenas 2010 [2]: 39; and RB 2011 [1], *For the Living*: 162.
54 RB 1980 [1], *Learning to Talk*: 17; and Vayenas 2010 [1]: 44.
55 See 'Managing the Art': 46–47 and 61 in this book.
56 Vayenas 2010 [1]: 114, 115, 117, 118.
57 *Note from RB*: In a letter I received on January 11, 2013, Nasos Vayenas writes: "I have been trying to translate some of your poems on poets ('Arthur Rimbaud', 'Sappho', 'John Keats'), but I find it very difficult; they resist. I am trying to translate poetry into poetry. I hope I will manage in the end."
58 Keats 1885: 54.
59 Vayenas 2010 [2]: 65.
60 Vayenas 2000.
61 See Vayenas 2000 and, for a comprehensive edition of the Greek works, Daskalopoulos 2003. For English translations of 12 such poems, see Nikolaou 2015.
62 See RB 2002 [1], 'Pour toi'.

Managing the Art

Richard Berengarten and Joanne Limburg

This interview was conducted via email in December 2001 and January 2002. The resulting bundle of texts served as the basis for my feature article 'Human Above All' on the first edition of *The Manager*, which appeared in *The Jewish Quarterly* (Nº 185, Spring 2002). Richard and I revised and updated this version of the text between November 2012 and January 2013.

JL

1

Joanne Limburg: How and when did you begin writing *The Manager*?

Richard Berengarten: *The Manager* started happening in 1978. The Greek poet Nasos Vayenas was living in Cambridge, doing research on George Seferis for his PhD at King's. He had written a poem in nineteen short sections, entitled *Biography*, which had just been published in Greece. He and I decided to translate it together. I had the benefit of his insights and explanations during translation, a fascinating experience.

Late one night, just after typing out the final English version of *Biography*, I found myself doodling in my notebook and writing (not translating) what seemed like more 'parts' of *Biography*, or rather spin-offs from it. These fragments came out effortlessly and at speed. Then, as a *jeu d'ésprit*, I had the idea of presenting Nasos with some 'new' sections of his own *Biography* – but pieces he hadn't written himself. I knew this would be in tune with his Borgesian sense of humour. Then I looked again at my doodles, and saw them in a new light. I realised that they didn't belong to *Biography*, that they were the first beginnings of something of my own.

These were the first inklings, self-announcements, of *The Manager*. Nasos's *Biography* was the trigger. I don't remember when the title arrived, whether then or later. But when it did, it announced itself cleanly and authoritatively. I never questioned it or needed to.

JL: The first thing one notices on opening *The Manager* is its very distinctive shape on the page. How did you arrive at this particular verse form?

RB: Nasos's *Biography* provided the immediate model for the *verset*, or as I call it, 'verse-paragraph'. In *The Manager* I think I've extended its range and flexibility. He told me he had adapted it from Seferis and the fifteen-syllable line of Greek oral poetry, for example the Cretan seventeenth-century masterpiece, *Erotokritos*.[1]

The verse-paragraph was a huge discovery for me. I only realised its full potential as I gradually worked at it, tracing its many precedents, partly through discussions with Nasos and partly through thinking more about other poetry and poets: for example, the fourteeners of early Elizabethan verse, Blake, Whitman, Ginsberg, Saint-John Perse, and Seferis. Since my student days, I'd been trying to develop a longer line for English, one that could be adaptable and flexible enough to bear the currents and stresses of contemporary speech-rhythms. Not just a *vers libre* line, but something more shaped, less loose, less flabby. When I asked Nasos where he thought Seferis had got *his* long line from, he answered unhesitatingly, "The Bible." Then I realised what should have been obvious all along: that Blake and Whitman had both derived *their* own long lines from the King James Authorised Version, and Ginsberg from the Hebrew or Yiddish Bible. So, curiously, it turned out that the Bible, in various languages, was the key to my own long line too. A little later, in *Black Light*, which was dedicated to the memory of Seferis, I imitated his long lines.

As I experimented with the verse-paragraph and tried it out in varying contexts, it gradually dawned on me that this was an extraordinarily flexible, adaptable and versatile instrument, well suited to handling anything from interior monologues, meditations on nature and expressions of intimacies to comedy, satire and social commentary. It could be a container for dramatic dialogue, straight narrative or description. It could equally well support specialist jargons, advertisements, business memoranda, fax messages, and so on. And it was capable of holding humour, parody, irony, sarcasm. In many ways, the flexibility of the verse-paragraph was the key to the realisation of my intention. This was primarily to present a kaleidoscopic composition made up of many apparently separate parts of contemporary life. And once that question of form had been sorted out, the rest followed.

JL: How far is *The Manager* autobiographical, and how far is the protagonist a persona?

RB: *The Manager* is a portrait (exploration, investigation) of its eponymous protagonist, who is a fictional character. I wanted him to be fleshed out, three-dimensional and individualised enough to appear plausible and authentic, but not as narrowed-down or realistically determined as the kinds of characters who appear in a great many novels. On the other hand, there's a strong novelistic element in the book. *The Manager* has occasionally been described as a verse-novel, and I don't mind that description, though I'd prefer simply to think of it as a 'long' poem. While the protagonist needed to be relatively actualised, he also had to be blurry or fuzzy enough to contain multiple possibilities and contradictions, and to be open to varying identifications and interpretations.

Specifically, the protagonist is a middle-class Englishman living through the final decades of the twentieth century. He's a manager in a large commercial organisation, operating somewhere in its middle ranks, with people 'above' him and 'below' him in the firm's hierarchy. Like many of his contemporaries, his world-view is fragmented and muddled. He has ethical and moral values, but he hasn't sorted them out very well in his own head.

I intended the persona of the Manager to be a typification of contemporary western life in the fourth quarter of the twentieth century. With the (spurious?) benefit of hindsight, it now occurs to me that my own need to discover (invent) this character may well already have been configured in the last lines of a short early poem, entitled 'For the New Year 1976':

> ... and so go forward into the last quarter of this century
>   as battered but resilient and somewhat joyful, assuming
> just as very little as most persons of this generation but
>   the renewable contract to earn and become the name Human.[2]

By exploring the Manager's subjectivity and behaviour, I wanted to find out more about *his* world (or do I mean *your/our/my* world?) through *his* eyes, and by examining *his/your/our/my* world, to find out more about our inner configurations and maps of a shared, intersubjective world. Outer and inner were supposed to open each other up, mirror each other. There's a passage in which the Manager looks at himself in the mirror.[3] And incidentally, I've always been interested in the blurry demarcations of pronouns as identity-markers and distrustful of their arbitrariness. In one of the 'Codas' to *The Manager*, there's a section on pronouns, including those of gender.[4] I saw my job as two-directional: to build up a view of the Manager through perceptions of contemporary life and of contemporary life through him. And if the end-result was to provide any kind of composite picture, it would accumulate out of worms'-eye details. There would be no need for overarching panoramic shots to provide splendid wide-screen God's-Eye views, as in Thomas Hardy's novels – except perhaps right at the end. There would be no narrator outside the speakers in the poem. And certainly no answers, solutions or finalities of any kind. The compositeness of the composition would be modelled (tapestried, 'mosaicked') through accretion of detail.

JL: Would you describe the Manager as a hero, an anti-hero, something in between?

RB: Whether as a hero, anti-hero or plain non-hero, I'm not really sure. What I wanted is easier to describe in negatives. I didn't want him to be either a cliché or out-of-the-ordinary: he could be *any* fellow, feller, chap, bloke, bod, guy. This idea couldn't stand up entirely, of course – and in class terms, not at all, since he's inexorably middle-class. But what did go through my head early in composition was that if *Everyman* was the typification of medieval Man, a good way to envisage or imagine an equivalent for our time might be an *anyman*. Such a persona would be uncovered (dis-covered?), not through any explicitly formulated agglutinative set of features, but as a serial configuration designated by disjunctions, alternatives, lapses, hiatuses, hints – and contradictions. Above all, contradictions. To expand this point, if *Everyman* belonged to an age when belief in a single absolute, generalised, all-inclusive and universal truth was *de rigueur*, then the attribute *Every* was entirely apposite in its authoritative, authoritarian insistence on inclusiveness. But in our day, when belief in any one single totalising universal reality has been knocked out both by modern physics and by competing and contradictory ethical values, then the attribute *any* seems considerably more appropriate. And if *Every* should be capitalised, then *any* should be small case, like the 'i' in e. e. cummings's poems. So the binary *or* replaces the inclusive *and*.

So while I articulately shaped this 'Manager' to embody or represent a kind of modern (or late-modern, or postmodern) type, I was also quite clear in specifically wanting him *not* to be quite a number of things. For example, he should be neither a Hollywoodian git nor a Woody-Allenian creep. Nor should he be a merely allegorical good-guy or two-dimensional simpleton, like the medieval Everyman. Nor, like a character out of Sartre or Camus, or Willy Loman in Arthur Miller's *Death of a Salesman*, should he be tragically pinioned – by his worries about the insufficiencies of his will or his willpower or his willie or his whatever – in a closed situation (*Huis Clos*). The Manager is of course neither Highman nor Lowman but Middleman. Not to mention Muddleman.

And isn't modern Middleman-Muddleman a goer, a gofer, an entrepreneur, a busybody, a haggler, a mover, a survivor, by default and definition? Whatever his faults and failings, he does have guts and gusto. *Ennui*, whether Art-for-Art's-Sake or Existentialist, isn't for him. Death is with him and lurks in him and he knows it will happen and he may be preparing for it in some corner of his consciousness, but it's not going to happen to or in him *quite* yet, that is, not if *he* has any choice in the matter. A choice which the Manager, in the early pangs of illusory and inflated self-belief in his own ego, thinks or at least hopes is actually his to make – as when he remembers being a child on the playground edge: "I was not made for death. I just *refuse* to die."[5] Later, when he harangues Death, perhaps he has moved on a bit in self-ironic understanding: "Do not approach. Not yet … For I have scarcely set out. / Have far too much yet to do. Have not proved myself, even anything."[6]

It's obvious that several layerings can be read into the title *The Manager* – through usages, puns, and etymologies – as well as into the name of the protagonist, Jordan Bruno. Giordano Bruno, remember, was a polymath, philosopher and magus. Names and titles like that can hardly *not* have multiple meanings. Think of Italo Svevo or Tristram Shandy or David Copperfield. And no prizes, nudge-nudge, for anyone who works them out. Clearly, Bruno isn't Prince Charming, nor was meant to be. He may go through phases of being and feeling blocked, trapped, self-absorbed, betrayed, self-pitying and depressed, as well as joyful, exuberant, happy, calm, etc. But he doesn't stop (get stuck, fixed, fixated) in any one of them. He fucks and fucks up. And he gets fucked and fucked up. But he moves on.

It became clear to me at some point in composition that whatever kind of muddle or mess the Manager might get into, he needed to be capable of introspection and thought, self-mockery and irony, and even sometimes reason, and at least *some* degree of self-determination and change. Even though he's a fiction, I wanted him to have 'an individual soul', 'an individual mind'.

JL: Though the Manager does undoubtedly have his 'anyman' aspect, there does still seem to be an autobiographical element to the poem. Could you say a bit more about that?

RB: The best critique I've come across of what could be called the 'biographical fallacy' appears in Northrop Frye's study of William Blake, *Fearful Symmetry*, in which he compares the biographical critic's attempts to explicate a work of art by referring its parts back to the often trivial details of its creator's life. He elegantly deploys the analogy of stripping of paint off a carefully made painting back to a bare canvas. "To dissolve art back into the artist's experience is like scraping the past off a canvas in order to see what the 'real' canvas looked like before it assumed its painted disguise."[7]

Inevitably, many features (aspects, facets, details, bits and pieces) of 'the Manager' have been modelled on my own experience, experiences, ideas and sensibility. How could they not have been? Equally, many features are quite distinct from anything in my biography. All this is to say that the Manager inevitably has something of me in him, but also something other than me. He isn't identical to or coterminous with any single version of whoever-it-is-that-I-am.

Very early in the various phases of composition, in spring 1979, I did a reading tour in the USA. At a reading in Ann Arbor, Michigan, I included some passages from the first few sketches for *The Manager*. The context was an open weekend poetry workshop in the university's adult education programme. Sitting in the back row of the audience was a tall man wearing a suit and tie with a fat Windsor knot, an unusually smart outfit for that kind of occasion. Because he was tall and at the back of the auditorium he had caught my eye, so I found myself projecting my voice towards him. At the end of the reading, he came up to me, shook my hand firmly, looked me full in the eye, and said, simply, "Thank you." And added, significantly, "How did you know?" I had no idea what he meant. "How did I know what?" I asked him. He said, "How did you know *my life*? That's me. That's my life. That's me you've been writing about."

Then it was my turn to thank him. I invited him for a drink and sitting at the bar he told me more about himself. His name was Ed Engle. He was a businessman who had just gone through a divorce. We became pen friends, and a few years later, when I spent six months working in South Bend, Indiana, I visited him. He owned a factory near Detroit which made small, highly polished metal parts for car engine pistons. He was probably the first *real* Manager I had ever met. I can't tell you how much his response gave me.

JL: Moving on from the poem's inception, how soon did the structure and form of the poem stabilise, and how and when did the main character settle? And what factors went into that?

RB: Two aspects of structure became clear pretty well immediately. First, at the micro level, the medium would be the verse-paragraph. Second, the poem would consist of discrete 'shots' or 'scenes', usually not longer than a single or double page. Photographic and filmic techniques, once I'd recognised them, were consciously woven in. So each section would present the verbal equivalent of a photo or what would nowadays be commonplace as a video-clip. I wonder if it could almost be said that I was making the verbal equivalents of YouTube takes but before YouTube had been invented? The scene might be exterior or interior or combine both aspects. If interior, it could present, for example, a state of mind, dream, fantasy, interior monologue. I felt I had Joyce, Malcolm Lowry, and Virginia Woolf on my side. Sharp focus was needed. And if blurry outlines were to be deployed, this would be by deliberate choice.

Working on each of these small components meant keeping two principles in mind. First, there was the identification, registration, clarification, honing, and polishing of the detail, of the minute particular[8] – the sketching and then the filling-in of the *this-here-now*, establishing the authenticity and accuracy of the 'part' – and doing all this in just enough depth and precision to specify it and enable it to come alive. And then, often considerably later, a sorting of the way in which this detail fitted or might or ought to fit into the overall pattern – and, on occasion, be rejected or excluded from it. Of course the main difficulty all along was to discover the shape, size and pattern (i.e. form) of this 'bigger picture', and how to model it (e.g. narrative, photo-album-collage, video, mosaic, tapestry, collage, bricolage, jig-saw, etc.) I throw so many alternative analogies here because not one of them fits totally.

JL: So how did the bigger picture begin to show itself?

RB: As I worked on *The Manager*, it grew and grew. Its shape kept changing in my mind. How it should 'develop' and how it should end were huge problems that I turned over constantly, debating with myself, with friends, and sometimes even with audiences at poetry readings when I tried out parts of it. And there were occasions when I couldn't see how it would or could ever end. Around the time when the potential scope of the poem was first shaping in my mind, when I was flooded with material for it, a brilliant twenty-year-old student of mine at CCAT, the poet Alan McConville – who not long afterwards died tragically of a brain haemorrhage – commented, "Richard, it sounds as if this *Manager* of yours is about the universe and other matters. That's just too much to bite off."

Well, there were plenty of times when I did get lost in it, immersed in it, when it took me over. I do tend to get transported by images and ideas, though perhaps that's what making poems is all about. Could one write poems without that?

I think this inability to see any end, at certain times when one is working on a poem – during any kind of creative project – is fascinating. Where is *it* going? Where am *I* going? Where are we going together, this thing and I/me – I through it, it through me? All one can do is simply follow the whatever-it-is, this inchoate thing that is urging for expression and clarification, be guided by it, and wait, patiently. As Theodore Roethke puts it: "I learn by going where I have to go."[9] One senses, somehow, that one isn't writing the poem so much as being written by it.

In his preface to the first edition, which appeared in Serbian translation in 1990, Anthony Rudolf, after Norman O. Brown, called the Manager "polymorphous-perverse".[10] Perhaps changeability itself is one of the keys to the multiple chambers of his being. There were times, too, when Bruno seemed to me an alter-ego, even a doppelgänger. He haunted me for many years. In general, I find it quite hard to say where autobiography as *fact* ends and fantasy, imagination, and fictional construction or reconstruction begins. Maybe this is a common experience for fiction writers. And querying whether stories, histories, and life-stories and life-histories – and roles, masks, and personae – are fictive, factive or factitious is a component in the poem itself. When the Manager looks into his mirror, his mirror-image tells or appears to tell him: "Time, Buddy Boy, you realised, a story is a fiction and life is the story and the story of the life is the fiction of a fiction made by sweet ole you not merely in order to live the damn thing, let alone die it or at least die in it, but …"[11]

JL: So for a good deal of the time you were feeling your way, in the dark, as writers often must. But if structure, as you put it, "kept shifting around", what about development? And how did you eventually establish the sequence that appears in the published poem?

RB: At several stages during composition, I found myself strongly resistant to all notions of development, both of character and of 'plot'. It wasn't so much that I'd 'lost' the plot, but that I didn't know if the poem should have one at all, at least in any linear fashion. I asked myself, as a kind of litmus test, "Have *I* 'developed' since I was, say, 20? Have *I* become any more intelligent, kind, profound, sincere, or wise?" I somehow doubted very much if I had. I found myself increasingly critical of the ways in which the notion of 'development' was being used in so many fields; the ways in which it was seen as the key to so many activities and disciplines; and, most of all, the ways in which it could too easily serve as ulterior justification for behaviour that was unpleasant, exploitative, cruel or barbaric. What is more, different kinds of 'development' always seemed to me to have their own defensive jargons, perhaps in readiness for the argument that the end justifies the means. There was 'evolutionary development', 'child development', 'educational development' and 'skills development'. There was 'developmental psychology' and 'developmental linguistics' and the development of consciousness and awareness. There was industrial, scientific, technological, social and economic development. Too much development, far too much. ... So development, to me, had itself got grossly over-developed. I seemed to be surrounded on all sides by 'development', pinioned inside it, and I was thoroughly sick of it.

By the late 1990s, I was devouring books by Zygmunt Bauman. When I started reading him, I found myself being bitterly sorry that I hadn't done so before. His writings clarified many of my difficulties in composition vis-à-vis *The Manager*. And especially, thanks to his brilliant *Postmodernity and its Discontents*, a series of heuristic flashes leapt through my head in rapid succession. What he clarified most to me was that notions of 'development' ('progress', 'advance', etc.) are enshrined in *all* modern (and modernist) philosophies – including capitalism, fascism and communism. What's more, these notions derive from a historical period marked by both imperialist expansion in space and positivist control over time. Out of this, I realised that my Manager is a character who resists all these notions. He's in revolt against the narrowing, pointedly teleological thrust of development. He will not be patronised. And he refuses to be colonised. I began to correspond with Bauman, and eventually he wrote a generous comment on *The Manager*, part of which appeared on the back cover of the first edition.[12] His comments meant an enormous amount to me. Incidentally, Bauman's thoughts on 'development' echo Octavio Paz's earlier analysis of "the twilight of the idea of revolution" and "the decline of the future".[13]

JL: It's clear, then, that the notion of development came to be anathema for *The Manager*, in its narrative form and central character, as well as in the process of its composition. But did any alternative structuring principles present themselves?

RB: Should a character in a poem or a novel necessarily develop? Change, yes; transform, by all means, yes; learn – well, one would hope so, especially from past mistakes (although somewhere or other I remembered Jung or Erich Neumann saying that one does not 'solve' problems, neuroses, etc., but 'transcends' them.) But must or even should one develop? Without even the merest hint of gloom or pessimism, the answer, surely, needed to be: not necessarily.

So for a long while, I toyed with the idea of publishing *The Manager* as a loose leaf album, in a ring-binder, or as a set of unbound pages in a box, like B. S. Johnson's wonderful novel *The Unfortunates*. The sections would then be able to be taken out and reshuffled into different orders. I still don't think this was an entirely stupid or fanciful idea. Many people, myself included, often read books of poems in random order, or even back to front. When the Cambridge poet Glen Cavaliero read *The Manager*, he confirmed this. He wrote me a letter which said: "I have now read *The Manager* all through twice – once forwards and then back (it works rather well that way, one sees it as a whole not just as an unfolding process)."[14]

But I finally rejected the idea of random or multiple sequencing. I think this was partly because I began to sense that there was some kind of pattern of movement, or change, or even (if one were to be pompous about it) 'narrative' or 'transformation' – going on in and through the book. I find it hard to intellectualise this. The feeling is still a visceral one.

JL: In what ways, then, do you think that the Manager does progress – or at least change – as a character?

RB: As I've suggested, 'development' isn't one of my favourite concepts. Could one say that he 'matures'?

JL: Then could I ask if his 'maturation' worked out, as you had intended?

RB: The author of a fiction can be the worst, least trustworthy, least authoritative of all its readers. That's one reason for listening to readers and critics. Not long after publication, I was in correspondence with the wonderful English novelist Nicholas Mosley, author of *Hopeful Monsters*, who wrote to me: "I find the end of *The Manager* intensely powerful and moving – like Dylan Thomas's raging against the dying of the light. But it is a savage paean of praise for life: the protagonist becomes a giant figure."[15] A similar response was forwarded via my publisher from Sir Peter Parker: "It strikes me as a remarkable leap, or leaps of imagination and, oh, he has got guts."[16] Responses like these suggest that there *is* a maturation – transformation – in the character. Comments like these validated intention.

JL: And what about the final 'buffer-piece'? With the two children playing in the street? How does that fit?

RB: As a complete change of scene. Here, we are hundreds, maybe thousands of miles away from the Manager himself, from any of his personal problems, his individual life, his little world. Perhaps hundreds of years away too. This is a panning out, a movie director's long shot. The children speak (or are learning to speak) a secret and perhaps new language. There are hints of pronouns in their words. They are "learning to talk".[17] I got this idea from the last scene of the great *Orfeu Negro*, set in Brazil, which I'd seen in 1962. That film ends with two children playing against a background of the sun going down. Or is it coming up? I'd like to think it's coming up.

JL: You've told me about the beginnings of *The Manager*, and the inspiration and influences behind its particular form. The front cover specifies that the book is "a poem". Could you say something about your interest in long poems and how this developed, as distinct from writing short poems?

RB: In Serbian and Croatian, the distinction between 'short (lyrical) poem' and 'long (narrative) poem' is made by two separate words: for short poem, *pesma* (Serbian) and *pjesma* (Croatian), which also means 'song'; and for long poem, *poema*. It's the same in Italian: *poesia* and *poema*. A pity we don't have a distinction like this in English, even though 'lyric' and 'lyre' are cognate and both embed the imagem[18] of music (sound, rhythm, instrument, melody, harmony, etc.). In the English-speaking world, the mental model of a poem that I think most people grow up with is a relatively short piece, and the conventional idea of composition is lyrical. This confusion is a pity because there seems to be little popular understanding that long poems 'belong' to everyone in the way short lyrics do, and aren't necessarily 'odd' or 'difficult'. There is a magnificent tradition of long poems in English, from *Beowulf* on.

In my own case, from an early age the writing of short poems came relatively easily to me, so much so that I've taken this mode more or less for granted, and have never found it especially worth making much fuss about – except when I sense that, for any reason, it's in danger of attack, or being distorted or belittled. Like most people, I enjoy poems and lines of the "M'illumino d'immenso"[19] and "Silent upon a peak in Darien"[20] variety. I've written plenty of sonnets, in varying patterns, and villanelles. Haiku and epigrams are scattered through my notebooks, nearly all unpublished. Even so, I've never been happy with any view of poetry that suggests that production of this kind of thing is the highest or most valuable thing one can aspire to: flawless gems, exquisite tiaras, crystalline carcanets, timeless instants out of time, mountainous moments, and so on. To rely on these kinds of miniatures alone to epitomise the ideal of poetry and of the poetic experience is specious, as if one were to read the whole of *La Divina Commedia* only in order to pull out pearls like "la bocca mi baciò tutto tremante".[21]

I've always wanted and aimed to write long poems as well as short lyrics. This has been an aim and challenge since I was in my teens. Many of my earliest attempts, even as a schoolboy, were long poems. Around the age of fifteen, I wrote a piece called 'The Household Gods', and a year or two later, I wrote other long poems at school, influenced by Alan Ginsberg. All of them are juvenilia, unpublishable. In the 1960s, when living in Greece in my twenties, I started a long poem about Orpheus entitled *The Orphead*. Only a couple of fragments survive from this,[22] but 'The Easter Rising 1967' (1969) also emerged in this period. In the 1970s, when I started getting interested in Celtic legend and myth, thanks to the influence of my first wife, Kim Landers, I wanted to write a long poem based on the Breton and Cornish story of the city of Ys and *la cathédrale engloutie*, but this turned out to be too much for me and I abandoned the attempt. All that survives is a prose piece.[23] Before the first edition of *The Manager* came out (2001), I published other long poems and sequences, including 'Avebury' (1971), 'The Offence of Poetry' (1973), 'Angels' (1976), 'Ode on the End of the Second Exile' (1976-8), the chant '*Tree*' (1981), 'Black Light' (1984), 'Against the Day' (1989), 'Day Estate' (1990s), and 'Croft Woods' (1998).[24] But *The Manager* was bigger and more ambitious than any previous attempts at long poems.

2

JL: *The Manager* has been a long time in the making. Could you give a fuller account of the story of its writing, and some idea of the timescale involved?

RB: I began composing in 1978. Except for a handful of small last-minute changes and adjustments, the text of the Elliott and Thompson edition, which was published in November 2001, was finalised around September 2000 – a span of nearly twenty-two years. So the process involved something of a journey. I didn't (couldn't) work on it regularly, only sporadically. The time it took to get *The Manager* out and the sporadic nature of composition were dictated by various considerations, most of them banal and best summed up as *force majeure*. This strangely long period of time in composition and editing was also connected to the finding of a publisher. So the full and intricate story of the writing and editing of *The Manager*, its advocates and supporters, and its publication-history, are entwined together. Any big project of any kind takes time. A long poem needs sustained periods of concentrated work. It has to be worked on, then left, then worked on, then left. It also has to be carried around in one's head while one is not sitting actually writing it. It quite often has to be forgotten and set aside too, so that it doesn't interfere with other things.

JL: So how did interference and interruption affect the writing?

RB: Writing poems doesn't pay the bills. Or rather, it never has done so in my case and I've never expected it to, even if I've fantasised about it doing so. The writing of *The Manager* kept having to be interrupted, in a whole series of jerky stop-start-stop-start patterns, simply because of the need to earn money doing other things. Moneymaking is something I've never been very good at or very interested in. The interruptions, of course, weren't *just* because of 'work', but to do with living-a-life: family, children, friends, holidays, hobbies, you name it, everything that makes the world go round. Life as a habit gets constantly interrupted by its need to be lived. It could also be said that life *consists of* interruptions: it can't avoid interruptedness, interruptions of interruptions, a never-ending series of interruptions of interruptions of interruptions, and so on, right up to and including that last interruption of all, one's own common but singular dying and death. What's more, until then, perhaps more so than our predecessors, we live in multiple worlds. We not only *multitask*, we *multi-live*.

So it could be said that the constant interruptions in the process of the writing of *The Manager* themselves constitute a kind of pattern, even *a patterning principle*. It could also be said that the insides and outsides of interruption-and-interruptedness-as-pattern have been carried through into the final product. An artistic work is bound to reflect and contain the act or process of its own composition. I think and hope *The Manager* does that. What is more, lack or absence of continuity is both what patterns it and what it's about. The action is broken up into episodes. Times within and between episodes are, as Zygmunt Bauman has put it, "flattened out."[25] The syntax in is often staccato and disjunctive. A lot of jerky full stops are used. The protagonist usually has (or experiences or projects) a sense of rush, hurry, anxiety, frustration, incompletion. Interruption as an explicit theme enters the text in several places, for example during a row between the Manager and his wife/partner.[26]

So I think the poem embodies and is also about this condition of being and feeling interrupted, this sense that everything that happens interrupts (and can't help interrupting) everything else that happens – in and through discontinuous episodes, accidental contiguities, uncertain contingencies, continual non sequiturs (i.e. non sequiturs and disruptions perceived as 'normal pattern'), occasional serendipities, and apparent synchronicities. And meshed into this, inevitably, goes the sense that events – occurrences, happenings, episodes, processes, and whatever patterns may run through or underlie them – are all, somehow, mysteriously, and for no special reason, *outside one's control*. Nor is it that they are *within* the control of any 'other' body or group, whether construed socially in terms of 'class', or intellectually – or even metaphysically – in terms of 'higher orders' – from any of which the Manager might feel excluded. It's rather that, if events are patterned at all, then it's by indiscernible forces, which a good deal of the time don't seem orderly or rational to anyone: "Oh Slattern of a Pattern, / Comptroller and Contortioner. Whore named More. Bond of Beyond. Father alias Further."[27]

JL: So does the Manager inhabit a meaningless universe without hierarchy, God or gods?

RB: Surely all one can say is, "Perhaps." I certainly don't think the condition the Manager exists in and operates through is either specifically pessimistic or nihilistic, according to, say, some Existentialist model such as Camus's *L'Étranger*. The world of *The Manager* isn't a meaning-void. I'd prefer to think of it as a condition jam-packed with possibilities and dangers, replete with ironies and returns, budding with openings and threats, blossoming with patterns in chaos, burgeoning with chaos in patterns, rippling with unseen avenues, showering undisclosed outlets … but this is beginning to sound like a shopping mall catalogue. *Sve je moguće*, they say in Serbian and Croatian. ("Everything is possible" – not "Nothing," not "Anything," but "Everything"). I was lucky to have been around when the conditions for this condition had already been clearly and almost prophetically marked out, at least as far as I was concerned, in fine, full ambiguity and ambivalence, in a poem by my friend and contemporary Peter Mansfield, entitled 'Credo', written when he was an undergraduate at Pembroke College, Cambridge, in 1962.[28]

JL: Would you say that *The Manager* was *about* the tearing of time into tatters?

RB: "Perhaps": again, that word. ... Or about the absence of any clear map of time? Or about times being flattened into anecdote and episodicity? Or about the recycling of linear time? Or simply about a man managing to get through his time, and out, carrying on regardless? And could it be said that in *The Manager*, interruption, hiatus, gap, *non sequitur*, absence, pause, caesura, and parataxis all convene to form a connecting, cohering, unifying principle in itself – because these all posit larger context and because they implicate an order? I'd like to think the latter is the case and that an implicated sense of order, or at least a search for order, is among the poem's core themes. Isn't the "blessed rage for order" what all poems are about?[29] So from the point of view of the Manager himself, might it equally be that an overall pattern does exist but that its workings are indiscernible, inscrutable, unfathomable?

JL: Further to 'timescales', I understand that you tend not to work on different projects serially, but rather on several long projects (as well as shorter poems) simultaneously, often writing, rewriting and returning to a particular project over many years. Could you say a bit about this way of working – how you came upon it, what it allows you to do?

RB: Again, this is partly though not entirely to do with *force majeure*. Most of the poets I know operate in this way, as do plenty of artists in other fields. I don't think I'm in any way unusual. Don't you work on a lot of projects at once?

JL: Not as a rule, but I know from talking to other poets that I'm unusual in that.

RB: In my own case, I think that if I had a particular project I was being *paid* to work on, I might simply drop everything else and concentrate on that. But poets aren't usually paid to write poems, and rather rarely get commissions, or work to exterior deadlines on poems. So, in effect, as well as working on different projects serially, each of the several long projects on which I'm working *in itself* becomes a serial. What's more, if I'm working sporadically on what I've marked out, prioritised, as *central* (in this case, a long poem), then the syndrome of Coleridge's "person from Porlock" will tend to govern just about everything that isn't part of that.[30] Then *life itself* turns into the person from Porlock, who keeps knocking on the door, any time, day or night, delivering junk mail, babies, viruses, windfalls, deaths, computer viruses, plagues, contracts, mad cow or foot-and-mouth disease, neighbours from hell, bankruptcy notices, terrorist attacks, car and train accidents, lottery tickets, lottery wins, bailiffs, immediate eviction orders – *you name it, these Porlock people can bring it …*

JL: I understand that a certain amount of collaboration was involved at the editing stage. Could you say more about that?

RB: Many friends contributed to the making as well as to the presentation, editing and publication of the poem. Anthony Rudolf was *The Manager*'s most loyal advocate. Nasos Vayenas had an important role, not only in its inception in 1978 but towards its end, too. When I saw Nasos again after a gap of some years, in Oxford in 1999, I was still talking about being unable (or not knowing how) to 'finish'. He said to me, simply, "Then, Richard, you must *un*finish it." This was a *koan*-like challenge.

Around the same time as I visited Nasos, editing was also going on with Peter Mansfield. He and I had already done a good deal of work together. As undergraduates at Pembroke College in 1963, we had worked together on the second number of an Oxbridge undergraduate literary magazine called *Carcanet*, which I had co-founded with Mike Duffett and others in 1962.[31] In the late 1960s, Peter and I co-translated a novel from Greek, *The Flaw*, by Antonis Samarakis. Over the years, from the 1960s to 2006, he worked on several of my books. And in the mid-1980s, he helped finalise *Black Light*. When it came to *The Manager*, as a superb linguist and a remarkably intuitive listener, he helped get details right. Towards the end, he did much more: he edited the whole book, a laborious and painstaking process. He pushed me to turn rough drafts into polished versions, made me excise dross or inferior material, cut down versions which I'd thought were already polished but which were in fact too long, and entirely removed what I sometimes thought were *beautifully* written sections, on the grounds that they were repetitious or did not fit, or because they belonged to an intrusive authorial or 'other' voice rather than one in keeping with *this* persona, *this* poem. He 'pounded the waste', chucking out and compacting the refuse. I bucked and baulked, but he was right and I knew it. I don't think I would have been able to see a good deal of this for myself. Of course, we argued points but, when it came to it, I submitted to him on most issues and didn't allow anything to be included that he disagreed with – though the ultimate responsibility remained mine as 'signatory'. Despite occasional infuriation, overall this was an enormously enjoyable experience, at least for me, and one that I learned a great deal from. Finally, most important, Peter helped me decide on the nuanced juxtaposition and ordering of sections.

This process of editorial discussion went on, too, well beyond the typescript stage and into the book's final making. Brad Thompson, the design-editor, who took enormous pains over each small detail, was keen to ensure that each double-page spread would look 'right' – and of course we couldn't know in advance the extent to which the visual impression of the typescript would match the page layout on his computer screen. When it came to it, at proof stage Peter and I had to add several sections back in – which we had only just taken out – and also adjust the order of several others, for visual design. Minor reordering continued into the second and third editions too, because new page formats and fonts entailed different pagination. So both content and structure were influenced by factors of design.

In these senses, then, a certain preparedness for instability and lack of 'finality' was built into the fabric of the text itself. Overall, this process was like cutting a version of a movie from its various takes. There was always the sense that other versions might be possible, that the text was never 100% 'solid' (bound, bonded), but as 'liquid', mercurial. The idea of liquidity is quite apt here, both literally and in connotations and associations that apply to money and investments. And couldn't the idea of liquidity be carried over, too, into the multiple and variable ways in which time can be patterned? 'Liquidising time' doesn't quite mean 'liquidating' it, though perhaps it does imply 'flattening' it. Anyway, as a result of these editings, a good deal of material was left over, some of it quite good. The best of it was collated in the two sequences 'Sketches With Voice-Overs' and 'Nine Codas' in *Book With No Back Cover*.

JL: Could you say more about the publishing history of *The Manager*? Various extracts came out in magazines, didn't they?

RB: Yes, a good number of extracts got published quite early on in magazines and anthologies, notably in 1983 in *boundary 2*, edited by William G. Spanos at SUNY Binghamton, which announced itself as "a journal of postmodern literature",[32] as well as in an issue of *Poetry South East*, edited by Barry MacSweeney.[33] To me, at that time, Barry's words of praise in his editorial were like the first tiny nuggets that a gold-prospector sifts out of a riverbed, even if now in retrospect they seem over-the-top:

> *The Manager* is a fabulous work. I wish I had room to publish more, or cash to print the lot. Its tense, hysterical edges (no insult) and jagged rhythms are just what we need in the eighties. More and more we need to record the breakdown, anger, frustration, paranoia and downright bloodiness of society. Richard has his writing hand on the thudding pulse. It will make a fine book.[34]

Then Elaine Feinstein included some extracts from the poem in a PEN anthology of new writing in 1988. I was also encouraged by some remarks in a review of Elaine's anthology by Carol Ann Duffy: "Some poets soar above straightforward craftsmanship. [The] extracts from *The Manager* by Richard Burns give a genuine frisson with their stark originality."[35]

JL: Turning to book publication, isn't there a curious story there? Didn't the first edition appear in Yugoslavia?

RB: Yes, I was given my first chance to publish a version of *The Manager* in Yugoslavia in 1990. I was probably the only English-language poet living in the country in those years. The secretary of the Montenegro Writers' Association wanted the text of a book from me, any book. The Serbo-Croat edition came out in 1991 in a fine translation by Vladimir Sekulić and Jasna B. Mišić,[36] with a generous introduction by Tony Rudolf. He pointed out that he thought it was a 'first' for an English writer, to have a book published in Serbo-Croat before being published in English. Then Tony showed the manuscript to the London literary agent, Giles Gordon, who took it on. Giles wrote me a letter on January 17, 1991, which started: "I suspect, quite genuinely, that THE MANAGER may be a masterpiece and posterity will regard it as such." I was gobsmacked. But he added that he didn't expect to find a publisher for it "… at this time. And possibly not last week and certainly not next week." But he did send it around all the major and fashionable British publishers. Several said they liked it, even admired it, but no-one would take it on. Some said that they didn't know how they could sell it to their own marketing departments. The book was desperately uncommercial. Eventually he gave up.

Then I gave up for a while too. I was going through a difficult time personally and financially, and this disappointment made things worse, especially after my hopes had been raised by Giles Gordon's letter. For several years I did very little writing. It's at times like that when you need your friends. Tony Rudolf tried to keep my spirits up. "Look, Richard," he said, "George Oppen spent ten years between writing one poem and the next."[37] Then Jerry and Mieke Hooker generously sent me a cheque to help me along,[38] and I received more valuable financial help from a private benefactor and from the Royal Literary Fund. So, gradually, my confidence picked up again. Antoinette Moses was an ally, arranging for republication of *Black Light*, under Aude Gotto's imprint at The King of Hearts, Norwich, in 1995.[39] Then, in 1999, Aude herself renewed her encouragement by editing and publishing the selection *Against Perfection*, including several extracts from *The Manager*.[40]

By then, *The Manager* itself had been rejected by as many mainstream publishers as had rejected Malcolm Lowry's *Under the Volcano* – and maybe more.[41] But in 1996, Tony Rudolf showed the book to David Elliott. At last here was an editor who believed in the book and was prepared to take it on. David was then working with Ib Bellew, who agreed to publish it. I was broke and had bills to pay, but these publishers – to me, unbelievably – were prepared to wait as long as it took me to complete the book. By 1998, I managed – yes, *managed* – to spend periods working on the book again, which was when I turned to Peter Mansfield to help me edit it. Our final version took a year to finalise.

Then Ib went out of business. But David joined up with Brad Thompson to form a new publishing company, as Brad put it, "specially to publish *The Manager*". Since then, three more editions have appeared: paperback and hardback editions from Salt Publishing in 2003 and 2008 and a new paperback edition from Shearsman Books in 2011.

3

JL: You use different registers of language in the poem – some parodying and satirical. Could you say a bit about the language?

RB: First, there was a need to get the voices 'right', not just the protagonist's but for all the speakers in the poem: their accents, tones, timbres, rhythms, registers, *argots*. This involved first 'hearing' each voice in my head, followed by a careful 'listening', authentication – linguist's skills – not to let my own overlays, constructions, or interpretations interfere. I think this point worth generalising. Part of the process of writing poems involves not so much 'self-expression' or 'developing an individual style' – which most critics, academics and pundits tell us we ought to be looking and aiming for – but, on the contrary, getting oneself and one's own linguistic prejudices and idiosyncrasies and styles *out of the damn way*. Samuel Beckett said that the reason he preferred to write in French was that doing so enabled him to write "*sans style.*"[42] Dismissing one's own insistent, irritating style-ego is the first key. Styles can become *bad* habits.[43]

Then, there's the fascination in the differences and widenesses of gaps between what Bernstein called restricted and elaborate codes,[44] and in the huge multiplicity of language-varieties that are present all the time both *out there*, in and among the voices of others, and *in here*, passing through the inner voices that concatenate inside one's head, for example in fantasy and dream – voices that may well be any poem's first sayers and tellers. And along with this goes interest in the sheer rapidity and unpredictability of shifts among registers and varieties. The comedian Kenneth Williams, whom I admire enormously, was a brilliant handler of these transitions. He could hike along a phrase or sentence in one register, somersault it hilariously into another, finally setting down his very camp camp, as it were, miles away. Part of the effect I was after in *The Manager was* comic, and I was pleased that several friends said to me after publication that they'd laughed out loud at certain points. I wanted the poem to express some of the ways in which arrays of unpredictable voices and noises, in choruses and solos, offset, juxtapose and counterpoint one another, in all aspects of life. And this links, of course, with what I've been saying about interruption. We're all constantly being bombarded by different kinds of language-use. It's most people's everyday experience – urban, suburban, even rural – pretty well all over the world. All you have to do is twiddle a radio knob or flip a TV channel. Speech coming in from a long distance is now all part of our immediate sound background. In the decade since publication, we've been wired up even more extensively: *www*, mobile phones, video phones, smart phones, iPads, Wi-Fi, Skype, etc. – and we quickly take each innovation for granted. *The Manager* tracks at least some aspects of that concatenation and conflation.

Obviously the most likely effect of all this variegated background noise is disturbance, screech, irritation, background hum, white noise, cacophony, babble, disjunction, split, gap. With that comes the need to multitask, plus a resulting anxiety that one *can't keep up*. But less obviously, this set of disjunctions is capable of transforming into surprise, delight, openings, discovery, serendipity – and even turn out to possess a set of discoverable rhythms and patterns of its own. And that pattern can be jazz. The jazz motif appears when the Manager is listening to an FM radio station when he's driving on the motorway.[45]

JL: You also have mock faxes, an email, adverts, a business memo, a newspaper horoscope, and even a CV in the poem.

RB: That's right. According to the theory of language register, performative aspects of a speaker's usage change according to medium, situation, and who is addressing whom. Idiolectal usage is influenced, even determined, by these factors. Every mode of language delivery is open to being explored in poems.

Tony Rudolf was right, too, in his introduction to the Serbian edition, in drawing attention to the ways in which the telephone in *The Manager* figures so prominently. It's not just that its appearances in the poem are intended to serve as part of the authenticating backdrop. Several sections in which the telephone appears as a medium are about *non*-communication rather than any kind or degree of success or satisfaction in this form of contact. Not getting through, getting the wrong number or wrong person, only getting through to an answering machine – or as we call it now, voice-mail – and so on, are all part of the poem's wiring. It was W. S. Graham, I think, who first wrote wonderful poems deploying telephone imagery, and I owe him a huge debt for that.[46] I wrote *The Manager* when mobile phones were just coming into mainstream consumer use.

JL: As one might expect, there's a good deal of business language in *The Manager*. Could you say a bit more about your use of this kind of language in the poem?

RB: As *The Manager* sets out to explore the subjectivity and behaviour of a contemporary businessman in both private and professional life, business-language has to be explored. Some of those aspects have been pretty well covered in the novel, ever since, say, Italo Svevo's *La coscienza di Zeno*, and even earlier. But I think it's relatively new in poetry, isn't it? In researching the poem, I read a lot of books on business management.

I have to confess to an ambivalent attitude to business-jargon. One thing that fascinates me about it is its gusto, its energy and even its voraciousness. Business greedily sucks every possible kind of vocabulary into its maw – for example, terminology from semantic fields such as war, sport, psychology, the sciences, technology, food, body language, and many more, all get replanted, grafted, culled, chopped up, recombined, and then rehashed and served up as quickly as possible and – hey presto, what do we have – cutting-edge buzz-words. In this sense, business jargon is parasitic, viral. It's enormously creative and energetic, highly metaphorical, and often slick, witty, playful. There's a poetry latent in all specialist jargons, and there's a good deal of surreptitious parodying of jargons in the text.[47] I hope some of the sheer fun of this manages (again, *manages*) to come over, for example, the pilot-speak in section 27.[48]

On the other hand, when it comes to the language of advertising and marketing that spins out of business, I think we tend to see ourselves as jaded, weary, cynical sophisticates who are all of us so knowing and so aware and so conscious of its whole gamut of subliminal aims and surreptitious intentions that we take no notice of it. We defend ourselves from it by means of irony, even though we know it affects us and conditions our buying behaviour, not to mention our dreams, aspirations, ambitions and so on, and even though by then it has become completely capable of liquefying and rejellifying vicariously in our consciousnesses, usually by invading, adopting and assimilating – i.e. co-opting – our irony itself, in order to seduce us all the more effectively – so that the original irony we have deployed as a defence spirals into ineffectuality and obsolescence, in the same sort of way as reinsurance does among small circles of financial brokers, and nobody notices until there's a scandal or a crash. Which is to say that using business language in a long poem like this has to involve multiple layerings of irony.

While in the poem I attempt to deflate business jargon wherever possible, as well as some of the apparently dehumanising aspects of PC-speak, pseudo-academic-speak, pseudo-sociological-speak, and so on, I'd hardly be after advocating any kind of linguistic purism to take their place, let alone any kind of 'clean up' operation. When irony's in question, these days there's too much complicity, too much connivance, too rooted an involvement, with-*and*-in-*and*-within the target of any attack, for any wholly believable mission-statements. (Incidentally, I think the interrelationship between irony and co-option is a huge issue that needs closer investigation.)

In 1990, around the time that the first Serbo-Croat edition was published in Montenegro, I sent a draft of the English version to Jeremy Hooker.[49] He wrote me a letter that made helpful criticisms, strictures and suggestions on weaknesses in the ordering, structure and content, most of which I hadn't fully worked out at that time and still needed to address. In that letter, he also pointed out "a linguistic versatility that is rare in any writing, and sometimes calls to mind Joyce, not by suggesting a debt to him, but by virtue of its control of language, its knowledge of words." So Jeremy recognised and validated what I had been aiming to do vis-à-vis voices and registers:

> The work has immense verbal richness, it delights in different purposes by different voices, and therefore has a considerable range of voices, a range far wider than that of *The Waste Land*. It is in the voices, above all – romantic, lyrical, sardonic, self-condemned by cliché, 'managerial', 'popular', 'bitter', tender, that *The Manager* at once composes and reveals, projects and diagnoses, a whole modern world with its conditions of life. ... I do not know

another poem, or indeed any writing, which is at once so expert in our modern consumerist specialist languages, and so witty in exposing their superficiality and heartlessness. You excitingly take great risks, you are closer to Blake of *The Marriage of Heaven and Hell* or the Prophetic Books than you are to the vast majority of your English and American contemporaries or even to Eliot of *The Waste Land*.[50]

Similarly, Anthony Rudolf mentions in his preface to the 1990 Yugoslav edition that 'The Manager' "… is 'just managing' in his personal life. He is not in control of it, preferring to control others." And he too refers to Eliot:

> The disjunctive pattern of this 'dissociated sensibility' (in Eliot's phrase), this life whose bits are hooked up only by the telephone – to which he is addicted – brings to mind the shadowy figures who flit in and out of the great predecessor's masterpiece, *The Waste Land*.[51]

JL: You have talked about *The Manager* being, *pace* Eliot, historical – of a particular moment in time. Can you tell me more about your attitude to Eliot? Would it be true to say that his influence is dominant? For example, the cover of the first edition shows people in the rush hour crossing a bridge. Isn't that a reference to *The Waste Land*?

RB: Yes, and a direct one. That cover idea came from the publisher David Elliott. He commissioned a photographer to stand on London Bridge during the rush hour and take shots of people hurrying by. The lines in question are from the first section of *The Waste Land*. "A crowd flowed over London Bridge, so many, / I had not thought death had undone so many."[52] This translates Dante's *Inferno* almost literally: "… si lunga tratta / di gente, ch'io non avrei mai creduto / che morte tanta n'avesse disfatta."[53] Incidentally, I can't help wondering if T. S. Eliot knew the translation by his relative Charles Eliot Norton, which seems very closely similar: "so long a train of folk, that I should never have believed death had undone so many."[54]

JL: Could you say more about how you view Eliot? And how this comes into *The Manager*?

RB: Eliot is one of the very few poets who have aroused any kind of "anxiety of influence" in me. Writing *The Manager* was partly a way of getting him off my back. Or rather, *The Manager* marks my attempt to 'answer' *The Waste Land*, at least to my own satisfaction if no-one else's. My aim was to write a 'big' poem that would 'articulate' the end of the twentieth century, in the same sort of way that *The Waste Land* had done for the 1920s and surrounding decades. A tall order. This inevitably meant following Eliot, modelling my work on his, learning all I possibly could from him, consciously submitting whatever individual talent I might have to his tradition,[55] and so on – while at the same time taking issue with some of Eliot's approaches and solutions.

I first came across *The Waste Land* at the age of sixteen in the lower sixth form. It seemed a masterpiece to me then and still does, despite all the knocks it has taken. Not all teenage appetites last, but this one has done so. Alan Sillitoe has a line in 'The Rats': "The Wasteland was my library and college."[56] I could say the same of Eliot's poem, though not of the working-class social context that Alan was brought up in.[57]

But for all my high admiration, there's plenty about Eliot's work in general and *The Waste Land* in particular that I never liked and can't abide. There's his atrocious class snobbery, and there are his élitist views on culture itself, and his attitudes to sexuality, all of them, in my view, linked directly to his anti-Semitism, which can't be wiped away with the apology that this was the 'merely' typical attitude of a man of his time and class, as Anthony Julius has shown convincingly in his book on Eliot.

Another of my objections to *The Waste Land*, this time primarily poetic – structural and aesthetic, even though it has ethical and moral implications too – is that with its final leap into prayer or blessing at the end, it jumps right out of all the questions and problems it poses and proposes. I think the chant *Shantih shantih shantih*, meaning 'inner peace' in Sanskrit, is too convenient by far.[58] Now, my objection to this line is not because I deny – or am in denial about – visionary experience. Far from it. What I don't like here is the suddenness of the jump into wordless peace. The line is a *deus ex machina*, and marks a cop-out, however subtly and possibly even quasi-ironically it might be controlled and contextualised. Eliot jumps off into religion, meditation, eternity, silence, as if to say, "Enough of language. *I can't do any more with it.* It isn't good enough for me. It's too coarse, too common, too karmic, too bonded and tied, too tortuous and tortured, too trammelled up in 'the ten thousand things'. Pure peace, pure vision, pure silence is better, and higher – a release!"

My objections to Eliot underpin several sections towards the end of the poem. For example, the middle-aged Manager implicitly pokes fun at himself and his own mortality by echoing lines about drowning in 'The

Dry Salvages', thereby parodying Eliotic notions of sainthood, saintliness and martyrdom.[59] Expert wriggler and avoider though the Manager may be, he does insist on operating *inside* history. I parody Eliot elsewhere too. For example his lines "To Carthage then I came / Burning burning burning burning / O Lord thou pluckest me out" in 'The Fire Sermon',[60] together with "Falling towers / Jerusalem Athens Alexandria / Vienna London" in 'What the Thunder Said',[61] are conflated and transformed to produce: "To Cape Town then I came. O Lord Thou. Dresden Nagasaki Sarajevo. Burning Burning Burning."[62] Here I deploy Eliot's own procedures (irony by juxtaposition), not only to parody him but also to make points which are different from his. Eliot's list of cities to me suggests his lamentations for the effects of time and degeneracy on 'high' civilisation. His is a plaint about corruption and decadence. To him, the barbarians outside the gates – and probably the Jews and other aliens within them – are very definitely *them*, not *us*. But the cities I list are specifically chosen as sites of senseless twentieth-century cruelty: racism, bombing, destruction, war, and civil war. We are all in these sites, together, all together. They belong to us all.

JL: What about Eliot and sexuality?

RB: The treatment of sexuality and his attitude to it is problematic throughout his work. Without demeaning Eliot's achievement by carrying out archaeological digs back into his biography, so far as I can make out, encounters with women seem to work positively in his poems only when they're approached on a symbolic level: in the rose garden, as it were. As for *The Waste Land*, all its sexual contacts and encounters strike me as being unhappy, sleazy, unfulfilling or depressing. I think that as a male embedded in a dualistic, puritanical tradition Eliot viewed *all* women as frightening, even terrifying. Though part of my education was set firmly inside a Protestant dualist tradition, I'm not a dualist by any means. For one thing, being Jewish comes in here. I may be wrong, but wouldn't you say that dualism is alien to Jews anyway?

JL: I'd say there's less of an emphasis on an essential physical/spiritual split, but Judaism certainly has its fair share of binary opposites.

RB: That's true, of course, to a degree. I'm thinking specifically of the body-mind split involving denial or denigration of eros. The Judaic tradition, at least as I've experienced it, has little trace of this.

JL: What about other influences, from drama, poetry and fiction? And what about your interests in psychology?

RB: Most of what I think of as 'interesting' influences in this respect are modern or modernist. As I've suggested, among the achievements of modernism in all its expressions was the discovery that when disjunction and disturbance are deliberately brought into an artistic work, when they become integral parts of it, then interruption *itself* becomes a structuring or ordering principle. Along with this, juxtaposition or overlay that is not necessarily logical or causal but, rather, apparently coincidental, results inevitably in parataxis and ellipsis. So non sequiturs – gaps (*écarts*), dashes, breaks, surprises and so on – themselves have a part to play in patterning, as does the unpredictability of consecutive utterances in any series of speech acts. Gaps themselves become not just gaps but seams in the fabric. They may baffle, and their disordering capacities may suggest irrationality, even madness, but they also imply a larger, as-yet-unimagined and perhaps ultimately untappable coherence, which is completely consonant with the theories both of Freud and Jung vis-à-vis subliminal consciousness, and the discoveries of post-Einsteinian physics and astronomy vis-à-vis the stuff and extensiveness of physical reality in space-time.

When it comes to drama, I think of *Waiting for Godot* and much else of Beckett, as well as of Pinter, especially *The Caretaker*, as being part of the brilliant and pioneering research that went on into discovering how such an ordering principle might work artistically. Both Beckett and Pinter have been strong influences in my thinking about dialogue, and even about speech itself. The staccato speech rhythms that occur, for example, when the Manager is experiencing a breakdown, or something close to it, embody these influences.[63]

As for poetic models, apart from *The Waste Land*, the other great modernist poem that absorbs and makes patterns out of apparently disjunctive fragments is *The Cantos* – whose title itself suggests, and perhaps even claims, that the patterns are *musical*. One section of *The Manager* pays direct homage to Pound, with its opening quote from Canto CXVI, "I cannot make it cohere," and "it coheres all right", as well as Canto CXV, "the light sings eternal".[64] Here again, an overall order is implicit and implicate. David Bohm incidentally clarifies that the etymology of the word *implicate* is 'enfolded' or 'folded inward'.[65]

As for prose fiction, the supreme influence on this poem is Joyce. One section in *The Manager* is a parody of Finneganese.[66] The passage occurs in the series of sections in which the Manager is experiencing a mental breakdown, or something close to one. During a session with a psychoanalyst or psychotherapist, the apparently 'crazed' or 'crazy' diction on the left-hand page is translated into the modulated views of the analyst on the right. Parody of course implies evaluation and, here, Joyce-speak is directly associated with breakdown – which, from a Laingian perspective, could also become *breakthrough*.[67] Nor is it an accident that this section ends with a passage conflating two quotations, one from Jung and the other from Marie von Franz, one of Jung's leading disciples, which make it clear that *breakthrough is possible*. "No alternative ... but to face into the dark approaching, unprejudiced and quite innocently, / And find out what its secret aims are and what it holds for you."[68]

JL: In the context of *Postmodernity and its Discontents*, and considering in particular the discontents, would you say more about sexuality and gender in The *Manager*? Much of the poem is concerned with the behaviour and perspectives of men, and with male sexuality. In *The Manager*, did you set out to write specifically as a male about a male?

RB: Yes. I set out deliberately to write about sex and sexuality from a male perspective. I mean this in the broadest possible sense: eros, fantasy, desire, projections, self-images, introjections and internalised images of the other, emotions, behaviour, and relationships. Of course, in *The Manager*, female personae speak too. For example, there are rows between husband and wife and intimate conversations after lovemaking, and there is a good deal of talking in bed.

A key influence in this respect was Doris Lessing's *The Golden Notebook*. I was struck by how powerfully and originally she had charted female sexuality and mental breakdown. I'd never seen these explored together so convincingly in fiction before, including the treatments in *Jane Eyre* and *Wide Sargasso Sea*. *The Golden Notebook* was a kind of giant beacon, a model to emulate – and a challenge too, because as far as heterosexual experience was concerned, I knew of no other work approaching it for her depth or range in the English language – at least in anything I'd read – from any contemporary or recent male novelists, or for that matter from poets of either sex – all of whom seemed stuck somewhere far behind her, perhaps with the exception of Ann Waldman in her celebratory chant-poem *Fast Speaking Woman*.[69] Apart from Joyce, I'd found little imaginative writing to do with sexuality that appealed to me or even seemed relevant or usable, from any male novelists writing in English. I'd long grown out of and away from the character and gender typologies of D. H. Lawrence and Henry Miller, for example. The only recent works of interest by male writers in exploring sexuality were, it seemed to me, homoerotic, for example Allen

Ginsberg's poems and John Rechy's novels. But my interest was in charting heterosexual experience.

Lessing's work was important to me in a third way, too. In her preface to *The Golden Notebook*, she writes that she aimed to write about a main character who was an *artist*. And she adds:

> Those archetypes, the artist and his mirror-image, the businessman, have straddled our culture, one shown as a boorish insensitive, the other as a creator, all excesses of sensibility and suffering and a towering egotism which has to be forgiven because of his products – in exactly the same way of course, as the businessman has to be forgiven for the sake of his.[70]

When I first came across this, I found her notion of artist and businessman as mirror-images – and perhaps *semblables* and *frères* – striking, challenging and provocative. It was a formulation that seemed more subtle and interesting than, for example, Arthur Miller's thinking about the world of business and commerce in *Death of a Salesman*, which seemed two-dimensional by comparison. And though I could never wholly accept Lessing's collation, especially when it came to thinking in depth about her word "products" (what does a businessman actually *produce*, except profit?), she did set me thinking about questions of aspiration, creativity, power, achievement, satisfaction, and fulfilment.

The Golden Notebook, then, gave me some indications of what might be possible. So I set out to take up its challenge in three distinct but interconnected ways. First, to write about male sexuality as Lessing had written about female sexuality, in as wide a range as possible of its varied permutations, as clearly, and, dare I say, as accurately as she'd done. Second, to write about mental breakdown. And third, I wanted to explore her idea of the artist and businessman as dialectally related mirror-images. All of these were factors that led me to explore the subjectivity of a businessman, including his sensibility, his suffering, his egotism – and his sexuality.

JL: So how did these concerns come to be expressed through *The Manager* in practice, in the subject matter and in your treatment of it?

RB: For a start, I wanted the book to be erotic, at least in part, and celebratory. Lyricism and eros are natural partners. In many passages of *The Manager*, eros is enjoyed simply, directly. Shortly after publication, I received an email from Jeremy Hooker. He wrote: "Did I tell you that I think '*The Manager*' is, among other things, the sexiest poem I've read for a very long time?"[71] That pleased me. I also relied on models of eroticism in other traditions: for example from *The Song of Songs*, and from modern poets I admire whose writings are unscarred by the Protestant body-spirit split, especially George Seferis, Pablo Neruda, and Octavio Paz. ... In 1996, Octavio returned to England for a reading with Charles Tomlinson at the Queen Elizabeth Hall, and I met up with him again afterwards with other friends of his for the first time in twenty-five years and for what was to be the last time. Three years earlier, Octavio published a last tour de force, his final affirmation of eros, translated into English as *The Double Flame*. He died in 1998. Paz and Seferis are both models for me in their approaches to sexuality. Neither of them is puritan or dualistic. Every line these poets write is simultaneously sensuous, sensual, erotic, sacred, *fleshed*. Seferis, for example, has these lines in his poem 'Memory, II': "as a woman's face changes yet remains the same / after she strips naked."[72] I would hope that something of the frank, open, steady and joyful clarity of that erotic gaze comes across in *The Manager* too.

I also found that comedy and eros make good partners. I think that there are passages in *The Manager* that can be read as simply comic by both male and female readers. Lyricism combined with comedy sometimes resulted in a kind of wryness, a recognition of pathos, perhaps even a complicit fellowship in sharing the condition of mortality.

Then anger, arguments, bitterness, frustration, pain, guilt and betrayal needed to be included. As did male attitudes to and about women, including both sides of that coin: on the one hand, male coarseness about women and insensitivity towards women (often, exorbitant, gross), and on the other, male sentimentality about women and idealisations of them (equally often, exorbitant and gross). There were also several areas that I wanted to look at which seemed to me 'difficult', that is, which I sometimes found it hard to confront in myself. Consequently, the process of writing was sometimes slow and even painful. One such vulnerable area is the male's longing for the mother, which still strikes me as being more or less inadmissible by most modern adult males. My 'Manager' *does* manage to admit this.[73] Another addresses that ambivalence in male sexuality between wanting power over a woman or women and wanting to be abandoned to a woman's power. And another is what a man can go through after a divorce – or after any relationship has broken up. Associated 'difficult' areas include male sexual possessiveness and jealousy, and the fantasies involved in the experience of jealousy. Some of this material may even be painful to read – for both male and female readers. I've been told by several people that some of these passages are 'too' close to the bone.

At one point, after the break-up of a relationship, the Manager cracks up. But he comes through, somehow 'still managing', to sing of the *Shekhinah*, and to call out "Life, my veil of splendour," and insisting, quoting the words of Seferis, "No it's not the past I'm talking about. I'm trying to talk about love."[74] So, all in all, I hope that *The Manager* presents not just the misery, suffering, embarrassment and pain attendant on sexual love, but some of its funny sides, its pleasures, its joys and compensations too, and even at times its revelations and transformative powers and effects.

JL: And have you found that female readers have responded differently from male readers?

RB: There has been a broad range of responses. The book has received praise and criticism from both female and male readers and reviewers. I think the men who like the poem have been able to identify fairly quickly and easily with the central character, at least to some extent – as in the early reaction I've mentioned from Ed Engle in 1979 and the later one from Jeremy Hooker. Obviously, 'the Manager', being male himself, isn't so easy for women to identify with. So I wonder if women readers who have liked the poem, have done so in slightly or subtly different ways from the men who have liked it. I don't know the answer to this, or even whether it's answerable. Elaine Feinstein has called it "a remarkable work".[75]

JL: Finally, you've mentioned influences from drama. There are clearly dramatic elements in *The Manager*. Has the poem even been performed?

RB: A one-off reading/performance was held on the final night of the fiftieth Stratford-upon-Avon Poetry Festival, on 24 August 2003, commissioned by the Festival director, Roger Pringle. Melanie[76] and I made a selection of forty-four sections into a script. I then made parts for three main voices. The reading took place on a Sunday evening and the actors, Jasper Britton, Alexandra Gilbreath and Henry Goodman, were members of the Royal Shakespeare Company. I gave myself a few bit-lines too here and there. On the Saturday night before the reading, Jasper played Petruchio and Alexandra played Kate in *The Taming of the Shrew*, which we went to see. So the whole experience was very exciting. On the Sunday morning we had only a few hours to rehearse. At one point in the rehearsal, I asked if a particular speech needed clarification. Gently but firmly, Henry Goodman told me to stop worrying, adding that as actors they knew what they were doing. It was their job to understand and interpret text. I had full confidence in them and was happy to keep out of the way.

The actors were brilliant. The entire experience was exhilarating for several reasons. First, to hear the text come alive thanks to their interpretations. Second, to know that the inflections and emphases I'd aimed at were actually *there*, in the text itself, not just in my head as authorial intentions. And third, to experience the audience's response.

JL: Thank you for this, I think we've shown how your view of *The Manager*, as its author, might help to inform and even illuminate a reader's understanding. The author isn't quite dead yet, as Barthes would have us believe.

Cambridge
December 2001 – January 2002
and November 2012 – January 2013

Notes

1. See also 44 in this book, note 40.
2. RB 1980 [1], *Learning to Talk*: 17.
3. RB 2011 [2], *The Manager*, section 88: 140–141.
4. RB 2003, 'Sketches With Voice-Overs' 7: 17. See also "the fourth person singular" in the short poem 'Mi dva', in RB 2011 [5], *Under Balkan Light*: 29; and 'Being aloof' and 'Pronouns' in RB 2015 [1], *Notness*: 20.
5. RB 2011 [2], *The Manager*, section 17: 28.
6. *Ibid.* section 97: 154.
7. Frye: 326.
8. The phrase "minute particular" is William Blake's. See Foster Damon: 280–281.
9. Roethke, 'The Waking': 104.
10. "Polimorfan-peverzan", RB 1990, *Menadžer*: 9. See also Brown.
11. RB 2011 [2], *The Manager*, section 88: 141.
12. Zygmunt Bauman's full (unpublished) comment was: "Many have tried, and many more will try, to crack the mystery of our condition, which is unlike any other we or our fathers or mothers have ever known before. Most have failed: our experience seems to escape any nets sewn of words which have been forced into stiff definitions. But images often say more and, unlike arguments, may be used as mirrors to hold up to the countenance of our experience. Richard Burns is master-supreme of images. His images speak, and they speak of truth that cannot be grasped in any other way" (RB, personal correspondence, December 1998).
13. Paz 1975: 131 and 132. Paz's comments predate Bauman's by at least fifteen years.
14. Glen Cavaliero, English poet (b. 1927), Fellow-commoner of St. Catherine's College, Cambridge. Personal correspondence, 2001, undated.
15. Nicholas Mosley, English novelist (b. 1923). Personal correspondence, 2001, undated.
16. Sir Peter Parker (1924–2002), English businessman and polymath, who pioneered modern management methods at British Rail. Personal correspondence, 2001, undated. See his obituary in *The Guardian*, 30 April 2002. http://www.theguardian.com/news/2002/apr/30/guardianobituaries. Consulted December 28, 2015.
17. A reference to the title of RB's second book. See note 2 above.

18 See RB 2013, *Imagems (1)*: 26: "I have coined the term 'imagem' with the meaning 'nexus, web, net, body, corpus, etc., of integrally associated ideas and images'. An imagem is composite, complex and polysemic. It also implies 'unit of imagery', comparable to the word mythologem ('unit of myth or mythology')." For further clarifications see RB 2012 [2], 'A Nimble Footing on the Coals – Tin Ujević, Lyricist: Some English Perspectives'. http://www.budilica.com/arhiva/3/richard-berengarten-a-nimble-footing-on-the-coals-tin-ujevic-lyricist-some-english-perspectives.html. Consulted December 14, 2015.

19 Giuseppe Ungaretti's shortest poem.

20 Keats, the last line of his sonnet 'On First Looking into Chapman's Homer'.

21 Dante, *Inferno* V, ll. 136.

22 'Orpheus Singing' and 'Noon' in RB 1972 [1], *Double Flute*: 26–27 and 38–41.

23 'Ys' in RB 2011 [1], *For the Living*: 97–103.

24 All published in RB 2011 [1], *For the Living*.

25 *Note from RB*: The image of a "flattening out" of time is deployed by Bauman to describe the experience of time in a postmodern society, which I think aptly suits *The Manager*. See 1997: 67 and 89–91. On his distinction between the 'event' and the 'episode', see in particular 91.

26 'Am I interrupting you', RB 2011 [2], *The Manager*, section 26: 40–41.

27 *Ibid.* section 87: 138–139.

28 Peter Mansfield, 'Credo': "It is not our business / we who have set out / to ask formulable questions / but in our passing to distil / answers from the lies of circumstance. // In the forest we must hear / behind the noise the young whisper / and scent not only this roebuck but him / in the next valley or the afternext / dissatisfied: // our bodies a nostril and a leap / our minds the only formless question / and acquiescence, in the ritual / of expectancy not hope / We are not liars. We are not priests." Text provided by RB. See also 43 above, note 13.

29 Stevens, 'The Idea of Order at Key West': 106.

30 The "person from Porlock" interrupted Coleridge's composition of his poem 'Kubla Khan'. Coleridge 1816, 'Preface'.

31 A few years later, *Carcanet* was taken over by Michael Schmidt in Oxford and gradually expanded by him into the well-known poetry publishing house.

32 RB 1983 [3], 'Thirty Extracts from *The Manager*'.

33 RB 1980 [2], 'Extracts from 'The Manager''. Barry MacSweeney: English poet and journalist (1948–2000).

34 *Poetry South East* 5, 1980: 'Intro'.

35 *The Guardian*, July 19, 1989.

36 Jasna B. Mišić, RB's second wife.

37 Personal correspondence, c. 1990.

38 Jeremy Hooker (b. 1941), Anglo-Welsh poet and critic.

39 Antoinette Moses (b. 1946), playwright, and producer of FLY (Festival of Literature for Young People), 2013.

40 Aude Gotto directed The King of Hearts, an independent gallery and arts centre in Norwich from October 1990 to December 2010. During this time she published several books of poetry.

41 For his agent's list of rejections of *Under the Volcano*, see Lowry: 419.

42 See Coe: 37: "In the first-ever-published full-length study of Beckett, *Die Unzulänglichkeit der Sprache* of 1957, Niklaus Gessner observes that he once asked the writer why he had abandoned English for French. The reply – which, characteristically, was given in French rather than in English – was 'En français, c'est plus facile d'écrire sans style.'" ["In French, it's easier to write without style."]

43 See also the remarks on the need "to eliminate any remnants of 'my own voice'" in 'Arijana's Thread', RB 2011 [4], *In a Time of Drought*: 77.

44 Bernstein: 262 (for index; see "linguistic code").

45 RB 2011 [2], *The Manager*, section 30: 46–47.

46 Graham 1970 and 1977.

47 For example, RB 2011 [2], *The Manager*, section 86: 135–137.

48 RB 2011 [2], *The Manager*, section 27: 42.

49 See note 38 above.

50 Personal correspondence, c. 1990.

51 RB 1990, *Menadžer*: 8.

52 Eliot 1972 [1922]: 29, ll. 62–63.

53 Dante, *Inferno* III, ll. 55–57.

54 Dante in Norton's translation: 28.

55 See Eliot 1961 [1917].

56 Sillitoe, 'The Rats', part 3, VI: 181.

57 Sillitoe's appraisal appears on the back cover of all English editions of *The Manager*, abbreviated from a personal letter, February 4, 1990: "I've just finished reading your book, and I think it's a wonderful and very special piece of work, something new, deep, and not beyond anybody's comprehension or enjoyment. It's a sad chronicle – love, death and renewal. But I'm still under its very strong influence, and can't be literary or specific about it."

58 Eliot 1972 [1922]: 43, l. 433.
59 RB 2011 [2], *The Manager*, section 97: 154.
60 Eliot, *op. cit.*: 39, ll. 307–309.
61 *Ibid.*: 41, ll. 373–375.
62 RB 2011 [2], *The Manager*, section 31: 48–49.
63 *Ibid.* sections 71: 114, and 75 and 76: 120–121.
64 *Ibid.* section 92: 146. See also Pound: 25–27.
65 Bohm: 177.
66 RB 2011 [2], *The Manager*, section 78: 124–125.
67 See Laing 1965, and Laing and Esterton 1970.
68 See Jung 1968 [1959]: 88–89; and Franz 1979 [1964]: 167. See also RB 2011 [2], *The Manager*: 168–169, note to section 78.
69 Waldmann: 1–47.
70 Lessing: 12.
71 Email, January 10, 2002.
72 Seferis 1969: 373.
73 RB 2011 [2], *The Manager*, section 62: 101.
74 *Ibid.* sections 98: 155 and 99: 156. See also Seferis 1969, 'The Thrush' III: 331.
75 *Ibid. The Manager*, cover comment.
76 Melanie Rein, RB's wife.

Aspects of the Work

Richard Berengarten and Ruth Halkon

The interview took place at Richard Berengarten's house in Cambridge during two hours of a dark January afternoon. When I arrived, Richard showed me into the sitting room of his house off Mill Road. He told me that it had once been a corner shop. An open door gave a glimpse of the writer's study, whose every available surface was crammed with books, both Richard's and those of others – his father's cello in the corner asserting the necessary, creative link between the living and the dead. What had started with a few questions about the release of the new *Critical Companion* to his writings, as our conversation found fluency and depth, gradually became an exploration and opening out of his works. I made a full transcript of the recording between February and April 2011. The text that follows was created in July 2011 by expanding and modifying the original interview through email correspondence with Richard, in a process of gradual and collaborative editing. So the result combines nearly all the original interview – especially its many-branching interconnected threads – with the richer expansion, detail and clarity that writing involves.

RH

1

Ruth Halkon: What was your reaction when you heard that the *Critical Companion* to your writings, with thirty-three contributors from around the world, was being prepared?

Richard Berengarten: I was delighted.

RH: How does it feel to read all these articles about your poems?

RB: The very fact that one has essays written about one's work gives one the sense that it is 'out there'. If other people are writing about it, one knows that there's solidity to the work and that it exists apart from oneself. That is satisfying because quite often, if one's writing isn't getting any feedback at all, one can feel lonely. Also, a good critic might offer slants or perceptions that you didn't realise were available. So that kind of reading enables a further deepening into your own work. It is very positive, since you're encouraged to do more, to go deeper and further.

RH: What is it like to have this kind of recognition and attention to your work?

RB: To have some attention is helpful. It encourages one to do still better. To feel that one has no recognition at all can be lonely. Though what one means by 'recognition' is interesting in itself. The world of poetry is very diverse and fragmented at the moment. There is a clear poetic Establishment, and this book does not make me a member.

RH: Would you like to join the British Establishment?

RB: Absolutely not.

RH: You said you see yourself as a European poet writing in English. Could you talk a bit more about that?

RB: I first made that statement on the cover-flap of *Against Perfection*, a selection of poems published in 1999.[1] There were several interconnected reasons for making it. First, my sense of myself and my writing has always been international. Second, I have travelled widely through Europe since I was a teenager and have lived and worked for long periods in three other European countries, Greece, Italy, and former Yugoslavia. Third, when I came to that formulation, twelve years ago, I did so reactively. Part of my reaction at that time was against provincialism and insularity, the Little Englandism associated with Philip Larkin for example, the nastier edges of which are racist. This went back to a series of questions I had asked myself at the beginning of the 1990s, soon after I returned from Yugoslavia, when I was doing a lot of thinking about identities and overlapping identities. The process was triggered by a letter from my stepdaughter Jelena, who was originally Yugoslav, but had acquired a British passport when her mother married me eight years previously. Jelena wrote to me when she was nineteen and working in Hong Kong during her gap year. She asked me, "Who am I? I suddenly feel ashamed of being Serbian." Clearly, she was asking a serious set of questions about her own identity. I had to think long and hard before I answered her.

RH: How did you answer her?

RB: My first answer was: never be ashamed of where you're from, because that's where your roots are. However, even to begin to be able to answer adequately, I was obliged to think through her question for myself. So I started puzzling about my own identity and formulated for myself a sort of hierarchy, a tree. At the top was 'being human'. I was thinking of 'being human' in the sense of the Biblical idea of man as 'a little lower than the angels' and the Renaissance idea of man as being noble and good, as reflected in Hamlet's speech "What a piece of work is a man" – where "piece-of-work" has the idea of *capolavoro*, 'masterpiece'.[2]

The next thing that struck me was: I'm a poet. Beneath the category 'human', for me it was clear that being a poet was the first of my other subcategories. I think that I would have been a poet, whatever my first language or whether I had been born male or female. I view my poetry as a vocation, a destiny. However Romantic that might sound, that's how I see it. After that, I'm male, not female. I enjoy being a male, but I have female *personae* in my poems too: the poem's voice is sometimes a woman's. Below that, I put the category of 'English language speaker', since this is my language. After that come things like my English nationality and my Jewish identity. Things like nationality and religion come lower down in the identity-set for me, unlike for Larkin, whom I think would have put his Englishness at or near the top. Anyway, my Englishness is mediated too through my being Anglo-Jewish, which instantly complicates my relationship to England. Identity to me then is irreducibly multifaceted. It is also, inevitably, hierarchised, morally and ethically.

RH: You've talked about your unwillingness to define yourself as an English poet, which implies an insularity and homogeneity that you react against. Surely the classification of yourself as a European poet leaves you open to similar accusations, though on a different scale?

RB: You're absolutely right. But it took me a while to see that. I have come to see that envisioning and claiming a European identity for myself is in its way just as partial, just as limiting, just as narrowly exclusive, and just as 'privileged' in the negative sense, as identifying myself with 'Englishness' would have been.

It's not just that the borders and edges of Europe are porous, or that as a language English is global, but that eurocentricity is no longer acceptable either, for many reasons. First, the people who live in Europe today come from all over the world, just as the people who live in, say, America do. Poetry is international, universal. Whether oral or written, poetry belongs organically inside every language and every culture. Like people, and like species of animals and plants, poetry is constantly migrating, transforming, mutating. These days, you only have to go along to any one of hundreds of annual international poetry festivals to discover that "no man is an island". We are all "a part of the main".³ Interconnected. To me, the implications of these simple facts are fundamental and far-reaching. They are a good deal more interesting and relevant than the ins-and-outs of literary fashion or any poetic squabblings in this or that particular language that people get het up about. My models for this way of thinking are William Blake, and, in a different way, Gerard Manley Hopkins, and also Walt Whitman – even though Whitman specifically identified his vision of universality with the potential of America, which if you misread it, as many people do, leads to an awful kind of all-American jingoism.

Being interested in universalism necessarily involves love of particulars too. I've recently written a short poem hinting at that, as part of my current work-in-progress on the *Yijing*, entitled 'In the spirit of Walt Whitman'. In that poem I talk about being interested in localities, villages, small things, the different things that people are and do, across the world – what Blake called "the minute particulars".⁴ This is related to what Hopkins means by "instress" and "inscape".⁵ So, details, localities, particulars, yes. But not nations. We are now all irrevocably international.

☙

RH: You strongly imply those ideas in the poem 'The Blue Butterfly', in which you describe your "pink, educated, ironical left hand", and then your "international bloody human hand", which is sanctified by the figure of the butterfly sitting on your finger.⁶ Why is the blue butterfly so significant, and why did you choose the hand as a synecdoche for your whole identity?

RB: The little blue butterfly that sat on my finger outside the war museum at Kragujevac came out of the blue, in every sense, and it was a life-changing experience. The butterfly 'chose me', in a sense – I felt, at the precise moment that it happened, that I was being 'called' to write. The imprint lasted twenty years, until I'd finished *The Blue Butterfly*. A long-lasting imprint, for such a tiny creature.

RH: Could you say more about the significance of the hand?

RB: The lyric, the 'Blue Butterfly' came straight out. One is gifted with such a poem. When it happens, it's the purest inspiration one can have. I wrote it in the evening and, come morning, I didn't want to touch it. That was in 1985. The theme of hands goes further back for me, though.

In 1979, when I was in my mid-30s, I'd gone to New York, arriving on St Patrick's Day to stay with a friend I had met in Venice, Johnny MacLean, and his wife. It was my first time in New York and the very first time I had ever experienced jetlag. We had gone out for dinner and drinks, and I was woken up in the middle of the night by a police siren. I was in a state of heightened excitement and, probably straight out of a dream, I wrote down some lines about my hands – all starting with the lines, "these hands are…" as a sort of pounding, drumming refrain. Curiously the motif of hands eventually found its way into 'The blue butterfly'. But not in any deliberate or deliberative way: the insect settling on my hand was a *datum*, a given, a gift.

More curiously still, that process is still going on. Later, I gradually, worked out a form for a sequence of poems about hands: a ten-line lyric, divided into two stanzas of five lines. Ten lines, ten fingers: two stanzas, two hands. I'm currently working on a series of chapbooks, each of which contains twenty of these hand poems. They've been published by a small press in New Zealand called the Earl of Seacliff. The series is gradually evolving into a book whose overall title will be *Manual*. The book will consist of the first hundred poems from the chapbooks.[7]

Hands are fascinating: they are the agents of the will, of the mind. They make, create and destroy; they play musical instruments and operate machines, which are themselves all extensions of hands. Hands are important metonyms for the whole human endeavour. I'm also fascinated by the *chakra* points in hands, and recently I've been learning *taiji* and getting into some Tantric and Daoist practices. Hands communicate energy. … And, curiously, it was only much later that I consciously connected the hands in *Manual* with the "writing hand" as the 'site' of *The Blue Butterfly*. So human hands, I discovered, are a recurrent preoccupation in my writing.

༒

RH: In the poem 'Tree',[8] you use the tree as a metonym, a symbol, in the way that you use hands – relating it to Adam Kadmon and Kabbalistic traditions, to Christian traditions, and then to Hindu and Tantric ideas. Why does this poem, and indeed why do many of your poems, have such a range of religious imagery? Do you consider yourself to be a religious poet?

RB: I do, in a way. Blake wrote that "all religions are one."[9] If you put 'all religions' together, you create a composite picture of the first attempts of humans to find *meaning*. 'Religio', the Latin antecedent of 'religion', means 're-binding'. The Indo-European root of the word 'religion' is the same as for words like 'yoke', 'join' and 'conjugal'. The poet is always trying to 'yoke', to 'join', to find connectivity, and that is engrained in the structure – and stuff – of metaphor itself, connecting different semantic fields. And of language itself, and of experience itself. Everything *is* connected and the poet realises these connections. Pound reminded himself of that, quasi-tragically, at the end of his *Cantos*: "It coheres all right – even if my notes do not cohere."[10] As Wordsworth says in *The Prelude*, "I mean to speak / Of that interminable building reared / By observation of affinities / In objects where no brotherhood exists / To passive minds."[11] "Observation of affinities" will inevitably result in perception of connectivity, yoking: *religio*. As is assumed in the entire endeavours of science and mathematics, there is pattern, and there are inherent, intrinsic laws governing pattern. This sense of pattern, connectedness, connectivity, is inherent in all poetry. The physicist David Bohm calls this "implicate order".[12]

So my interest in religion is nothing to do with pietism or holiness but in the way it brings ideas, thoughts, images, phenomena together, because that's what I think poetry is all about. If you don't look at the great religions, you're missing out. The great religious texts of the world have all inspired great poetry: some of the Bible and the Vedas, not to mention the epic of Gilgamesh, and also the brilliant Daoist teachings that are both religion and philosophy, especially the Laozi and the Zhuangzi. It seems stupid to limit oneself and one's work by not looking at religions.

RH: How does this interest in different religions link to your earlier claim that we are all irrevocably international?

RB: My interest in different religions, as well as languages and cultures, suggests not only a sense of identity that 'nationality' can ever quite encompass, but a composite identity I would call *universalist*, in that I see that poetry is relevant to everybody on the planet – of course operating through their particular culture and history, but not limited by those particulars. I think the most important thing in the twenty-first century is humanity. As I've said, I think this has to be combined with what Blake called the "minute particulars".

RH: What about one's sense of 'rootedness' – belonging?

RB: A well-explored and conventional idea is that a good or great poet needs to be 'rooted' in the 'soil' of the country in which he or she was born, and that his or her poems, like those of, say, Whitman, William Carlos

Williams, W. B. Yeats, or the plays of Synge, must therefore celebrate that land. Williams writes a book called *In the American Grain*. And Hugh MacDiarmid celebrates this kind of patriotism with a four-line lyric: "The rose of all the world is not for me. / I want for my part / Only the little white rose of Scotland / That smells sharp and sweet – and breaks the heart."[13] The sweeter smell of this kind of patriotism is, of course, something we can all relish – despite its sometimes teetering on the edge of sentimentality. We can respect it and we indulge in it. But the negative side of patriotism is nationalism, which attributes the particular qualities of that group of people to the soil – and this mentality is precisely the one that can end up with racism vis-à-vis whichever people who don't belong to that group. Worse still, the power of 'soil' leads to that of 'blood and soil' (*Blut und Boden*). We know very well, and to our cost, what the Nazis made of that.

More than that, I think we need to move beyond it, beyond nationality, beyond nationalism, which we know is dangerous. The origin of both words, incidentally, is in Latin, *nascere*, 'to be born'. The Slavonic languages have a more or less identical pattern: In Serbian, Croatian and Bosnian, for example (all of which used to be called 'Serbo-Croat'), the word for 'nation' is *narod* and for nationality *narodnost*. The word *rod* means 'birth'. So your parents are your *roditelji* and your birthday is your *rodjendan*. But *narod* means not only 'nation' but also 'people', 'tribe', 'race' and even 'religious group'. So *narodnost* comes to mean, in practice, something like 'ethnicity'. But consider what extremes of violent emotion and inhumane actions were provoked in the wars that broke up Yugoslavia in the 1990s, *because* people's thinking, belief systems and behaviour were actually rooted in those terms – and limited by them. I lived in former Yugoslavia, as you know. We should retrieve warning lessons from what happened there.

RH: If that's the case, then, who should you as a poet speak to, if you cannot speak to and for just 'the English'?

RB: I'm not so sure that we can know exactly who 'the English' *are* these days. And anyway, the English language speaks to vast numbers of people across the globe. As it is, I want to speak to and for all kinds of people. The main editor to the *Companion*, Norman Jope, wrote in his introduction that my work operates within many different "canons",[14] and I'm delighted with this observation. I go to Greece and my book of poems dedicated to George Seferis, *Black Light,* has been translated 'back' into Greek[15] and a Greek writer says that it gives her a frisson of her own childhood.[16] It could be argued that my poems translated into Serbian belong to a Serbian and south Slavonic as much as a English Serbophile (or 'Yugophilic') tradition. There's an Italian writer who says that I'm a Mediterranean poet;[17] and a Jewish poet says that my *Blue Butterfly* celebrates Jewish identity in a new, proud way.[18] Nobody has said that I'm particularly 'English', but I think some of my poems, such as 'Croft Woods', are very English indeed. I'm now working on a single long sequence of poems, a long-standing project, which is based on the *Yijing* and is intended as homage to the Chinese cultural tradition.[19] Does that give you an idea of where I'm at? I would call myself a 'universalist' if one could take out of that term any suggestion of ego-tripping. I've explored the notion of universality in several texts, most recently in the epigraph to the new edition of *The Manager*,[20] and at the end of the introduction to the 'Volta' project.[21] I would advocate 'universalism' as the next move that needs to be made in the wake of post-modernism.

୬

RH: You write in *The Blue Butterfly* about the dead, who are voiceless, and the experience of walking on their skulls buried beneath the soil, and about how your poetry gives them a voice.[22] You also mention the way that your poetry gives voice to those anonymous dead in mass graves around the world. Then, in your essay, 'A Grove of Trees and a Grove of Stones',[23] you write about the dangers of severing the connection between the living and the dead – the severing of this connection allowed the Nazis and Serbians to massacre others. You say that, in order to avoid such atrocities we should remember the dead, remember the past and avoid repeating their mistakes. Then, in the poem, 'The Voice in the Garden', you also write about their connection to the living: "[T]he dead have not gone elsewhere. They are here / inside us. ..."[24] In this way, you seem to suggest that our past, the past of our ancestors is integrally bound up with – bound *into* – our present. Have I got that right?

RB: Yes, you have. Why are the dead central and important in my work? One of the strands in my relation to the dead has to do with post-Holocaust (post-*Shoah*) consciousness. I first discovered the facts of the Holocaust at the age of thirteen, when I was taken to a theatre production of *The Diary of Anne Frank* by my mother. (I've written an essay, a kind of personal memoir, on this, which hasn't yet been published, entitled '"My" Anne Frank'.) That event coincided with the onset of puberty and with a series of shifts and changes in all the outward and inward aspects of my life. One is very open and impressionable at that age. The play affected me profoundly, it moved me, incomparably. The fact that all those people were captured and killed spoke to me very directly, as it would speak to anybody, but particularly too, because of my Jewish identity. I found myself thinking that Anne Frank was a *fellow* of mine, my kin. And then I found myself writing *to* her in the teenage journal that I started, soon after seeing the play and after reading the *Diary*. It was the beginning of my poetry. The dead at that point seemed living to me, and I felt the burden of those people who had been killed for no reason other than that they were Jewish. Since they could no longer speak for themselves, who would speak for them?

Later, I read English at Cambridge. One of the great things about the Cambridge degree (as you know) is that it gives you a sense of the historical panorama of English Literature from around the time of Chaucer to the present day. You gain a sense of tradition, and the moment you start exploring tradition, you begin to understand what the dead have contributed to us. To me at that time, Eliot's essay 'Tradition and the Individual Talent' seemed to hit the nail on the head: a new writer modifies tradition; therefore tradition is alive in that writer. So, when I was an undergraduate, I began to understand that if I were to become a poet myself, I would have to absorb that tradition. And one way you communicate with the dead is through the act of reading. Let's say I'm reading George Eliot's *Daniel Deronda*. That book is immediate to me, that dead writer's ideas and thoughts enter my present. The great lines of poetry from the past are very much presences for me.

At that time I also started thinking about how we use past, present and future, in a linear frame, to set up distinctions that confer a particular version of reality. But the presence of the past is as important as the pastness of the past, and the future lurks in the present as well. George Seferis, who is a master for me, says "the living are not enough for me ... / I have to ask the dead / in order to go on farther."[25] Sometimes contemporary discussion or news can seem banal and a bit meaningless, compared to the voices of the dead, the voices of great poets for example.

RH: Tell me more about this poetic communion between the living and the dead?

RB: When it comes to poetry, and its transmission and absorption, I sometimes have the curious sense of linear time being set in reverse, of time's arrow taking a different set of directions: the sense that, somehow, poetry is addressed not only to readers in the present and future – but that there's a curious way in which poetry is addressed to the dead too. I've seen this happening at funerals: I remember a daughter of a man who had died standing up and turning to the coffin as she spoke – she said 'you' to the coffin – as Shakespeare's Antony does to Julius Caesar – just as if her father was alive. And at that moment, so he was for her: his presence was alive to her and in her. I wonder if the realities of present, past and future are far more intricately interconnected than we think. That is a huge subject: on the one hand it takes in issues developed in post-quantum-theory physics and on the other the theory of synchronicity.

A good recent book on this from the point of view of a quantum physicist is Huw Price's *Time's Arrow and Archimedes' Point*. He offers different models for the directionality of time's flow. This is a respected and tough-minded academic philosopher, not a mystic. As for Jung's concept of synchronicity, I think this is of equal importance for our understanding of the world. There's a mass of exciting literature on this, including books by Marie-Louise von Franz and, more recently, Roderick Main and Joseph Cambray. I think poets should be alert and alive to these issues. For one thing, they're exciting. Our present scientific understanding both of how consciousness works and of how events and phenomena in the world are correlated is in its infancy. We need to bring together the discoveries of physics and of psychology. The poet's role is crucial. Incidentally, you mentioned *The Blue Butterfly*, and the way that it is connected with the dead. As I've mentioned, that book was based on a powerful experience of synchronicity. The book is consciously and articulately addressed to the living, the dead and the unborn.

RH: Your friend Octavio Paz said something similar: "For the first time in our history, we are contemporaries of all humanity."[26] Why do you think that this idea is so prominent, has become so relevant now, rather than, say, a hundred years ago?

RB: That's a good question. And your gloss on that statement of Octavio's from *The Labyrinth of Solitude* accords with my own reading of it. I'm not sure whether Octavio was actually intending to include the dead in his phrase "all humanity", but for myself I think "all humanity" must include the dead and the unborn, as well as the living. He may or may not have meant the dead.[27]

RH: The phrase "contemporaries of all of humanity" suggests that.

RB: Yes, it does. Octavio wrote that around 1949. In the nineteenth century it became fashionable to collect antiquities and folklore. All over Europe, you had people like the Grimm brothers in Germany, Vuk

Karadžić in Serbia and Francis Child in the British Isles, collecting folklore and folk songs and oral tradition, which at the time they called 'antiquities'. Through the nineteenth century, and into the twentieth century, up to the time of James Frazer, and far beyond, the notion of the 'primitive' comes into scholarship, especially the new disciplines of anthropology and psychology, as a core ideological element. You find it in Edward Tylor's *Primitive Culture* in the 1870s and even as late as Eric Hobsbaum's hugely overrated and superficial studies on banditry published nearly a century later, in 1959 and 2000 – the assumption that we Europeans or Westerners are unquestionably more 'civilised', and so implicitly 'more human', than those 'primitives' whom we study. But Lévi-Strauss exploded that kind of thinking in his book *La Pensée Sauvage*. In English this book is known as *The Savage Mind*, which is almost as unfortunate in its pejorative associations as a title like 'The Primitive Mind' would have been. But the English fails to capture the far richer *double entendre* of the original. In French, *pensée* means both 'thought' and 'pansy', while 'sauvage' means not only 'savage' or 'primitive' but also 'wild' as distinct from 'tame'. So the French title is rich and beautiful. It also means 'The Wild Pansy'.

RH: So what changed?

RB: Around the time of Lévi-Strauss, there was a realisation that so-called 'primitives' are people of no less intelligence, no less human than 'we' are. And this central idea has been far more fully developed since the Second World War – particularly in the wake of the Nazi Holocaust – especially through the Universal Declaration of Human Rights, adopted by the United Nations in 1948. The idea of *humanitas*, of *anthropos*, of *covečnost*, *čovečanstvo*, of *mankind*, had been growing for centuries, of course, but this is when it is first articulated and adopted, as it were, universally, by the community of nations outside of particular religious creeds: that we're *all* human, and there's no group of people less human than any other. In the core of the Communist tradition there's also this fine belief that everyone is equal, that everyone deserves an equal chance. This is a profound discovery, a moral advance – despite the fact that Communists have done vile things, that vile persecutions were committed under Communist regimes, just as under Fascist ones – and under democracies too. If you think back through the history of colonialism, for example of the treatment of Maoris and Aborigines by the English, of millions of people in Africa by the Europeans and north Americans, of the Evenks and Evens and other Asian peoples by Turkic tribes, and then by Russians, of all indigenous Americans by white

European settlers – the length of the list of persecutions and exploitations is just horrendous. The core of this behaviour is a mindset that condones the treatment of 'other' people as though they were sub-human. But, clearly, they're not. Any kind of persecution of particular groups isn't just morally wrong and stupid and evil; it represents an intellectual and imaginative failure – to understand that humanity involves all humans. My humanness and your humanness are linked. Archbishop Desmond Tutu says this when he talks about the concept and practice of 'Ubuntu' in South Africa.[28] Actual *practice* of the idea of 'all humanity being one' is relatively new.

RH: Isn't the idea of all humanity being one similar to the Christian idea, love thy neighbour as you love yourself?

RB: Who is one's neighbour? The history of Christianity makes it clear that some neighbours were considerably more neighbourly than others. Now, though, it is *anybody* who is human. Anybody and everybody. One of the great things about humanity at the moment is that we see ourselves as part of the same human race.

Not only that, every poet has some interlocutor in mind, some ideal reader or listener. For me, incidentally, an interlocutor is by definition singular, for two reasons. First, because poetic communication is always necessarily directed out of the fulness, the completeness, of one person's humanity into the fulness/completeness of another's. Secondly, because the act of receiving a poem can only be done by an individual, in the core, as it were, of an individual's uniqueness.[29] So, with this in mind, I wouldn't want to suggest that a poet should write for anyone he or she doesn't want to write for. But even taking that point, I think it's a pity if a poet of our time doesn't grasp the full power and gentleness of the word 'human' in its fullest and most recent range of connotations. This idea first surfaced spontaneously and with full force for me in a short poem I wrote in January 1976, to celebrate the last quarter of the twentieth century.[30]

2

RH: Your poem 'Avebury' begins with an "ancestorless" man standing among the stones of the stone circle.[31] Through a progression using sculpture – you begin with the Willendorf Venus, via the Nike of Samothrace to Michelangelo's Prisoners – you draw a path through history, connecting the ancestorless men to his ancestors by showing him the past.

RB: That's a lovely way of putting it. I think I was really feeling my way then, I was magnetised by the images. I couldn't have put it like that, but it's an excellent observation. By "ancestorless", by the way, I meant something like 'without any deep sense of history'.

RH: One of the contributors to the *Companion* mentions that they're all sort of faceless: the Prisoners are half-formed, they have no features, and the Willendorf Venus's face is covered by her hair.

RB: This is a critic and poet called Neli Moody. And it is an interesting essay.[32]

RH: Do you think her observation is correct, and if so, is it significant? Are you aiming at some kind of universalisation or, rather, universality, by missing out the features that would identify these sculptures as individuals? Or is something else going on?

RB: Do you mean because of the facelessness of the Prisoners and the Nike?

RH: Yes, and of the Venus too.

RB: Well, all of them do have their faces or heads hidden or cut off or lost, though I don't think I was in any way consciously selecting them on that basis. The two "musicians" in the last of this series of five fragmented sonnets that are embedded into the poem are the Cycladic flute player and lyre player, marble figures, both in the National Museum in Athens. That Cycladic style is very refined, very abstracted, and the figures have an almost Brancusi-like quality. Their heads are there, but no features are visible.[33] [*RB shows me a plaster replica of the Willendorf Venus.*] The Willendorf Venus is very different: she's much more fulsome, physical, earthy. She has her head bowed over her breasts, tucked down towards them, almost nestling there. She seems completely self-involved in her own innerness; the whole of her is intent on the fertility aspect.

Rachel Levy's book *The Gate of Horn* was an important source for me in writing 'Avebury', especially the chapter in that book on 'The Mother Goddess and the Dead', from which a lot of my ideas and images in the poem are developed. The patterning on the Willendorf Venus's bowed head obviously represents hair, which has been wound around her head, and possibly plaited; and the style is called 'beehive' hair. She has no features, *because* her head is bowed and what's being concentrated on are the breasts, the hips, as in other figurines of that period, like the Venus of Dolní Věstonice

– a photo of which incidentally is on the cover of *Manual 4*, together with my hand next to the original sculpture in the museum in Brno.[34] These statuettes, from around thirty thousand years ago, are obviously goddess figures. Both Erich Neumann and Marija Gimbutas have explored these figures in major studies of the fertility goddess.[35] Are you saying I'm trying to reclaim some sort of individuality, or to deny it, with the sequence of 'fragmented sonnets' on these figures?

RH: You do give them some individual features, for example the Nike with her "incredible arrogant breasts".[36] She's ready to fly. You give her a kind of personality. But does the fact that she's faceless mean that she's something many people could project themselves onto and identify with?

RB: I'm not sure about that. I'm not sure that that idea was conscious enough in me at the time I wrote those little pieces for me to be able to say now with certainty that I was connecting facelessness with some kind of 'universality'. If anything, I would have thought that if I'd been doing that, it would have been a rather reductive kind of universality. The face, and especially the eyes in the face, are after all the keys to our humanness – according to Emmanuel Lévinas anyway – and I'd go along with his ideas concerning the face.[37]

Perhaps it'd be interesting to explore another way of looking at it too. At that time, I was exploring a kind of fragmented, paratactic, gnomic diction, derived partly from Paz and partly from Charles Olson – and further back, of course, from Pound's *Cantos*. In retrospect, it's clearer to me now – even if only a little clearer – that the approach I followed in writing 'Avebury' was to allow statements to well up through me, out into the poem, rather than imposing too much conscious patterning on them or over them. Which is not to say they weren't closely 'worked', but rather that I didn't analyse (i.e. over-analyse) them.

Rather than the face, what I was more strongly interested in those figures, as a male, was the female anatomy. The line, "incredible arrogant breasts" to me is erotic – the male desiring the full femaleness of that figure. These are fertility figurines: they're meant to be erotic.

RH: You offset that by referring to Michelangelo's Prisoners, and their "genitals / trapped / under unhewn rock".[38] Isn't the key thing about them the fact that they're half-formed, "trapped in unhewn rock" – almost as if they were a half-formed poem that has been discarded?

RB: I'm not sure if they're 'half-formed'; I rather think of them as being fully formed already, but under or within the rock, as it were, so 'not yet expressed'. I see them as being imprisoned, "trapped", not allowed out, or rather, not *yet* allowed out. For me this has a decidedly powerful, direct sexual meaning. The trapped genitalia means what it says: that their sexuality is trapped too. Michelangelo had no qualms about exposing male genitalia – and celebrating them explicitly – in many other sculptures. But here, what's true of the figure's genitalia is also true of his head. This is how I interpret his sculptures in this particular series. Here, both head and genitals are trapped. Two aspects of creative energy are confined: the sexual/procreative *and* the intellectual/spiritual. So I think you're right in suggesting that these forms can also be read as statements about the artist's struggle to 'free' his figure from its matrix of rock – if that is in fact what you are suggesting. And couldn't these figures also carry an implicit historical meaning, long before any full-scale republican movements ever appear on the European scene – I mean the political and social struggle for freedom?

RH: Yes, these figures could indeed signify the struggle of the artist to free the idea from his brain and reveal it on paper or on canvas or wall or in stone – and the failure inherent in this struggle to realise the artist's conceptions.

RB: The fragmented sonnet about Michelangelo's Prisoners is balanced by another about the two phalloi on Delos.[39] On this Cycladic island, as part of the ancient temple, there are two huge phalloi on top of columns. One is proud and erect, rampant, but the other has been cut off. Presumably it's been vandalised at some point over the last two and a half thousand years. In spring 1968, when I went to the island and saw these figures, there was a viper coiled near them, rearing its head and flickering its tongue. The entire experience was decidedly, powerfully phallic. As for the phallos that was cut off, it reminded me again that symbolically castration and beheading are related. There are various myths about a god being beheaded or castrated, Attis, Adonis, etc., and it's thought that these are variants of the same motif, both of them to do with the cutting off of life – whether of the male individual himself or of his capacity to procreate – and the theme of the seasonal sacrifice of the young god to the chthonic female forces, to ensure nature's fertility.

RH: This discussion takes me to another Michelangelo sculpture, which appears in your poem 'Croft Woods', the Rondanini Pietà. You describe this figure as being "dug" out of the rock.[40] Craig Woelfel says that this image suggests that, although part of the sculpture comes from the artist, the rest is already inherent in the material.⁴¹ Does this apply to poetry too? Do the words come from someone or something else?

RB: I think there's a Platonic element in the image of the sculpture. I'm no longer a Platonist, if ever I was one, but Plato's core idea that in matter there are encapsulated 'perfect' forms is powerful. The further idea that we extrapolate from that, even though Plato himself dismissed artists and poets, is that it's the artist's and poet's job to 'release' the form, which *is* the poem or sculpture. It's the same with the Michelangelo sculpture. It's the sculptor's job to chip away until the sculpture is released. As, for example, in his David, the perfect epitome of personal, physical and political freedom. Is that what you're talking about?

RH: Yes, and the way this relates to poetry.

RB: I do think there is an element of that. That the poet at work is motivated by a "blessed rage for order", as Wallace Stevens put it in 'The Idea of Order at Key West',⁴² – "order" to him being something that is both "implicate", i.e. already out there, as well as in here, *in-hering*, in the Bohmian sense, but also that needs to be reached for, to be reached out for and attained in the form of the poem that emerges. That is, of course, if it can ever be attained at all. To Stevens, the order he rages after is *implicitly* the achieved, resultant form that emerges out of the matrix it has been embedded in. And the matrix in that great poem of his is not rock but the sea. The next lines, the last lines of the poem, go like this: "The maker's rage to order words of the sea, / Words of the fragrant portals, dimly-starred, / And of ourselves and of our origins, / In ghostlier demarcations, keener sounds." That's just fantastic! We're a long way from sculpture here. But the idea that the poem, or any kind of made artefact, emerges from its matrix, is identical to what we've just been saying vis-à-vis sculpture. This is consonant, too, with organicist models of the processes of artistic creation and scientific discovery both beginning in gestation, and a sort of self-brooding, way below the level of conscious awareness.

RH: Yet the lines in this poem "She was the single artificer of the world / In which she sang," suggest another idea, of the poet as an active creator, a maker, consciously and skilfully shaping the material rather than following it.

RB: Yes. The image of the matrix suggests other metaphors you could follow too. For example – to follow that metaphor itself, that is, of 'following' – the artistic process *does* consist in 'following': I've used the title 'Following' for a group of poems in a fairly recent book, with precisely that idea in mind, and it's one that's central to my poetics.⁴³ One is not imposing one's self *on* the material; one is actually working *with* the material, through it, in fellowship and harmony with it, coaxing it, blending with it, asking it what it wants to do and how and where it wants to go.

Hands are important here too, as in any artistic process, because they aren't pushing, but feeling their way and allowing something to move and grow. The carpenter goes with the grain of the wood – hence another aspect of that lovely title *In the American Grain* by William Carlos Williams. So you follow the organic qualities of the material. ... I talked to the sculptor Rosie Musgrave about this and the same principle applies. She works in and with the grain and texture of the stone. She knows all about stone. The different qualities of particular kinds of stone, and the uniqueness of each individual block. That sculpture is one of hers. [*RB points to a symmetrical stone sculpture in an alcove in the room, a circular form set in a square, measuring around 46 cm in height and length, and with a depth of 8 cm. On the side, some words rise out of the stone: THE OCEAN REFUSES NO RIVER.*]⁴⁴ Out of this rock she has carved an immaculate form. We're back with Plato, in a way. Expressed in Jungian terms, the poem itself is an archetypal configuration, and the process of writing is a clarification, blowing away the mists, verbiage and confusion – and the surrounding scaffolding or envelope or shell – until the poem's form is revealed. Hatched. As if the form is what the poem itself wants to assert, through the poet.

I keep on finding this in other works as well. Three images come to mind, one musical, one architectural, and one scientific. The first could be any Bach fugue. It's not just that in Bach, content and form are married in the purest possible way: it's that their content is *itself* perfect form and vice versa. If you think of some tunes or motifs in music, there was a time before they existed. I've written about this in a poem.⁴⁵ The other examples are both here in Cambridge. One is King's College Chapel. If you look at the fan-vaulted ceiling and the way that everything connects and coheres, it's hard to imagine a time before it ever existed. It seems eternal, there's some kind of mathematical perfection to it, as though it had always been there – as though it was 'discovered' rather than 'built' or 'made'. In nature there are these fantastic forms. The third example is the structure of DNA. It's a discovery, the double helix, it's there already and it's beautiful, and very simple. After a discovery like this has happened, one thinks gosh, it's always been there. I think that applies to works of art. Imagine a time before Shakespeare's *Hamlet* was written. It's almost as though once it's written it enters into some sort of space that is, as it were, elemental, fundamental, as far as consciousness is concerned. I think when one is writing a poem – what one is trying to do when one is writing a poem, even a small poem – is like that. I'm trying to think of another example. Take 'Life' by George Herbert. It's a gem of a poem, it's perfect, it's faultless, flawless, as if it had always 'been there' … Ah, here's that poem about music that I was looking for. It's from a sequel to *The Manager*. [RB reads 'Once, hearing music'.][46]

RH: You do evoke that feeling of awe that one sometimes faces in the presence of great art or music – the disbelief that any mortal could make this, contrasted with the knowledge that he did.

RB: What I wanted to add here is that the key to all these patternings, what they all have in common – music, architecture, sculpture, poetry, scientific discovery, the structure of matter itself – is ultimately mathematical. Spencer-Brown in *Laws of Form* talks about the way we think of mathematics as being able to reveal the structure of the world.[47] Yeats wrote: "Measurement began our might. / Forms a stark Egyptian thought, / Forms that gentler Phidias wrought."[48] These lines are to do with the way that massively powerful and geometrically perfect forms and harmonies were discovered in ancient Egypt and then modified and humanised in Greek sculpture. Again: geometry, music, architecture, sculpture. We can add poetry, because poetry is based on rhythm and measurement too. 'Metre' means measurement.

Marie-Louise von Franz follows Jung in thinking that number is itself archetypal. You can't actually touch 'number'. But every child over the age of four knows what it is. Number is out there. Numbers, plural, are out there. You can count them on your fingers, your digits. But number is digital and virtual and abstract too. It runs computers. It's in your head. It links the inner and outer worlds, the physical and psychic realities. Roy Harris, who was Professor of General Linguistics at Oxford, considered number to be magical.[49] And von Franz links number both with the physics of time and with patterns of synchronicity in ways that no contemporary poets, at least none that I've come across, have even started to study seriously. I find all these connections very exciting. And Jung's theory of synchronicity is of course rooted in the *Yijing*, and largely derived from his studies of this ancient Chinese masterpiece. … These are some of the factors that motivate and underpin my poetry. The book I'm working on at present, a kind of homage to the *Yijing*, is tied up with all these issues. It's had an even longer gestation than other long poems, like *The Blue Butterfly*, which have taken from ten to twenty years from their first arrival to their completion and final publication.

RH: Why such a long time? Is the evolution of a poem a long gestation and labour with a gradual birth?

RB: The gestation-and-birth imagem works very well. And here, I think there are several other things worth saying. First, there's no prescribed term and I'm not in a hurry. Nor am I so desperately bothered about what goes on in the contemporary poetic world, or so involved in it or dependent on it, that I feel I have to get a volume out every year or so, to keep up a presence on the literary scene, or in time to go in for this or that prize or competition, or anything of that kind. In that sense at least, the pace I work at and the way I work is determined by patterns I create and impose on myself. Secondly, if one is aiming at durability, and also to produce long works, both of which I am, one needs to give oneself space and time.

In many ways I think of myself as a lyric poet, I'm quite interested in making short poems. But I'm also interested in long poems, and that's why the poems about hands, that I mentioned earlier, form such an elaborate sequence. Many of the great poets have written long poems – Browning, Tennyson, Milton, Eliot, and many many more – and those are the people I model myself on, rather than the Larkins or the Seamus Heaneys of this world. A third factor, which isn't self-imposed but the result of necessity, is simply to do with the exigencies of living. Like most people, I have to earn a living; I don't have a private income. When you have a day job, a money job, you're constantly being interrupted. So you have to store stuff rather than simply writing it out in white heat. You have to plan your writing times, and treasure them. And you have to build interruption itself into the writing process.

RH: Do you welcome the interruptions of having a day job, an everyday life, or do you see them as a distraction from your poetry?

RB: Interruption seems to me a very interesting thing. It can be very negative, but there is a way in which artistic creation needs to allow interruption, since what interrupts is, by definition, spontaneous and 'other'. Interruption, I think, is linked in with the notion of the guest and the host – and Derrida is very good on their interdependence, incidentally, in his book *Of Hospitality*, co-authored with Anne Defourtmentelle. The guest who is invited in is someone who is *welcomed* as an intrusion. But the distinction between intruder and guest is complex and subtle. For one thing, you have to be careful about interruptions, including self-interruptions, since they can distract you from what you're doing, but sometimes they can be very valuable.

RH: What do you do when a line of a poem or an idea is itself the interruption – appearing while you go about your money job, or during other aspects of your life. How do you ready yourself for this guest?

RB: That's a great question. From one point of view, I aim to write a great deal of the time because I want to allow the ideas to surface, quickly and without much, if any, premeditation or planning. You have to catch ideas on the wing, and while they're hot – even if it's not always in white heat – otherwise it's too late. Ideas and themes get forgotten and disappear. So I'm always jotting down notes and ideas and lines, and sometimes quick drafts of entire poems. I have thousands and thousands of notes of this kind. I record them in big spiral-bound notebooks and have a massive collection of these notebooks by now. This is my raw material. I keep one of these notebooks by my bed in case I wake up with an idea in the morning or in the middle of the night. The material that goes down includes records of dreams. Quite a few poems of mine come out of a dream-matrix. And I always take a notebook with me whenever I go out, and especially when I travel. Travelling itself stimulates the flow of inner images and ideas because outer images go flashing by very quickly and they interact energetically with one's inner themes and motifs. At first one notices what one is interested in but then one also gets surprised by things that one hadn't noticed or expected to notice or thought of noticing. The point is that these inflows are interruptions too. So, as I've suggested, interruptions are positive as well as negative and one has to treat them as a host treats guests. Even so, this kind of gathering in is only part of it. Actual composition involves slow, quiet, patient and careful solitary work on and with this raw material.

RH: Can an entire book be an 'interruption'?

RB: One book that was written more or less in white heat one summer was the sequence *Black Light*. It consisted of twelve poems, and much later on I added one that I'd written at the same time but hadn't at first been sure of, to make thirteen poems. Curiously, the short prose piece I'd been unsure of at first and had thought of rejecting turned out later to be the part that clinched and lifted the whole set.[50]

So that book itself arrived as an interruption: that is, as something unexpected and sudden. I managed to keep most *other* interruptions away at that time – that is, further interruptions of the first interruption – in order to maintain the impetus and flow. If you're *constantly* being interrupted or are interrupting yourself, it's hard to maintain any kind of flow at all. I'm very good at self-interruption. A woman I had a relationship with many years ago called it my 'W.E.P.', by which she meant my 'Work Evasion Programme'. It was a good way of putting it, and I worked that, ironically, into *The Manager*.[51] I think we've all got our work evasion programmes, and I'm very lazy in that way. But any long work inevitably involves interruption, so the ability to hold something in your mind over a long period is essential in all composition. If it's a long thing, an ambitious thing, and you have a day job, you can't write it to deadlines as a journalist would. When all is said and done, there are no deadlines in poetry, apart from the inner ones you impose yourself.

3

RH: Could you talk to me about the poetic voices your poems use? Many of your poems take on the voices and identities of others. I was thinking about the poem 'Don't send bread tomorrow', in which you adopt the voices of those who know they are about to be killed at Kragujevac.[52] Often there are multiple voices, none of which can be identified as your own. In contrast, the poem 'May' seems intensely personal and I found myself close to tears when you were describing your sister Sarah, who was born deaf, dumb and blind, and so unable to react to your father's music.[53] How does it feel to put such an intensely private poem in the public domain?

RB: The voices of others coming into the first poem you mention are actually documented voices from victims, and I retranslated the little messages they left and then wove them into the poem, as though they were a kind of chorus. It has just occurred to me as I say this, there's a chorus of female voices in *Murder in the Cathedral,* which was a play I acted in at school and was profoundly moved by. You have consecutive individual voices coming out of the chorus – I've never thought of that influence before. I think the voices of others are important *because* one is following them, one is receiving them. Also, I quite often have a sense of the otherness of the poetic voice that is welling through me, the othernesses of the poems that come to me. There are many voices. I work a lot with dreams. Some of these voices come to me from dreams and I remember them. The voices of others enlarge the scope of a poem and humanise it. Nothing bores me more than those awful poems that are absolutely ubiquitous these days in nearly all types of writing, from the avant garde to the traditionalists – the poems that go 'I, I, I'.

The insistent dominant 'I' can be an irritant and often the site – and indication – of a bad poem. And bad faith. A good poem often involves an opening to the voice of the other, not an insistence on the 'I'.

RH: What about 'May'? That's an 'I' poem.

RB: True. 'May' was fairly rare for me because on the whole I don't go for 'confessional' poems. I rejected the Lowell, Berryman, and Plath tradition, the 'I, I, I' stuff, when I was quite young, for reasons I've just mentioned. And anyway, I don't go along with the ideas that a poet should be thought of as a patient confessing shameful secrets or a penitent confessing sins, any more than a reader should be construed as a therapist, or counsellor, or priest. ... But something welled up in that poem, 'May', which was bigger than me. Once again, that poem, rather than being to do with opening up my privacies, I think of as connecting with the voices of the dead. And I don't feel any sense that what is going on in the poem involves revealing autobiographical detail that may be shameful or better kept secret or hidden.

There's also a way in which the exploration of subjectivity may reach a point when you touch the intersubjective. When I was a Cambridge undergraduate in the early 1960s, I went to F. R. Leavis's lectures. Leavis had an idea that he called 'the Third Realm'.[54] There's the first realm, that of objectivity – science deals with that. Then there's the second realm, that of subjectivity, for example dreams. The third realm is that of literature, and that's a realm that combines subjectivity and objectivity. Now, while I think Leavis's formulation is a useful way in, to start considering the borders between the private and the public in poetry, I would want to go more deeply than that – to layers that probably no Cambridge literary academic would ever broach. For it's not just that Leavis's 'Third Realm' consists of the intersubjective, but that the intersubjective is the clearest indication of the archetypal.

The intersubjective clearly has a kind of 'objectivity' of its own. Let's say one is watching *Othello* in the theatre. My sixth form English teacher gave me this example back in 1959. In the theatre, at the moment when Othello is accusing Desdemona of adultery and is about to strangle her, someone in the audience shouts out "You bloody great fool, don't you realise she's innocent?" This is a subjective response, but it's one that everybody in the audience is feeling at just that moment, and has sympathy with, so it becomes intersubjective.

RH: So are you saying that 'May' was not a confessional poem?

RB: I'm saying that confessing is not its key. I hoped it would touch layers of intersubjectivity.

RH: What particularly moved me was the way you described your father. Your father's music resonates through the poem. Even though the music fails to awaken the daughter, it awakens something in the reader.

At this point the interview breaks off, as Berengarten shows me photographs: of his father Alexander, who had a musical instrument shop in Shaftesbury Avenue, and was one of the first people to import the jazz saxophone into the UK; of his Aunt Rose, who sang in Hollywood and dubbed the stars; and two photos of his father's brother, Seymour, the uncle who went to Hollywood as a musician, one photo on set in a group with Rudolph Valentino, and the other with Buster Keaton Junior and Norma Talmadge. Berengarten shows other photos of his father, who died when Berengarten was three years old; of his mother, Rosalind, who attempted to keep the family musical instrument shop going after her husband's death; and of Berengarten as a small boy, posing with musical instruments and, aged thirteen, as a Bar Mitzvah boy.

༄

RH: To completely change the subject. You lived in Italy when Ezra Pound was there. Did you meet him?

RB: I did and I didn't. That's a fascinating question and I still have to write about it fully. The question itself encapsulates a good deal of my complex and ambivalent stance not only vis-à-vis Pound but also other major Anglophone modernists. Some though not all of the story is covered in a memoir I wrote in 1996, entitled 'With Peter Russell in Venice 1965–1966', and I've made a start on the remaining aspects, which take a more critical and less sympathetic perspective of these modernists, in another so-far unfinished memoir entitled 'Two Drachmas for a Pound'.

I was living in Italy and teaching in a little English language school in Padua, at roughly the same point that you are at now – that is, shortly after coming down from Cambridge – which would have been in late 1964. It was my first job after graduation and I'd found it thanks to an elderly Venetian poet, Diego Valeri. He'd been a lecturer on a course I'd attended in summer 1963, in Bressanone, on an Italian Institute student grant, organised by the University of Padua. I remember going up to him at the end of a lecture and shyly saying to him, in my schoolboy French – because I didn't speak

Italian yet: "Excusez moi, professeur, je suis aussi poète." He must have found that quite funny, but he was a perfect Venetian gentleman, utterly charming, and very kind. He helped me to get that job, which I started in September 1964 in Padua. Then in January 1965, I received a letter from Peter Russell, an English poet living in Venice, inviting me to visit him there. So I took the bus from Padua to Venice to visit him, and learned from him that Diego Valeri had suggested he contact me. At first I thought Peter might be homosexual. He had a great swathe of white hair running from back to front along the middle of his head, like a badger. I thought it might have been dyed, but later learned from him that it was where he had torn his hair out after his bookshop in Tunbridge Wells had gone bankrupt, and the hair had grown back pure white. When I got to know him, he turned out to be very – promiscuously – heterosexual. He and I talked all night.

That meeting with Peter was a turning point that took my life in a new direction. I was twenty-one and he was forty-two, and he introduced me to the living world of poetry. We decided at the end of the conversation, over some strong coffee the next morning, that I would come and live in the bigger apartment he was about to move into, and that I would ask my girlfriend from Cambridge, Kim Landers, to come out too.[55] Peter was a Poundian, and he had moved to Venice partly to live near Pound. In 1950, he had edited a book of essays called *An Examination of Ezra Pound*, when Pound had been incarcerated in St Elizabeth's hospital as a lunatic, and this book had been one of the influential factors in securing Pound's release. It contained essays by writers such as T. S. Eliot, Edith Sitwell, Allen Tate, Ernest Hemingway, George Seferis, Wyndham Lewis and Marshall McLuhan. When Kim and I lived at his place in 1965, Peter was on close terms with Pound and Olga Rudge, his partner, and he kept going off to visit Pound on the Giudecca. He would come back and tell us stories about how he had sat there all afternoon and how Pound had said little or nothing. We lived in Castello, in a fine top floor apartment in the Campo de la Bragora, not far from the Riva degli Schiavoni and Piazza San Marco. It had an *altana*, a balcony on the rooftop, from where on clear days you could see as far as the Dolomites, even though Venice was usually too misty.

We would often see Pound and Olga Rudge walking together on the Giudecca, on the other side of the Grand Canal. But Peter never took Kim or me with him to see Pound. In 2002, when I went to see Peter, who was dying in the Casa di Riposo in Castelfranco di Sopra, a little town in the Tuscan hills, he said suddenly, completely out of the blue: "I never took you to see Pound." I said, "No, you didn't." And he said "Well, I didn't, and that's that." I had often wondered why he didn't take me, and still do. I think he might have been worried on the one hand that I would be too iconoclastic, and possibly abrupt, because Kim and I at that age were querying just about everything.

At the beginning of the 1960s, my crew in Cambridge were terribly irreverent, in a way you couldn't imagine from undergraduates now. We were exploding out of the '50s. We weren't worried about getting jobs. We knew we could and would, if we wanted them. There was no unemployment likely for Cambridge graduates. So we were a curious contradictory mix of cockiness, privileged assumptions and unconscious snobbery on the one hand, and insecurity, brashness and uncertainty, desire to please and rebelliousness on the other. We were used to hierarchies, and we were flouting them, even while contradictorily respecting and accepting many of their structures. At that time I thought of Pound mainly as an iconoclast. Perhaps Peter was worried that I'd talk to Pound without due respect, as though he were anyone, rather than a great figure. I may have been naïve, but it did seem odd to me at the time that a person famous for being an iconoclast in his youth should himself end up by being revered and being bowed down to. Perhaps this was to do with a strong element of immaturity and youthful immodesty on my part. But celebrity culture still irks me, though I'm a little wiser in the ways of the world these days. The other thing was Pound's fascism and his virulent anti-Semitism. I believe that Peter Russell whitewashed these, as he often pointed out that Pound had had many Jewish friends and had never been personally anti-Semitic towards any of them. Perhaps Peter might have been worried that, if he took me to see Pound, I might have brought up 'awkward' Jewish issues with him, even though I was only twenty-two at the time. It remained for Alan Ginsberg to do that.

Kim and I did actually meet Pound once with Peter, among a group of people during the interval of a concert at La Fenice, the fine old Venetian theatre that was destroyed in a fire a few years later.

My 'relationship' with Pound is very complicated. As John Gery says in his essay in the *Companion*, I approached Pound in two ways: both directly, through his poems, and indirectly, filtered through Peter Russell, who was his disciple.[56] I've never been able to be a disciple of any kind to anyone: I don't think it's in my nature. Aside from that, my own complex ambivalences vis-à-vis Pound are those that many poets of my generation have towards him. Added to this, or rather, a key part of it, is the problem of his anti-Semitism, which was virulent, vile and is utterly to be rejected. This is an interesting question when you look at American modernism, because many important Jewish poets were influenced by him, and among them are major modernist figures: Carl Rakosi, George Oppen, Charles Reznikoff, Louis Zukofsky, to mention only a few, let alone many later poets. There is this genuine problem in relation to both Pound and Eliot, though their anti-Semitism is expressed very differently. Eliot's anti-Semitism is analysed brilliantly in Anthony Julius's book, where links with literary form are explored too. I reread Pound only occasionally now and I've come to question him more than ever before. These days, much of his prose writing seems bombastic and hollow to me, even though you can't possibly get away from his genius as a poet. Anyway, that was part of the Italian experience.

Cambridge and London
January–July 2011

Notes

1. "Richard Burns has lived in Greece, Italy, the USA, and the former Yugoslavia, and has worked in the Czech Republic, Latvia, Poland and Russia. ... He writes: 'The English language has always been a source of joy and fascination to me, but I would much rather think of myself as a European poet who writes in English than as an "English" poet.'" RB 1999: back flap.
2. Act 2, Scene 2, l. 303.
3. Donne: 108.
4. See Damon: 281–282.
5. *Note from RB*: See for example Hopkins, writing of snow: "All the world is full of inscape and chance left free to act falls into an order as well as purpose: looking out of my window I caught it in the random clods and broken heaps of snow made by the cast of a broom." (230). And writing of clouds: "What you look at hard seems to look hard at you, hence the true and the false instress of nature. One day in early March when long streamers were rising from over Kemble End one large flake loop-shaped, not a streamer but belonging to the string, moving too slowly to be seen, seemed to cap and fill the zenith with as white shire of cloud. I looked long up at it till the height and the beauty of the inscaping – regularly curled knots springing if I remember from fine stems, like foliation in wood and stone – had strongly grown on me. It changed beautiful changes, growing more into ribs and one stretch of running into branching like coral. Unless you refresh the mind from time to time you cannot always remember or believe how deep the inscape in things is" (Hopkins: 204–205).
6. RB 2011 [3], *The Blue Butterfly*: 8.
7. *Editors' note* (added later): for the *Manual* chapbook series, see: RB 2006 [3], 2007, 2008 [6] and 2009 [4]. *Manual, the first hundred* was completed in 2012 and published in 2014.
8. RB 2011 [1], *For the Living*: 117–130.
9. Blake: 148.
10. Pound, 'Canto CXVI': 27. See also 79 in this book, note 64.
11. Wordsworth, Book 2, ll. 401–405: 31.
12. See Bohm.
13. MacDiarmid, 'The Little White Rose': 461.
14. Jope: 1; and see the 'Editors' Introduction': 10 in this book.
15. RB 2006 [2].
16. Filippakopoulou: 196–197.

17 "Berengarten belongs to all of us: he is Greek, Italian, Yugoslav. In short, he is Mediterranean." Nicolao: 46.

18 Wilson: 371.

19 RB 2016, *Changing*.

20 "Among plural narratives a poem's singularity relies on contexts. Its tissues, textures, intermeshings and codings are not only its own. I follow Octavio Paz in believing that 'for the first time in our history, we are contemporaries of all humanity.' Such a belief postulates an enlightened and magnanimous universalism that is threaded in impassioned love for minute particulars. While firmly rooted in modernism and fully acknowledging the achievements of the modernist masters, such a belief can no longer make concessions to the canny and clannish exclusiveness of traditional modernist and neo-modernist avant-gardes. A poem should be to mean as well as mean to be." RB 2011 [2], *The Manager*: 161.

21 "The 'Volta' project ... issues an implicit claim, made gradually more explicit here, that multilingualism and diversity constitute our defining contemporary linguistic, cultural, literary and poetic reality. In attempting at least a preliminary outline of some guiding principles for a viable future poetics, this anthology, including this essay, may form part of a larger communal project. Such a poetics might be called universalist. It could also be called the poetics of the border/line." RB 2009 [1].

22 RB 2011 [3], *The Blue Butterfly*, 'War again' and 'This country weighs so heavy': 16 and 53.

23 RB 1989.

24 RB 2011 [5], *Under Balkan Light*, 'The Voice in the Garden': 73.

25 Seferis 1969, 'Stratis Thalassinos Among the Agapanthi': 279.

26 Paz 1967: 182.

27 *Ibid.*: 182. *Note from RB*: Anthony Rudolf pointed out to me in December 2014 that by "we" in this statement, Paz means "we Mexicans". For many years, I have construed "we" to mean "we humans".

28 Tutu, Archbishop Desmond. In Enright and North (eds): xiii. See also RB 2013, *Imagems (1)*: 11.

29 See RB 2002 [1], 'Pour toi'.

30 RB 1980 [1], *Learning to Talk*, 'For the New Year 1976': 17.

31 RB 2011 [1], *For the Living*, 'Avebury': 23–50, esp. II: 26.

32 Moody: 125.

33 RB 2011 [1], *For the Living*, 'Avebury' X: 34.

[34] See RB 2009 [4], *Manual, the fourth 20*; and also RB 2014, *Manual, the first hundred*, frontispiece.

[35] See Neumann: esp. 95, 96 and Gimbutas 2001 [1989]: esp. 31, 51, 141 and 198; also, 1996 [1974] and 2001 [1999].

[36] RB 2011 [1], *For the Living*, 'Avebury' VI: 30.

[37] See Lévinas 2000, 2003 [1] and 2003 [2].

[38] RB 2011 [1], *For the Living*, 'Avebury' VII: 31.

[39] *Ibid.*: IX: 33.

[40] RB 2011 [1], *For the Living*, 'Croft Woods': 197–210, esp. 205.

[41] Woelfel: 231.

[42] Stevens: 106.

[43] RB 2003, *Book With No Back Cover*: 13–53.

[44] See Musgrave.

[45] RB 2003, *Book With No Back Cover*: 'Nine Codas' 7: 46.

[46] *Ibid.*

[47] "The discipline of mathematics is seen to be a way, powerful in comparison with others, of revealing our internal knowledge of the structure of the world, and only by the way associated with our common ability to reason and compute." Spencer Brown: xiii.

[48] Yeats, 'Under Ben Bulben': 399.

[49] "Counting is in its very essence magical, if any human practice at all is. For numbers are things no one has ever seen, heard or touched. Yet they exist, and their existence can be confirmed in everyday humdrum terms. Numbers are instantly available for every counting operation, like spirits that can be conjured up at will." Harris 2002 [1986]: 133–135.

[50] RB 2011 [1], *For the Living*, 'Ambassador (An Old Man in the Harbour)': 174–176. *Editors' note*: a later [bilingual English-Spanish] edition includes yet another poem, the sonnet 'Night Bathing'. RB comments: "This poem, which was started in summer 1982, was not completed until summer 2011." See RB 2012 [1], *Black Light / Luz negra*: 42–43 and 82.

[51] RB 2011 [2], *The Manager*, section 26: 40.

[52] RB 2011 [3], *The Blue Butterfly*, 'Don't send bread tomorrow': 6–7.

[53] RB 2001 [1], *For the Living*, 'May': 177–184.

[54] Leavis: 36.

[55] Kim Landers and RB married in 1966. They separated in 1979 and then divorced. They remain friends.

[56] Gery: 146–149.

I Must Try This Telling

RICHARD BERENGARTEN AND SEAN RYS

This text is based on a conversation that took place between Richard Berengarten and Sean Rys before an audience in the Old Little Theater on the University of California campus at Santa Barbara, on April 11, 2012, following a reading of poems by RB. The reading included poems from *The Balkan Trilogy*,[1] notably the title poem from *The Blue Butterfly*. Both events were planned and introduced by Professor Kay Young of the UCSB English Department. Sean Rys made a transcript of the conversation between June and September 2012, which both poets edited and amplified between October 2012 and July 2013.

SR

1

Sean Rys: Richard, thank you for agreeing to speak with me about *The Balkan Trilogy*. I thought that we might begin our discussion by turning to the origin point once more. That is, your seemingly random or chance encounter with the blue butterfly. You mentioned in an earlier exchange that Carl Gustav Jung's writing on synchronicity has informed your own thinking and writing around these events. Bearing in mind what Jung terms "meaningful coincidence",[2] how do you now view this chance convergence in light of the great body of research and three books of poems that it has engendered?

Richard Berengarten: The butterfly settling on my hand outside the memorial museum in Kragujevac in 1984 was a changing point in my life. That little butterfly turned out to be a very heavy creature indeed. It took me twenty years to get its weight off of my finger – my writing finger. In other words, it took me twenty years, perhaps slightly more, to write the books in *The Balkan Trilogy*. That event was the trigger for that writing. If it hadn't happened, I doubt if any of those books would have got made. 'The blue butterfly', together with 'Nada: hope or nothing', was as you say the starting point.³ These two poems arrived as gifts. They came, almost unfiltered, straight out of the experience itself. But even as I was writing those two poems, I realised there was a lot more going on under their surface.

So I changed my life. I went to live in Yugoslavia – because of that experience. I managed to get a job there in 1987. My friends said to me, "Why are you going to live in Yugoslavia ... Yugoslavia? What on earth are you interested in doing that for?" I said, "Chasing Butterflies. 'La chasse aux papillons'." That's the title of a 1960s song by Georges Brassens.

SR: To what extent did your relocation to Yugoslavia shape the direction of your writing?

RB: Massively. I went to live there for *The Blue Butterfly* to get written. I wanted to live in that space: to experience it, to discover its ground, ground myself in it. People talk these days about geo-cultural, geo-historical, geo-political zones. And all these factors came into my decision to live in Yugoslavia. But there are geo-psychic zones too and, somehow, that factor was the most important of all. By then, I knew that there was a good deal more behind the two poems that had emerged so spontaneously. By 'behind' I mean latent, as-yet-unexpressed, pushing at me, in me, through me, for expression and articulation. I was aware that the butterfly and the soul are one and the same in ancient Greek: ψυχή [*psyche*].

I'd like to be rather circumspect about what I'm going to say next, because I don't want to make any kind of huge claims here, and certainly not of any 'mystical' sort: I felt that the butterfly landing on my hand was a signal from the dead. That's the way I experienced it. I felt that the butterfly called me from the souls of those men and boys, and women and girls, who had been massacred by the Nazis in their reprisal against an attack by Serbian partisans and royalists on a German platoon. A hundred Serbian civilians were executed for each German soldier killed. Nearly three thousand people were shot. To me, the butterfly was a messenger – or itself a message – *from* them. At that moment, that was startling, puzzling, upsetting. But I experienced it both matter-of-factly and as a burden, a job to be done. That's why I've said it was a very heavy butterfly. I experienced a *call* to write about those dead Serbs, Jews and Roma. There was an injunction: to write about them and for them, perhaps even *to* them. And I mean all dimensions of the word 'call'. In saying this I'm thinking of what Stanley Cavell writes about the call of the 'other'.⁴

So could it be that I was being called by the soul or souls of those sacrificed Serbs? I felt I had a sort of responsibility to them. I want to say this modestly and not in an inflated way. I don't feel inflated about it. That's how I experienced it.

SR: Can you speak more to the influence of Jung in understanding these synchronicities?

RB: Jung's theory of synchronicity offers the most accurate way I've come across of understanding what happened to me. His various definitions of synchronicity as "meaningful coincidence" depend on an event in the outside world corresponding – or, if you like, chiming or resonating – with an inner experience or state of mind. The sense of meaning (i.e. of meaningfulness and depth) to the person experiencing the event is one of the criteria he specifies for a synchronicity.[5] For me, the tiny blue butterfly landing on my writing finger at the site of a Nazi massacre fitted these parameters.

In retrospect it's also clear that this event/experience could hardly have been more apposite in terms of my own personality and dispositions at that time. While I experienced and interpreted the event as utterly *extra-ordinary*, it was almost as if it had been 'tailored' for me, a 'perfect fit'. As an English Jew, born in London in June 1943 – less than two months after the destruction of the Warsaw Ghetto – in my teenage years I had grown up with the overwhelming shadow of the Holocaust looming like a spectre over all horizons of my ancestral past. I had already tried several times to write poems relating to the Holocaust, and in my own eyes had failed in all of them – except one, the long poem 'Angels'.[6] So that butterfly coming to perch on my finger was already loaded with meanings for me.

SR: Could you elaborate more fully and precisely on *what ways* this event constituted what Jung calls a synchronicity? What is the full range of indicators, of "criteria"?

RB: Jung defines synchronicity as "an acausal connecting principle".[7] There's no way that the connection between the blue butterfly landing on my finger and my condition of mind at that time could be understood, mapped or explicated in a causal frame. For the person experiencing such an event, a particular patterning of combined experiential responses forms a clear set of indicators of synchronicity. I'd characterize these to include all of the following: a sense of resonance, of chiming, of calling and being called, as I've already suggested. Then, the sense of 'import' and 'importance', of a heuristic opening, of personal discovery, all the more powerful for being sudden and unexpected. And then, the establishment of direct connectivity (conjunction, *coniunctio*) between personal layers and transpersonal or archetypal layers of consciousness. Hence, an overall sense of an exponential and simultaneous increase in depth and an opening of horizons, combined with meaning and meaningfulness, purpose and purposefulness. So, overall, a *charge*, in all senses of that word: an energy current, a boost, a thrusting forward, a challenge, and a sense of obligation and commitment towards *doing* something: i.e. a creativity, towards a making that is a becoming, a becoming that is a making. For me, the 'doing something' and the becoming were the making of a poem, a book that is a poem. And every one of these factors was present. All of which is to say that, for me personally, the arrival of that butterfly came as a gift, an epiphany.

SR: What you've been saying reminds me of Paul Celan's notion of the poem as a "making-toward", or a conversation encountered along the way.[8] Does this resonate with your experience of writing *The Balkan Trilogy*? Is the writing of the poem also an arrival?

RB: Yes. Celan's concept of 'conversation along the way' and writing as a process of deepening one's understanding – I think that's true. I also think that different *modes* of understanding come together in the various stages of writing a poem. For example, with *In a Time of Drought*, I wrote that in a sort of white heat. It was an experience of being *inspired*. I wrote it in a very short period, in the middle of working on *The Blue Butterfly*. And that intensity even got carried over into its revisions, through my correspondence with Peter Mansfield.[9] The figure of the rain maiden worked strongly on me, in me, through me. I knew that I was dealing with mythological material – Jung would call it archetypal material – and even at the time I recognised that that myth, that archetype, had somehow latched on to me, caught me, called me, landed on me, in me. It was as if it had taken me over, as if my personal, individual voice was irrelevant to the telling. So the best things I could achieve in the composition of the poem had to be, first, to see it through to the end and, second, to eradicate that personal voice.[10] What's more, embedded in working with that material, both during the writing of the poem itself and later in compiling its glossary and notes, I was doing a good deal of linguistic and mythological research into the origins of the folk practice, as far back as I could get.[11] I was exploring scholars like Roman Jakobson, who had written brilliantly about the etymologies of the names of the characters in the customs.[12] I traced the material back to 1818 and Vuk Karadžić, the first Serbian authority, who was a friend of Goethe – and to one of the brothers Grimm,[13] to

Frazer's *The Golden Bough*,[14] to the Bulgarian scholar Mikhail Arnaudov,[15] to the Russian Ana Plotnikova,[16] and various other nineteenth century and twentieth century authors. I also intuited that I was dealing with material that related to the Persephone myth, and later got particularly excited when this hunch was corroborated. I discovered two Russian scholars, Ivanov and Toporov, who had written of etymologically cognate material being "typologically parallel", and cleverly managed to hint at considerably more than that – i.e. at long-range influences through time.[17]

Even more interestingly, at least to me at that time, as I gradually got more and more deeply into this intricately interwoven *imagem*,[18] many strands and facets that kept appearing spontaneously in my own thoughts and experience, turned out actually to be part of the legends themselves. I kept discovering extraordinary correspondences between stuff that belonged to the *materia* itself and the themes that were working through me – which I was discovering in myself in the act of writing, without knowing that it belonged to the *materia* too. So that was a way of 'conversing', in Celan's terms, which meant different layerings of conversations: convergences and divergences. It meant layerings at intuitive and visceral levels – simultaneously intuitive and visceral – when the poetry was pouring out of me. So the conscious mind had to try to catch up later on. I also think the welling up of deep material could be construed as a continuation or a working-through of the patterns of synchronicity that we were talking about earlier. The *materia* appeared both inside me and outside, around me. I had many experiences involving those kinds of recognitions and connections during this period, gestated by the writing of the poem and by the research I was putting into it.

That leads to another point, which involves the entire question, so often posed, about authorial intention. Northrop Frye reminds us in his book on Blake, *Fearful Symmetry*, that the artist, the poet, is somebody who actually *sets out* to write a work. Doing this is a conscious act. It's not an accident, it doesn't just *happen*. It's hard work. It's driven by intention, will, ego, choice, deliberation, all of those elements.[19]

Even so, at the same time, there are aspects that the poet is in contact with but doesn't and can't control. As Shelley said: "A man cannot say 'I *will* compose poetry.'"[20] So the whole question of intention is an interesting critical and psychological issue. Ted Hughes broaches this question from an interesting angle in his famous *Paris Review* interview. He says something like this: a poet writes what he or she intends to write, but a poet may also be writing what he or she intends *not* to say, which still somehow *needs* to get said.[21] We could extend this to suggest that a poet may not only be saying what he or she doesn't *intend* to say, but also intends *not* to say. An interesting contradiction, this, flowering into paradox. It may even be that you find – depending on what kind of psychology you adopt – archetypal material welling up *despite* the poet. If you're a Jungian, you might want to say something like 'shadow material' or 'anima material'. If you're a Freudian, you might prefer to say 'repressed material'. What do you think about this? How far are we 'responsible' for what we write?

SR: The use of 'responsibility' in this context has always troubled me, as it seems to indicate an objective control that doesn't entirely ring true. So I would agree with Shelley's response as a starting point: the compositional act has more to do with making oneself multilaterally receptive – it's not an act of brute force or ego or even a matter of 'willing' the poem into being! If we accept Shelley's accompanying claim that poetic composition corresponds 'inversely' with inspiration, and if we ultimately think of the poem as a trace recording of its predicating source(s), it places demands on the poet to more consistently cultivate these moments of inspiration when they *do* occur. Is this a form of responsibility? I'd like to think that it is …

RB: Yes, absolutely. Though I don't entirely agree with Shelley here, because he's one-sided, and so he simplifies things. There's another aspect to making poems that he doesn't touch. As you hint, by talking about 'inverse correspondence' and 'trace recording'. Shelley says: "when composition begins, inspiration is already on the decline."[22] In my experience, that isn't always true. If I 'catch the moment right' – or moments – or if they catch me – inspiration *pours* into composition, brims into it, and composition contains the moment's momentum like a cup or bowl until it fills up. In its abundance it may of course overbrim, overspill, even overwhelm its container. I think Shelley is talking about that sense: "My cup runneth over." In any case, will and intention work as 'secondary' principles with and *through* this primary upwelling and outpouring, and are fully engaged in it. For conscious will and intention do play a vital part in composition, as we've seen from Northrop Frye's comment, both in directing energy into and through the work, and in making patterns, setting up structures and choosing forms for the energy to settle in. The Chinese call this energy *qi*.

I agree too with what you say about the poet's 'responsibility'. Its preliminary keys are a constant and, as you say, "multilateral" receptivity and readiness: willingness rather than will; alertness not assertiveness; preparedness rather than pushing or pulling. Being *responsible* means, in the first instance, being *responsive*, which in turn precipitates *response, responding*.

Overall, 'taking responsibility' means training oneself in all of these skills, which eventually become second nature. And this training involves daily practice and lasts a lifetime, as it does for any art, craft, skill [*metier, mestiere, τέχνη, techne*]. These days I think of any such practice as a kind of *wu wei*, often translated as 'actionless action', 'effortless action', 'non-action', 'non-doing', etc. By this I mean that in preparing for the arrival of a poem, one *does* nothing. That is to say, nothing, literally *nothing*, is what one *does*. And in the doing of nothing, one enters what from the outside might appear to be a kind of unfocused haze. But what's actually going on, in the connecting interior rooms or subterranean caverns and corridors of consciousness, is a multilateral alertness, to echoes and resonances, a quiet listening patience. A musing.

Even so, when a poem does arrive, 'out of the blue' as it were, at that moment, one moves at lightning speed, to catch it. This is the art of the hunter, an imagem that Ted Hughes explores in his essay 'Capturing Animals'.[23] The doing of *nothing*, a still waiting, transmutes suddenly into the doing of *everything*: one moves from inaction into highly focused, spreading and infiltrating action. Fast!

So to me, the *onset* of a poem involves hearing, tuning in, listening out for and allowing entry to its voice (singular) or voices (plural), and then following – at top speed. Between *allowing* and *following*, a harmonious chime rings out, as between wineglasses. More often than not, I've a prior plan, a mental pattern, a containing *Gestalt*, often formulated tentatively through number, perhaps even an architectonics. Number is vital in all senses. But given this context, I train myself *not* to exert any other prior control, *not* to spy out or expect anything in advance, *not* to focus too sharply or intently, but rather to be open, hospitable and welcoming to the 'other' voice if and when it comes – or voices. This process also necessarily involves openness to being *surprised, astonished*, which also mean openness to receiving a gift. I've explored this reality in several short statements on poetics, in *Imagems (1)*.[24] There can of course be no active 'expectation' of a heuristic moment – which would be a self-contradiction – but there is a readiness to respond to it and resonate with it.

This kind of contextualising applies entirely to the extraordinary 'arrival' of my butterfly. There was a 'twiceness' to this arrival: first the creature *on* my hand; then, later, the poem emerging *from* my writing hand, the same hand.[25] The poem called 'The telling, first attempt' is about what you describe accurately as 'multilateral receptivity', in the first arrival, though it could also apply equally to the second:

> Now my ears awakened in an alert
> attentive and percipient listening
> to scoured shells of voices, wholly prised apart
> from those dead mouths, pouring their testament
> onto spring wind, stirred by the instrument
> of the butterfly on my finger, glistening.[26]

I often experience a poem's presence or likely proximity *synaesthetically*, as is evidenced in the rhyme "listening" / "glistening". But of all the senses, aural indicators and clues for this process strike me, usually, as being even more 'primary', more intimate, more apt and accurate, than visual ones. I often first register the otherness of the arriving poem as words and rhythms *sounding* inside me. So the butterfly as "instrument" here contains not only the idea of 'implement' but also that of 'music'.

SR: In addition to being 'primary', don't these aural indicators also resonate on deeply *primal* wavelengths that have little or nothing to do with the upper stratum of semantic meaning? Another aspect of this has to do with the fact that the poem is felt (it acts upon us bodily) before it's understood, and that sometimes this felt experience of the poem can overwhelm the gravity of its declaration. Hopkins is often this way for me, as is Whitman, and certain poems by Stevens as well. In my own work, I've found that following the prosody of words *first* as they collide or come into contact with other words makes possible a whole range of latent correspondences that blind allegiance to narrative linearity wouldn't have allowed. In this process, I also find guidance in the dual movement of the word *inspiration*, which indicates both an opening outward to the 'air around' and a drawing or receiving of it inwardly (inhalation). What a great metaphor for the poem!

RB: I think you're right to emphasise aurality. And I have a similar response to all the three poets you mention, though in markedly different ways – simply because their prosodies are so different. Musicality in Stevens is paramount because most of what he does is based on playing meaning off against the burden (ground) of the iambic pentameter. Hopkins's sprung rhythm is *intended* to deviate from this pattern. ... And hearing really is primary. In poetry, we attune to aural layers that are far 'deeper' than semantic meaning. And in this respect it's fascinating to compare hearing and sight ontogenetically. I've written a statement on this: 'On Poetry and Sound: The Ontogenesis of Poetry'.[27] The human foetus develops hearing in the third trimester of pregnancy. Sight develops only *after* birth. What's even more astonishing – and exciting – is that recent research shows that a foetus 'recognises' the sounds of his/her mother language (that is his/her own mother's language). This means that a human being begins to *learn* and *remember* the sound patterns of his/her language well before birth.[28] So the native language starts to be learned *pre*natally! This strikes me as being an enormously rich area for poetry and poetics, one that's scarcely yet been broached, let alone recognised by most practitioners.

I particularly like the idea of speech-sound patterns being primary in poetry, phylogenetically as well as ontogenetically. I think these must have originated in prehistory even before semantic meanings ever occurred in the brains of our hominid ancestors. And I wonder, and of course we can't know this, how did speech itself arise in the human species? I mean, in evolutionary terms? Could it have been that early human or proto-human anatomical development of the vocal chords and supra-laryngeal tract meant that the tract was large enough and long enough for this hominid to make certain sounds, and play with them, improvise with them, and that this sound-play was a stage on the way to triggering what we now call meaning? Philip Lieberman's research across this huge field is stupendously exciting. And I find it fascinating when we start to think about, for example, reduplication in this context, especially as it occurs in baby proto-speech and child speech. These are after all the beginnings of all sorts of interesting sound patterns that we poets work with as part of our stock-in-trade, our *melopoeia*. There are a lot of words in all languages that reduplicate.

2

SR: To return to the text, *The Blue Butterfly* begins with a fascinating tension created by the movement from the lyric space of "stagnation" in one of the early poems,[29] to the dense and perhaps what one might call the 'commercial' language of the 'Two documents',[30] which is a poem, as you note, crafted out of the standing orders and reports issued by Franz Böhme …

RB: Yes, though I would say that 'commercial' is not quite right. It's militaristic. It's fascist and dehumanised …

SR: Right, and speaking to that, one of the things that I'm interested in is the way in which you've re-contextualised the language of these found texts by introducing into them the formal constraints of a poem, by breaking the line, by introducing prosody into language that is inherently 'militaristic'. Could you speak about the form behind these poems?

RB: I introduce documentary material into *The Blue Butterfly* because history is important to me. As I said earlier in my reading this afternoon, in connection with *The Manager* and T. S. Eliot, I'm not really interested in 'jumping out of history'. Of course, I'm interested in what Eliot calls "the moment in and out of time"[31] and "the timeless moment",[32] for sure. As timeless moments come and go, one allows for that, one builds it in. Who isn't? But in this book I'm equally interested in *engaging* with history. *The Blue Butterfly* engages with a historical event.

As for the finer points of lineation in the two poems that you mention, they're basically 'found poems'. I took two documents from German official missives during the Second World War about policy towards Serbs: about how reprisals should be calculated arithmetically, how prisoners should be dealt with, and how many should be shot. It was important that the poems should operate, like the original commands, in a very neutral, cut-and-dry way. The lineation doesn't really matter, it was relatively arbitrary, or rather, it was based simply on breath-pause positions in English. I wasn't applying any kind of lyric there. I suppose I was creating an anti-lyric. Because when the curt, clipped, deadpan tone and content, the factual officialese of these documents is taken out of its original context and thrust into a poem, so that it gets juxtaposed against utterances that are self-evidently poignant, then the absurdity and monstrosity of the language of officialdom become clear. There's nothing new about this kind of contextual juxtaposition. It's the key to all satire, as for example within and across pairs of rhyming lines in the English heroic couplet, as perfected by Dryden, Pope and Johnson. You could say, it's parataxis as satire.

The context where I do apply the technique of the found poem actually to *achieve* lyric is in another poem, which also comes near the beginning of the sequence, 'Don't send bread tomorrow'.[33] This poem documents messages left by men and boys who knew they were going to be slaughtered. Their messages were scribbled on bits of paper, and some of these were found on their bodies after they were killed. I made a collage of those and juxtaposed them (once again, juxtaposition being the key to the technique) against stanzas of my own, recording photographic 'shots' from a visit there years after the massacre, which punned ironically on the word 'shoot'. I couldn't think of anything more personal than these statements by men and boys who knew they were going to *die* in the following twenty-four hours. These are all very powerful documents of human courage. To me, the power of those statements *exceeds* personal lyric – unless of course it could be said that the lyric is by definition that which exceeds the personal.

If the English translations of these messages are poignant, the quality of the vocabulary – its precise calibre, its moral fibre – in the Serbian original, is little short of breathtaking, heartbreaking. So, in *The Blue Butterfly*, I integrate documentary in different kinds of ways.

SR: I certainly see your point about contextual juxtaposition drawing attention to the monstrosity of programmatic speech, especially when the issuing of such language results in the widespread annulment of human life. Yet I also want to believe that the end result of these poems is something other than satire. It seems more to me! Doesn't the lineation, even if declared arbitrary, begin to rupture or turn the sentence? And doesn't this rupturing become aware of itself, and doesn't that awareness lead to a kind of reanimation? To my mind, recontextualising language of this nature and placing it under the formal pressures of the poem starts to imbue it with an underlying *melos*, and this music becomes the possibility of repair.

RB: That's interesting and not something I'd thought of before. Perhaps all sorts of things are going on here. What a found poem does, I think, is lift language out of a certain context and put it somewhere else. And the very lifting it out of context, and saying, 'Let's look at this' could be said to be art, in a way. The key is recontextualisation. And also 'otherness', getting through and away from the personal 'I'. Even so, I don't think that getting away from the 'I' can be forced, programmatically.

SR: Right.

RB: Another perhaps not-so-obvious aspect of this question of contexts is that my notion of poetry is based to a large extent on Romantic theories of inspiration, as has been suggested, pretty clearly, by our previous mention of Shelley, 'responsibility', 'will' and 'intention'. Even though I modify and qualify these ideas, this means that I believe the 'voice' speaking in a poem isn't necessarily – and certain not entirely – that of ego consciousness. And though ego consciousness necessarily enters into the patterning (crafting, making) of a poem, there's an otherness, an elseness, to it right from the moment of its first appearance, which I take as axiomatic. *Je est un autre*, as Rimbaud said in 1871.[34] And that's different from the kind of discourse that you and I are having now – which is not poetry, but discourse *about* poetry. In this kind of conversation on a topic, we do our best to be relevant, rational, attentive to what the other is saying – and to avoid non sequiturs. Even so, we know that conversation of any kind depends to a large extent on non sequiturs and proceeds by means of them: interruptions, diversions, spirallings, and recursive clarifications, not to mention misunderstandings. Without non sequiturs, a conversation would have no mental leaps, surprises, discoveries or vitality. How might our discourse now move into poetry? Well, I'm not sure exactly where the borderline between poetry and non-poetry is. It's subtle. If you and I really hit it off, in terms of the mental vibrations between us, and we were really attuned to each other, we might find that something like poetry started happening as we were talking to each other. Now that would be *very* exciting!

SR: It certainly would be! And I wonder if shifts of this nature happen more often than we think – perhaps they're just another form of the empathetic moment that occurs when two people engaged in a dialogue arrive at a moment of shared understanding, when they finally come to inhabit or stand-*under* the speech occasion of a fellow human being.

RB: I find this idea exciting, poetry achieving empathy – or, rather, achieving the condition of becoming the language of empathy – marked by shifts that 'linear' thinking doesn't and can't encompass. Rupert Sheldrake would say, perhaps, that a 'morphogenetic' or 'morphic' field is set up, which in turns creates a 'morphic resonance'.[35] And doesn't this link implicitly too with what you've been saying about music? Kay Young explores the connection between music and empathy very profoundly and in just this way in her book *Imagining Minds*, especially where she focuses on musical and sound motifs in *Middlemarch* and *Daniel Deronda*, claiming that these *transcend time*.[36] This, surely, is the scope of poetry too.

SR: I think she's right. Music in its most primitive configuration is little more than an exercise in repetition with degrees of variance. And yet, these repetitions are so deeply vested in cultural and anthropological memory that their soundings tend to invoke in us a ritualistic (and often spiritual) longing for otherness. In music, the certainty of return is a promise of renewal – a promise that stands against western notions of time and death. Is there a corollary in the language arts?

RB: The corollary is obviously poetry itself, which shares an enormous number of features with music, above all sound in non-identical repetition, or rhythm. Of course, language itself is rhythmical; and language – as poetry – meets music in song. In some south-Slavic languages, the words for 'song' and 'lyrical poem' are identical: Serbian *pesma*; Croatian *pjesma*; Macedonian *pesen*. Incidentally, I think we need the qualification 'non-identical' in our discussion here, because nothing could be worse than identical repetition, which would be total monotony, a Sisyphean hell. It's probable that identical repetition can't actually exist: any two so-called 'identical' identities or beings are bound to differ slightly, even in the minutest of details. But without non-identical repetition, there's no life. Rhythm is life's base. Binary alternation, breath, the heartbeat, systole and diastole, the cycles of day and night, of moon and tides, of the earth's ellipse and seasons, are all based in non-identical repetition. In *Repetition and Identity*, Catherine Pickstock explains how non-identical repetition in both space and time is a necessary constituent of the thinghood of things themselves.[37] What's more, in and through us, the rhythms of non-identical repetition don't invoke *only* longing. They embed wellness, harmony, order, pattern, 'knownness', trust of and in our bodies, our beings, in the actual, physical world. Since rhythm and repetition actually *constitute* our world, in us they set up *Sicherheit*, a fine German word that combines the meanings of *safety*, *security*, *surety* and *sureness*. So non-identical repetitions combine and oscillate between thisness and elseness, between the *hic et nunc* and alterity.

SR: What happens when the poem begins to move by means other than intervals of repetition? I'm thinking here of the blue butterfly as an associative mechanism throughout *The Balkan Trilogy*, one that gives rise to innumerable departures, both on the page and beyond it. If repetition connotes safety and security, where do alternative measures of narrative movement – ellipsis, parataxis, non sequitur – place us within the contextual frame?

RB: I wasn't disagreeing with what you said about rhythm and otherness. Some combinations of rhythms, chords and tones do inspire, for example, awe, the thrill of the numinous, the chill of the eerie, the sense of an other-than-human presence, even of a more-than-human order. I meant only to point out that rhythm is fundamental to *Sicherheit* too. The different effects of major and minor musical chords on the hearer indicate both these parameters. ... I also think that juxtaposition itself implies connectivity and patterning, whether evidently 'meaningful' and 'ordered' or 'accidental' and 'random'. And if there is connectivity, dialectics inevitably come in: it may be to do with either sameness or contrast, similarity or difference. As for the recurrence of the blue butterfly at multiple points during *The Balkan Trilogy*, the repetition clearly involves return to the predominant motif in varying contexts, but each one different, each one new. And I like the idea that each recurrence in a new context opens up new connectivities, or at least their potential, both on the page and off it, that is, in the reader's mind. In my understanding, this is what symbols do. A symbol is a complex nexus of actual and potential meanings 'operating' at many levels in the psyche and mind, but 'originating' at formative layers of consciousness. A symbol is multidirectional, never reducible to the single or even bipolar directionality of the sign.

I like the idea that apparent non sequiturs indicate not only difference, sudden jumps, surprise, dissonance and so on, but may also hint at a larger contextual frame, an unrealised or subliminal or implicit connectivity, perhaps something like David Bohm's "implicate order" – by which he means not *implicit* but *pleated* order, i.e. one 'containing folds', 'in-pleated'.[38] I think that kind of thing happens on stage, say, in a Beckett play, or a Pinter play, for example, where the kind of speech that is coming out from the actors is actually banal and prosaic, yet there's a powerful, locked energy in the dynamic between the two speakers. Plays like *Waiting for Godot* and *The Caretaker* are like this. The characters' surface language is to all extents and purposes antipoetic – drab, inconsequential, vapid, full of clichés – full, one might say, of absences. But the dramatic charge gives a huge, echoing, polysemic resonance to the speeches. Where does this charge come from? I think non sequiturs are the key and that the resonance lies precisely in these paratactic gaps and hiatuses *between* utterances. Paradoxically, both despite and because of the surface disconnectedness, we suspect – or glimpse, or discern, or want to discern – a deeper, underlying connectedness.

SR: Since your reading of 'implicate order' as 'pleated order' connects with digression (non sequitur), do you think deployment of digression and/or non sequitur also functions as a stratagem for suspending time (delaying death?) in the fictive? If so, this *modus operandi* would seem to correspond with the ritualistic nature of repetition in music, its desire for return, which may be equated to a stance against western rectilinear time.

RB: Bohm explains that, etymologically, 'implicate' actually means 'in-pleated'. The fundamental properties that generate – and bind – what he calls the implicate order and make it meaningful are those of relativity. Relativity also means relatedness, connectivity. Meaning itself is (or rather, is based in) relatedness, connectivity. Curiously, this idea, this theme, is the key to all metaphor too, as Wordsworth's imagem of the "interminable building" produced by an active imagination necessarily assumes.[39] This connectivity is also to be equated with Pound's belated discovery that "it coheres all right, even if my notes do not cohere."[40] It's clear too that discoveries like these inevitably involve a realisation of the value of human modesty within the grand order of things. Pound would arguably have been a far better, far less flawed poet if he had worked this out before his Fascist excesses, not left it till his last *Cantos*. But Pound was brilliantly gifted all along in *implying* connectivity through paratactical juxtaposition. Once you start connecting things up in non-linear fashion like that, you're not limited to balancing your life or vision inside the narrow bandwidth of sequential time. You set up – or rather, recognise, or rather, suggest or invoke a *field* – of dance, music, song, poetry. And what you recognise is that this field is the one that you're already in! Nor, I think, do you necessarily dance *against* death – if 'against' is meant in a simple antagonistic sense. The word 'against' could also mean 'towards', as in Spenser's line, "Against the Brydale day" in his 'Prothalamion',[41] as well as 'reliant on' in modern English, as in the phrase "to lean against a wall". I pick up this contradiction in a poem entitled 'Against the Day',[42] as well as in the title of the book in which that poem first appeared, *Against Perfection*. So the dance – of poetry, music, ritual – can be *with* death, that is to say, with death as a partner. Isn't this, perhaps, what the butterfly does?

3

SR: Your poems are deeply rooted in spiritual and psychological inquiry, in striving after the ineffable. They also inhabit a very physical reality and unfold against an historical backdrop, drawing in at times to celebrate the mundane occurrences of daily life. How do you negotiate these sometimes discontiguous terrains?

RB: The poetic, for me, is closely connected with and engrained in a sense of the radiance of the commonplace. This idea is embedded in my poetic philosophy. I've a poem called 'Only the Common Miracle',[43] and in *Under Balkan Light* there's a two-line poem which goes: "Voices in the mirror call / The commonplace is miracle."[44] I believe strongly that the commonplace is irradiated with wonder, delight, energy, power, beauty – and that's something that I'm learning more and more these days, now that I'm writing poems that are connected with – no, better, I should say, *rooted in* – Daoism and the *Yijing*. As a learner of *taiqi* and *qigong*, I definitely have that sense sometimes, when I'm doing *taiqi*, of a kind of radiance – the radiance of the ordinary.

SR: Is that for you the place where the poem is engendered? And does the poem involve finding the 'normal' world to be something other than the 'everyday' – I mean 'everyday' in the sense of merely 'banal', 'ordinary'?

RB: In a way, yes, to both these questions. But neither the language nor the experience – nor the world itself – *stop* being or belonging to the everyday. They are still the everyday. They consist of it and in it. For things are still what they are: "a rose is a rose is a rose."[45] And they are *just* what they are, nothing more or else, but they're also simultaneously invigorated, irradiated with energy.

As for poetic language, it doesn't necessarily have to condense or deviate from 'everyday' speech. In the positive sense, an everyday quality can give a poem an intimacy, a personal flavour – as, say, in George Herbert's line: "I made a posie, while the day ran by."[46] What could be more ordinary, domestic, down-to-earth than that? The claim of poetry to use (return to) the *koine*, the common tongue, to "language, such as men do use",[47] and the "language really used by men",[48] in any case reverberates powerfully throughout literary history. Think of Dante choosing Tuscan not Latin and – in their particular local varieties of English – Wordsworth, Whitman, Synge, William Carlos Williams. ... And not just "such as men do use", but women too. ... Nor does the poem's arrival necessarily mean sudden extraordinary mental leaps or dramatic heuristic flashes. The mundane world's being-noticed often 'happens' very quietly and undramatically. I explore some experiential aspects of this sense in several poems, including the rhymed lyric 'In the room suddenly', which focuses on the experience of listening to music,[49] and the last verse of 'The telling, first attempt' in *The Blue Butterfly*:

> All was ordinary, still – and yet, otherness
> without seam. The world did not sheer away
> but was its very self, no more nor less
> than ever, but tuned now to its own being,
> and the heard and seen were hearing, seeing,
> spirit within spiral, wave within way.[50]

Paradoxically, then, the music of the poem, the music that *is* the poem, *both* transforms the world *and* leaves it to carry on as before, though following the experience of the poem, the world appears more finely 'tuned'. But this sense only opens up, when the 'I' leaves off pushing and insisting. Does that correspond with your sense of what is poetic, of what is the charge?

SR: Celan spoke of "an addressable Thou"[51] and Rilke famously apostrophised his Angel in the *Duino Elegies,* defining it as "that being committed to the recognition of a higher order of reality in the invisible."[52] Yet there are almost certainly those poets for whom the otherness of the addressee is more hermetic, perhaps even an echo of the poet's own voice.

RB: Right. In my own case, when I talk of the 'other', I don't mean a narcissistic or egoist echo. I'm closer in spirit to Rilke, Celan, Mandelstam, and George Eliot – and Lévinas. I've a lot of poems about the imagined other, especially sonnets, where the reader is explicitly identified and addressed as the poem's imagined other. I also have a text on this addressee, entitled 'Pour toi', whose theme is precisely this.[53] Sometimes I even envisage that reader – other, interlocutor – as being 'present' on the 'other side' of the page I'm writing on, while I'm actually writing. At other times, I imagine the reader reading the text of the poem I'm writing, in hundreds of years' time. ... And of course, between the poet and the reader, death does intervene – simply because the reader may come along many centuries after the poet. For this reason, as I say in *Imagems (1)*, poems are "space-time travellers".[54] Shakespeare knew about this, and this theme is key to his sonnets: "So long as men can breathe or eyes can see, / So long lives this, and this gives life to thee."[55] And François Villon knew it: "Frères humains, qui après nous vivez." [Brother humans, who live after us.][56] Paul Celan knew it. And Osip Mandelstam in his essay 'To an Interlocutor' says that we all have friends, everyone has friends, we talk to our friends, we write to our friends, but the poet doesn't do that – the poet does something else. The poet is a person stranded on an island who sends a message out in a bottle.[57] So the poem is addressed 'to whom it may concern', possibly years and years after his own death. *The Manager* actually has the dedication "To whom it may concern". The person who picks up the bottle, whoever he or she happens to be, opens it, takes out the message, and finds that 'the message is addressed to *me* – because I am reading it!'

My internal configuration of that particular experience, in its most wonderful way, is tied to the story of Miklós Radnóti, the Hungarian poet.[58] Radnóti was a Jew, and as a prisoner at the end of the Second World War, he was being force-marched by the Germans down into Serbia and then back to Hungary. He kept a notebook, and in the inside front cover of that little school exercise book, he wrote – in French, and in English, and Serbian, and Hungarian – a message, to say that whoever finds this book, it is the property of so-and-so. And then he was shot! And the poems in this notebook were 'shot' too. They were gone for good. But after the war his grave was dug up, and the poems surfaced again, through death, *after* death. That's just amazing. Radnóti's reader exists – we readers exist – *on the other side* of his death.

SR: Carolyn Forché writes about Radnóti in her introduction to *Against Forgetting*, where she marvels that a poem might be the last record of a human life.⁵⁹

RB: She's right. But I'm making another point, about poems as connectors between life and life, between consciousness and consciousness, across death, despite death, in defiance of death. Think, too, of texts that were deliberately buried, whether to be preserved for posterity in this world or as passports to the next, or both – surfacing thousands of years later. I'm thinking of *Gilgamesh*, of the Dead Sea Scrolls, of the Mawangdui texts of the *Yijing* and *Dao De Jing*.

There's something else I'd like to add here, though – because I wouldn't want it to be thought that I'm the kind of poet who simply believes that the poem consists entirely of what you might call 'the haiku moment'. You know, that moment of rapture or thrill where the hairs on your arms stand up on end. I'm interested in lyric, of course, but also in long poems, and as I said earlier, I'm interested in history – in time and in space, and therefore in the architectonics of poems, of poems as buildings and streets and cities. I'm interested in the poem as big construct. Now, supposing you take that motif literally, to construct a poem *as* an 'inhabitable space', *as* a town or a city, as William Carlos Williams did in *Paterson,* or Charles Olson with Gloucester in *The Maximus Poems*, or Dylan Thomas in *Under Milk Wood* – you can't have wonderful apartments and beautiful buildings at every point in these poems, any more than in a living city. You've also got parts of those poems that aren't so wonderful. Bus stations? Slum areas? Refuse dumps? So even by that analogy, I think there's space, there are spaces, in long poems, big poems, for what might be considered, conventionally, the 'non-poetic'.

4

SR: Since we've been discussing the possibility of the poem-as-dialogue, perhaps we could turn to a poem that appears near the end of *The Blue Butterfly*: 'Conversation between a blue butterfly and a murdered man at the entrance to the underworld'. What I find remarkable here is how the dialogue speaks to us from a place referred to in the poem as "an edge, / a brink, *without-within*, one that is best / described by *notness*, by negations of / what may be defined".[60] Now, I know you've been working on a book of what you call 'metaphysical sonnets' with the curious title *Notness* ...[61]

RB: Yes, that title is an anagram of the word 'Sonnets'. And actually I've just completed this book. When I discovered that, simply by fooling around, I understood that I'd hit on something interesting. Incidentally, at first I actually thought I'd coined the word *notness*, but apparently the neologism belongs first to Dylan Thomas, who used it in 1933, and then to Henry Miller, who did so again in 1945.[62] But I extend the word's meaning in a non-pejorative way. One of the main themes of this sequence is that being and non-being – *isness* and *notness* – whirl around inside each other within the core of the moment – within the infinitesimally small *now* – in much the same way that subatomic particles (which are simultaneously *not-particles* but waves, and equally *not-waves* but particles) whizz around in the nucleus of an atom.

SR: Bearing that in mind, as well as the quote I've just mentioned, might the more general claim hold true too: that all poetry operates on an 'edge' or 'brink' between the expressible and the inexpressible? That is, might we consider the poem itself to exist in a constant condition of 'without-within', so that we reach a kind of paradox in which the eternal present/presence evoked by the poem is systematically undermined by the failure of language to reanimate what it names?

RB: I see what you mean, but from one point of view, at least, I think precisely what a good poem does *is* to reanimate what it names. That is to say, in a poem, the Saussurean *écart* between *signifiant* and *signifié* is bridged, re-forged, rebuilt. There's no inevitable or necessary failure in poetry: the poem makes – and constantly remakes – the world. Or: "In the beginning was the Word."

But from another point of view, language by its nature can't control, cover, touch, etc. – or even graze or skim – *everything*. So I think what you're saying is very powerful, and it reminds me of that trope in Zhuangzi about the trap (or net) and the fish. When you catch the fish, you no longer need the trap. When you catch the meaning, you no longer need the word. Trap and word are containers that you leave aside when you've caught what they're designed to catch.[63]

I think more could be added here. For example: in Daoist terms, if you understand this, it's scarcely the beginning of understanding. Because you can carry on discarding, in just this way – and according to the Daoists, discarding *is* the Way, the *Dao*. For when you've caught the idea contained in the meaning, you can discard the meaning. And when you've understood the idea, or think you've understood it, you can discard ideas too. ... And then, when you've discarded understanding, and discarded thinking, and discarded the ego-trip of thinking that you understand – then perhaps you may begin to realise that in the core of everything there's a nothing, as at the heart of an onion. And, conversely, in the core of every nothing, there's everything. ... And once all this has dawned on you, you may begin to realise too that there's no 'core' either, nor are there any 'surfaces' or 'depths', or even 'distances' or 'time', only a dance in which everything and nothing are constantly swirling around, transforming into each other, like subatomic particles in a Feynman diagram.[64] Then, once you've absorbed all this, you discover that you've hardly even begun to set out on the way, the *Dao*.[65]

And incidentally or coincidentally, somewhere in the course of all these transformations, you also realise what every poet knows: that words are imperfect instruments for registering and communicating reality, for netting meanings. As you say, there's always the sense with words that they leave something unsaid. They can't 'capture' the meaning, or thing, or experience in its entirety.

So when I accidentally discovered or, rather, following Dylan Thomas, rediscovered the word *notness*, I realised that I had in my grasp a word for this *nothing* at the heart of *everything*, one that relates to *thisness*, *nowness* and *hereness* in the same way that *nothing* relates to *everything*. So could the paradox at least partly be that this word *notness* perhaps itself actually succeeds in encapsulating what cannot be capsulated, even if only in part? That it does touch or at least comes close to touching the untouchable? That it at least borders the unsayable?

SR: That's a fascinating premise. And I want to say that there's a paradoxical energy at work in this language play that mirrors some of the larger questions confronted in *The Balkan Trilogy*. Is paradox a way of seeing-beyond language?

RB: Can we see or even cry 'beyond'? Or would it be more accurate to say that we may have the gift to sense it, to intuit it, in much the same way that a dowser is able to locate subterranean water, but can't explain how? I'd like to clarify that I don't think poets need to set out to be 'visionaries' who aim at 'surpassing' language in order to try to reach some mystical 'other' state or 'higher' state. I like the Daoist teachings because they say, and keep saying, that there's nowhere to go but *now-here*. Nowhere else. And *elseness* is itself engrained in the now-here. The Daoist injunction is nothing else but "Go here," which in English turns out to be deliciously paradoxical because the verb *go*, especially in the pithy imperative, implicitly carries the meaning *away from here*. To go *to* the *now-here* therefore embeds a contradiction and is itself paradoxical. And to go to the now-here and be fully in it is hardly easy, as anyone who has done any meditating knows. It takes practice, devotion, and discipline.

As poets we're locked into language. And even if we have the sense of the ineffable, of that which we cannot reach and still less touch, we're constantly coming back to language, which pulls us back to the palpable.

It's worth remembering too that Zhuangzi doesn't say that we throw away the net or trap for good. If we want to catch more fish, we'll need to use it again, or make another one. ... So long as we're alive, we carry on in our blood and bones and skins. ... We don't slough them off once and for all to attain 'higher states' – though who knows what mightn't be possible for a Daoist master? And as for the vast majority of us, so long as we're alive, we need food, and that food might well be fish. And so long as we're alive, we keep coming back to using words.

SR: The metaphor of the two-way bridge is apt. I've also seen the poem referred to as a "trajectory" by Octavio Paz, which I rather like.[66] Both instances remind me that poetry is fundamentally a linkage-*between*, which may also explain Paz's accompanying claim that "poetry is our only recourse against rectilinear time – against progress."[67] This seems true to me ...

RB: For Paz, the keys that oppose poetry to diachronic time are rhythm, repetition and cyclicity, all of which bring poetry closer to the experience of time in rite or ritual than in sequential history or linear logic.[68] This brings us back to what we've been saying about non-identical repetition. This also tallies well with the imagem I've already suggested: of a poem as a weft mapping and criss-crossing language along the axes of both diachronic and synchronic time – *and* patterning the stuff! Extend that two-dimensional model into three and more, and you begin to have something interesting.

SR: Somewhere along the line I got to thinking of the poem as existing in a condition of 'ablative presence', and this was especially true in my reading of 'A conversation between the blue butterfly and a murdered man at the entrance to the underworld.' Does this resonate at all with your experience of writing it?

RB: The distinction between the two voices in this poem got quite carefully mapped out at an early stage, and attention to that, once established, governed a good deal of my attention in the course of composition. The man, the dying man, talks in fourteeners. I think the fourteen-syllable line sets up an interesting pace, flexion, rhythm. It was tried out by some of the early Elizabethans, though in a rather rat-a-tat, bouncy, jangly way. So, in the 'Conversation' poem in *The Blue Butterfly*, on the one hand you have a long line that's rather prosaic, that holds rather well the patterns, rhythms, and inflections of contemporary English speech, while on the other you have the speeches of the butterfly rendered in iambic pentameters. This means that the mode in which the butterfly speaks is more 'vatic', more 'traditional', more sonorous. Now, that may or may not be noticed on the surface, but it's part of the craftwork that has gone into this poem's making. The two modalities are made present in the form, or rather brought into presence by and through the form.

In setting up this dialogue, I also found that it did move into questions of absence and presence, in various ways. For one thing, in terms of its entire subject matter, questions about which reality we're in, and whose reality, take us back again to the quotation from Zhuangzi that is one of the three epigraphs to *The Blue Butterfly*: "Once I dreamed I was a butterfly. Fluttering around, I was completely involved in being a butterfly and was unaware of being a man. Then, suddenly, I woke up and found myself myself again. Now I don't know whether I was a man dreaming I was a butterfly, or whether I'm a butterfly dreaming I was a man."[69] The fact that in this particular poem, the dialogue between the man and the butterfly takes place at the 'instant' of the man's dying, relates directly to – and spins out – Zhuangzi's multi-dimensional, koan-like question: as if to say "Is this all – has this all been – a dream? And if so, whose? The man's? Or the butterfly's?" (Which also, incidentally, forms the airy substance of Prospero's speech in *The Tempest*: "We are such stuff, as dreams are made on, and our little life / is rounded with a sleep.")[70]

My blue butterfly, though, in keeping with the Greek and European tradition that I'm steeped in, doesn't quite share the human speaker's mortality, but is inescapably identified with ψυχή [*psyche*]. This soul-butterfly / butterfly-soul hovers over and around the gate that divides this world from the underworld, as its keeper and guardian. The butterfly, then, simultaneously belongs to both zones and neither zone. And regardless of whatever the butterfly 'really' is or may be in itself, the reality is that to the man at and in that instant of his dying, that butterfly appears as a psychopomp, a soul-guide. In Chinese and European traditions alike, for obvious reasons to do with its changes into different states, the butterfly is interpretable as a 'symbol of transformation'.[71]

SR: The butterfly as soul-guide, yes. And that's a powerful trope throughout the three books.

RB: There are at least three plaited strands here: butterfly as soul-guide, as messenger from the soul, and as soul itself. ... And the other question to be asked here is: how long is an instant? How long is the singularity of a 'now'? This is a long poem, eleven pages, so the instant of dying is stretched out, almost as if linear time had come to a standstill, or been flattened out, or collapsed, at this point. Well, at the instant of death, linear time is no longer relevant. In envisioning this very long drawn out 'instant' of dying, I suppose I was trying to peep into, or prise open, or scry, or stretch my hearing, as far as I could – though not one of these verbs, by the very impossibility of the task, could ever quite fit adequately – into what goes on in that moment between life and death that the *bardo*s of the *Tibetan Book of the Dead* talk about.[72] With no 'authority' whatever, I was trying to push that boundary as far as I could.

In doing that, something happened: I found that the butterfly made gnomic utterances which I didn't expect and still don't fully understand. And which I don't regard as 'my' invention, you know, or as 'my' poetics. It was as if the butterfly was dictating to me.

5

SR: Let's return to something you said earlier about the poem perhaps existing as a document of record for something that has happened. The poems in this trilogy, for instance, represent the historical event or events they're documenting ...

RB: ... happened in the world, yes ...

SR: ... which I find compelling considered against the very long postscripts that end the book, your research notes. How do you manage these two sides, the creative side and also the documentary side, within the book?

RB: I suppose that it's partly to do, for myself, with a certain kind of obsessiveness. And with what you were saying earlier about having a conversation with oneself. My procedures go something like this.

First, the poem itself emerges, as the primary text, as fully experiential, as a kind of writing that engages me entirely. As I experience it, the writing of a poem isn't usually driven first and foremost by the head, and certainly not by the intellect alone. It's not just abstract or theoretical. It involves other kinds of energetic engagement that are directly experienced as embodied – emotional, intuitive, physical – all of which work synthetically, and synaesthetically, with and through the shaping intellect. The word we have for this synaesthetic faculty-of-faculties, this overall faculty that is more than the sum of all its parts, is Imagination. It's what Coleridge called "the esemplastic power",[73] deriving his idea from Schelling's notion of *Ineinsbildung*.[74] Both Coleridge's and Schelling's term means 'the forming or making together into one' of opposites – again, a making, a doing, that involves a *coincidentia oppositorum*.

After the poem has emerged in this way, and been worked on carefully, and placed in what for me is its 'final' context, a book – after all these procedures – I also want to ruminate on it, to 'understand' ('stand-under') what I've been doing. And this is the point when the analytic intellect comes in. So footnotes and postscripts are first and foremost my – perhaps rather futile – attempts to try to pin things down. Futile, because explication and explanation can never clarify the whole picture in the way that a poem can encapsulate it. Explications often tend towards simplification, while meanings in poems are multi-layered, complex, polysemic.

But I do it all the same.

And this brings me to the second reason. Thinking about poems and exploring them intellectually outside and after their composition, and researching whatever it may be that lies around them and behind them, deepens and broadens my understanding of the field they're embedded in; and this process can in turn lead to more poems, so that the already-made poems themselves become *part of the field*, and an oscillating and never-ending two-way relationship develops between the generating of new poems and the field out of which they emerge. Isn't this Wordsworth's "interminable building" again, which I've already mentioned?

The third reason I include notes and documentation is that the making of a poem for me is often a powerful, formative, heuristic – and primary – experience in its own right; and, incidentally, not necessarily at all one that "takes its origin from emotion recollected in tranquillity".[75] This being so, intellectualising a powerful experience is synonymous and coterminous with distancing myself from it, or rather, containing it in a detached, separated form. And this self-distancing in turn means freeing myself up to be open and ready to new poems.

As for these three Balkan books, there are many names, contexts and references that most English-speaking readers are unlikely to know. So in these books, my notes are there to allow an interested reader to explore unfamiliar places and zones.

SR: I love the implied idea here that books are evolving entities, and that different readers will encounter the same text under different frames of reference.

RB: Yes, even an apparently 'fixed' text has a mobility. For example, it gets translated, performed, quoted from, selected from, abridged.

6

SR: Turning now to *In Time of Drought*: in the postscript you describe how in the act of the poem's making you arrived at "an attempt to eliminate any elements of my own voice".[76]

RB: Yes. We've touched on aspects of that issue throughout this conversation, haven't we?

SR: Right. This seems to resonate with something that Eliot said elsewhere about the progress of the artist being a continual self-sacrifice, or an extinction of one's personality.[77] Since it is precisely your experience that drives the meditations in *The Blue Butterfly* and *Under Balkan Light*, what was it about these particular books that led you to push your voice into the margins?

RB: I agree with Eliot here, although I don't see this process in terms of a Christian abnegation, as he implies, perhaps of the same kind and order as that of his saintly Christian figure of Thomas à Becket in *Murder in the Cathedral*. Perhaps I can come back to that. As well as Eliot, one could think of Samuel Beckett, who said: "En francais, c'est plus facile d'écrire sans style."[78]

My desire to do something like this in that particular book did have to do with the same kind of shedding. Since I was a student, fifty years ago, I've made it my business to work painstakingly on craft, and as a result I suppose I'm skilled in a number of different poetic modes. Added to which, musicality has always come quite easily to me. Could that have been because my father was a musician, even though he died when I was very young? At any rate, it's not hard for me to write well in certain styles. But then, I think, there comes a certain point where one wants to shed 'styles' altogether. One says to oneself: "I don't need this kind of stuff anymore," you know. "I just want to be simple, to listen to the poem and get my ego out of the way." This sentiment was voiced wonderfully by George Herbert in the seventeenth century. He has these lines in a great poem called 'The Forerunners': "Lovely enchanting language, sugar-cane, / Hony of roses, whither wilt thou flie?"[79] Now there's melody! He's got it all there, and he's *good* at it. He knows how to do it, how to achieve grace, elegance, beauty. But this poem of his is about *rejecting* all of that, and moving on. So in the same poem he writes "Farewell sweet phrases, lovely metaphors." It is as if he says: "No. I want to write for my God, simply and purely."

Now I'm not a Christian, and am far from being any kind of monotheist, but not altogether dissimilarly, what was going on for me in composing *In a Time of Drought* was the desire to get the trappings of my own ego, my own personal stuff, out of the way, because I knew that I was in touch with something more powerful. Again I come back here to a Jungian model: something archetypal. In retrospect, I think it's accurate to put it this way: not being dominated by ego seemed to be part of what was 'required' of me – whatever or whoever I am, or is, or was – by the poem itself. To put it more crudely: this poem simply didn't need to be filtered through my own bullshit, my personal crap. What it needed was clarity and resonance, not cleverness, not personality. My friend Peter Mansfield, who helped me work on the polished drafts in extensive email exchanges, entered fully into that intention with me.

SR: Because I read this as such a rich, musical book, I'm led to believe that it's music that enters your work once the ego and personal pronoun 'I' come out. Is this your feeling as well?

RB: The idea that music enters once the ego partially 'dissolves' – or rather, when the borders of the ego become porous – is true. This takes us back to Kay Young's wonderful essay on *Daniel Deronda*, doesn't it?[80] But how do I define that quality of the work that is *not my personal* self?

SR: Right! And that's a clever reversal of what I'm trying to pin down here. … How *does* one eliminate personal voice from a poem? And what happens when you *do* strip it away, when the 'I' is abandoned, along with its egocentric demands on the poem – what stands in its place? I ask this because the relative absence of a centrally-located 'I' in this book suggested to me a correspondingly fuller emphasis on the qualities of rhythm and music.

RB: If that is what happens here, I'm delighted. I can't answer for this particular book: that's for a reader to do. But in general, I do believe you're right in linking the loss or dropping of ego-concerns with a greater likelihood of being able to open up to fuller, deeper and richer resonances, and, as a direct consequence of that, to opening up to everything that *music* and *musicality* imply. Another way of putting this is that only when the 'I' is dropped is it possible to be amenable and attentive to the voice of the *other* – of Rimbaud's *autre*. Or, if you like, when one's personal voice is 'vacated', then the *transpersonal* has a chance of appearing. "Be not afeard; the isle is full of noises," says Caliban, "Sounds and sweet airs, that give delight and hurt not."[81] The Caliban in each of us hears and responds to this kind of music more effectively than any self-driven inner rationalist or materialist. Even so, we're still faced with the question, who is it that does the dropping? I would say it's still the individual, but one who's got wiser, deeper, and more attuned to what's going on within and without himself/herself, who's no longer so bound up in ego-consciousness.

Even so, there's another aspect to this discussion that we haven't broached yet. I think we may need to be a little more attentive to how we talk about the 'I' and the 'non-I', the ego and the non-ego. And perhaps it wouldn't be a bad thing to qualify, modify, and even to contradict some of the ways we've been talking about these areas until now. For example, I don't think the tropes of 'stripping away' or 'pushing into the margins' or 'casting out' the 'I' are entirely accurate or helpful. The 'I' isn't a layer of paint. Nor is it a taboo creature or spirit, a demon or monster to be 'cast out', in the sense of 'exorcised'. (Caliban is a "monster" to the callous and thick-headed Trinculo and Stefano.) What I mean here is that I don't think the ego can or should be stripped or peeled off, or cast out, or anything like that, if this procedure is construed as a simple act of will. Here, we're partly back with Shelley's objections to 'will' as the prime driver. But it's not only that. It's because it's precisely the 'I' that *exerts* that kind of will. So the exercise of banishing or cutting out the 'I', if *merely* willed, is necessarily carried out by that same 'I'. Here's a double-bind, a self-deception, a psychological trick we can all too easily play on ourselves, to enable us to think we're wiser than we really are. There's a glaring tautology here.

SR: Yet it also strikes me as the most available way of speaking about an 'elimination of voice', especially since the presence or absence of an identifiable speaker tends to be so completely tied up in the kind of impressions a reader will formulate.

RB: Perhaps. But to take this point a little further still – will, intention, determination, etc., not to mention survival, *depend* on the ego and its strength. Deprive a child of ego, deny a child of 'I', and you deprive that child of survival skills and possibly of sanity. Consolidate the child's ego, and you build confidence, opportunity, creativity, trust, and capacity for love.

As for poetry, without an initial experiencing 'I', there's no experience and no poem. Deny the initial experiencing 'I' and the entire humanity of the poem – its feeling and its feeling tone, the sympathy and empathy between 'I' and 'other' – get lost. I draw attention to this not just in the context of our discussion of a particular poem or poems, but because, as I see it, there are fashions and orthodoxies in contemporary poetics to do with these issues of ego. I think we need to see these issues clearly and not be beguiled or cheated by intellectual hegemonies of taste. I'm thinking here especially of the idea of the 'death of the author' and the invention of the term 'scriptor' by Barthes, which was followed by Foucault, as well as Derrida, in the late 1960s and through the 1970s.[82] Their ideas were swept into Anglophone poetry, especially through the L=A=N=G=U=A=G=E poets, as part of an ideologically motivated programme, so that getting rid of the 'I' was *de rigueur*. And the poetics that emerged independently in England through Jeremy Prynne and the so-called Cambridge school and other groups wasn't dissimilar. Some of these poets exert powerful egos. I think we should be wary of trusting, let alone accepting any statements of theirs about 'abolishing' the ego, and we should view that as a rhetorical trick, one that's all the more suspect when they and their disciples and adherents don't see it as such. By this I mean that *forcing* the 'I' out means it goes back into hiding and gets more and more devious, which results in even bigger ego trips, and correspondingly bigger self-deceptions and more strenuous denials of those ego trips by the perpetrators.

SR: This is certainly one possible consequence of "forcing the 'I' out", but is it the only one? I also wonder if eliminating the personal voice from the poem makes possible a return to polyvocality, or at least invites into the poem the kind of transpersonal material typically filtered by an ego-bound or controlling 'I'.

RB: Yes, of course it does. But I think we need to be especially wary here, since there are so many traps dictated by contemporary hype and intellectual fashion that are all too easy for the unsuspecting to fall into, and if we aren't careful what we shall end up with is specious, ersatz, bogus.

For a start, eliminating the personal or narratorial 'I' may be appropriate, called for, necessary, even inevitable, in genres such as drama. Suspending or dropping the 'I' can work well in other genres too, for example in third person narratives, including epics, ballads and novels. As I've mentioned, that solution worked well for my purposes in *In a Time of Drought*. This poem is best described, I suppose, as a set of ballads or cantos, even though I added a personal memoir in the voice of the 'I' in the 'Postscript'.[83]

But anyone who knows the slightest tricks of rhetoric knows that pronouns can replace one another and that they operate in fundamentally binary sets, which are often 'marked'/'unmarked', as do active and passive voices of verbs. So it's dead easy to hide the 'I', and *pretend* that it has been 'transcended', when it has only been suppressed or disguised, quite possibly for manipulative or propagandistic ends.

What's more, without 'I', there's no 'Thou'. Which means that without 'I', there can be no love poetry, and no devotional poetry. No psalms. No hymns. Nor a poetry of lamentation or genuine protest. Ultimately, then, you can't have *lyric* poetry at all without an 'I'. What an impoverishment. The strictly *grammatical* issue here is that if it is *de rigeur* to ban the 'I', relationality itself is put under full frontal attack. Relationality itself is dependent on distinctions (demarcations) between persons, pronouns, *personae*; and when these get fudged, blurred, squeezed or squashed, the result is that individuality, difference and otherness, not to mention respect and affection for them – and hence freedom itself – all get thrown out too. Complete *depersonalisation* ensues. A linguistic issue hence becomes a social, moral, psychological and metaphysical one. And since lyric itself then has no ground to stand on, it evaporates, escapes.

There can be no recognition and acceptance of distinctness of one from another without persons. I would go further than this and say not only are lyric, relationality and sociability under attack, but also *human bodies*. The 'difficult' poetry we're talking about is bodiless, faceless, eyeless (I-less), personless. Without bodies the five senses have no home, and there's no eros, no desire, no love. Universal elimination of the 'I' is therefore anti-human, and according to the paradigmatic model of historical reversal, the L=A=N=G=U=A=G=E poets and their followers, by very dint of so strenuously denying the 'I' in order to absolve themselves from bourgeois sentimentality, and by insisting on the so-called materiality of language, ignore its humanness and its capacity for interiority and desire. And their concept of 'materiality' in any case seems crudely utilitarian – based on nineteenth century mental models, as if the discoveries of quantum physics meant nothing.

So, the net result is that the polar opposite of your implication becomes true. Polyvocality gets undermined. The transpersonal is unattainable. All that is left is language: pettiness not poetry, hype not hope. Triviality and preciousness. Language belongs to human beings, who have bodies, brains, hearts, lungs and voices. Poems aren't brainless or heartless or voice-less. They're written by real men and women who intend (mean) to write them, not by 'scriptors', as Barthes and Foucault claim. Nor is writing (*écriture*) primary, as Derrida claims, in its 'control' over humans. I agree with Catherine Pickstock's assault on the pre-eminence Derrida accords to *écriture*:

> Unlike inspiration from the Muses, there is here no knowing invocation of the impersonal Derridean god: *writing*. Derrida's emphasis on the commerce of absence and death with writing causes him irresponsibly to discount the way in which *all language presupposes engagement with living bodies*.[84] (My emphasis, RB).

She continues:

> Such writing acts automatically, without reference to place or time. It is a universalizer in a nihilistic mode. There is no subject. There are only objects, death(s).[85]

I also agree with what Nasos Vayenas says of some of these writers and their followers in his critique entitled 'Identity and Poetic Language', part of which I've co-translated.

> Can it really be that literary writing is a field where … every trace of the writer's individual identity, all attempt at expression, has been obliterated? … Regardless of the extent to which language may have its own will, and however extensive may be that part of language which the poet is unable to control, the part that the poet *is* able to control is what actually moulds the part that is uncontrollable into poetic discourse. This part, the part of the language that *can* be moulded by the poet's expressive will, is formed by the nature of the poet's spoken discourse (*parole*). No poem is a real poem unless it possesses the character of the poet's spoken discourse, which is shaped by the poet's deeper self and which in turn shapes the voice in the poet's text.[86]

The author is *not* dead. It's the author who gives authority: authority is the author's behest and bequest. More: the author is authentic. The author's voice is what authenticates the poem. The poem is authenticated in having had an author, with a distinct, distinctive, personal, human voice, and a set of directed, willed intentions, even if we don't know his or her name, or anything else about her or him, other than the surviving poem.

As for the dissolution of the 'ego', when it comes to the processes we've been talking about, the word *shedding* has cropped up, and I believe this may be more helpful and more accurate than *stripping*, etc. *Shedding* implies the imagem of a gradual, organic process, one that (as Jung says) tends to happen in the second part of human life,[87] a natural letting go of ego-concerns, a falling or dropping away, like leaves from an autumnal tree.

And perhaps yet another way of thinking about this is that no shedding happens at all, that rather the ego becomes more firmly based, and more fully contextualised, in a deepened self, until its dissolution in death.

If I look back now at *The Blue Butterfly*, the first book in *The Balkan Trilogy*, its starting point certainly wasn't an abnegation, denial or repression of ego. The experience that became the matter of the subject poem was very much *mine*: the butterfly sat on *my* finger, on *my* writing hand. And if I now read this title poem as if it were written by someone else, a salient exercise for any writer, I can't help noticing that the word "me" or "my" occurs in it ten times: an emphatic reiteration. On the evidence of this, then, I would say that the transcendent experience of synchronicity that we've been talking about in relation to the making of this poem didn't abolish ego-consciousness but, on the contrary, first consolidated it and strengthened it. My conclusion, then, is that identity, far from being obliterated, gets more firmly rooted, consolidated (grounded) and deepened through this kind of experience. What's more, I don't believe the disappearance of the ego can be forced or commanded, whether by fashion or any other kind of dictate. In this context, the willed obliteration of the ego doesn't make good sense at all, in any sense.

SR: The final question I wanted to ask about the trilogy has to do with the larger ethical implications facing the language arts as they approach social atrocities of this magnitude. On one hand we have Theodor Adorno's famous, oft-quoted remark "To write poetry after Auschwitz is barbaric."[88] On the other hand, Brecht's "Motto": "In the dark times will there also be singing? / Yes, there will also be singing. / About the dark times."[89] And my question, for you, when navigating this sort of material, is where you find yourself between Adorno's recourse to silence and the Brechtian call to song as a form of witnessing?

RB: I'm contra-Adorno. I've written my response to his remark very clearly into *The Blue Butterfly*. I can't possibly doubt Adorno's sincerity or his integrity. I consider him a serious thinker, although not one I'm attuned to in the sense that he appeals to me viscerally, in my core. I honour him and I honour his integrity. But I think he's *wrong*. And quite apart from the fact that his statement has been taken out of context, and, anyway, he modified it later – the reason I think that he's wrong is that after Auschwitz, we *must* write. We have the duty to articulate, to do as much as we can to understand, to deepen and clarify our understanding of evil. And the function of language remains to understand, to articulate understanding. So I'm going to end our conversation with a quote, if I may, from a poem that was intended as my implicit response to Adorno, although I've written more poems since then returning to the same theme: that poetry has a moral purpose in relation to human stupidity, barbarity, cruelty and capacity for evil. Poetry stands against them.

I call this poem 'The Telling', and there are three parts to it, which I call three 'attempts' at telling. This is the 'second attempt'. Now the whole assumption underlying this title and subtitle is that the 'attempt' – any attempt – to express the inexpressible, whether it is to verbalise the horrific, like the massacre of nearly three thousand people at Šumarice, or the ineffable, like the butterfly settling on my writing hand at the site of that massacre – is bound to fail. But, still, the aspiration has to be there. For this contradiction turns out to be the paradox without which poetry can't happen.

> Nobody could stay unmoved in this place,
> not blench at all, not flinch with at least some
> tightening of skin, muscles of throat and face
> or watering of eyes. *We who live on*
> *might have been them.* There's no prerogative on
> pain. Cruelty's commonness makes us all dumb.
>
> Numb silence, though, is no answer to evil.
> To remain tacit, to call up no speech on its
> repeated occurrences, is to grovel
> before it, as to some pre-ordained essence
> demanding just as complete acquiescence
> as the rotation of seasons and planets,
>
> and that won't do. Fail or not, I must try
> this telling ...[90]

April 2012 – July 2013
Santa Barbara, Tucson and Cambridge

Notes

1. *The Balkan Trilogy* consists of *The Blue Butterfly*, *In a Time of Drought* and *Under Balkan Light* (RB 2011 [3, 4 and 5]).
2. Jung 1969 [2] [1960], 'Synchronicity: An Acausal Connecting Principle': 417–531, esp. 426, 435 and 439ff.
3. RB 2011 [3], *The Blue Butterfly*: 8–9.
4. Cavell, 'What Is a Thing Called?': 65–85. See esp. 84: "[O]nly I could reach to the other's (inner life). ... It calls upon me, it calls me out. I have to acknowledge it. I am fated to that as I am to my body; it is as natural to me."
5. Jung, *op. cit.*: 485: "The synchronicity principle asserts that the terms of a meaningful coincidence are connected by *simultaneity* and *meaning*."
6. Written between 1974 and 1976. See RB 2011 [1], *For the Living*: 52–56 and 221.
7. Jung, *op. cit.*
8. Celan: 396: "Poems in this sense too are underway: they are making toward something. Toward what? Toward something standing open, occupiable, perhaps toward an addressable Thou, toward an addressable reality." See also RB 2002 [1], 'Pour toi'.
9. RB 2011 [4], *In a Time of Drought*: 103.
10. See 'Arijana's Thread', RB 2011 [4], *In a Time of Drought*: 73–77, esp. 76–77 for RB's statements on composition.
11. RB 2011 [4], *In a Time of Drought*: 81–101.
12. Jakobson 1985 [1] and [2].
13. Grimm: 334–336.
14. Frazer: 69–70.
15. See Arnaudov: 155–201.
16. See Plotnikova: 100–103.
17. Ivanov and Toporov: 106–108.
18. See RB 2013, *Imagems (1): six statements on poetics*: 26. "I have coined the term 'imagem' with the meaning 'nexus, web, net, body, corpus, etc., of integrally associated ideas and images'. An *imagem* is composite, complex and polysemic. It also implies 'unit of imagery', comparable to the word *mythologem* ('unit of myth or mythology', or, as defined by the *Oxford English Dictionary* online, 'fundamental theme or motif of myth or other discourse')."
19. Frye: 326. See also 50–51 in this book.

20 Shelley 1923 [1840], 53: "Poetry is not like reasoning, a power to be exerted according to the determination of the will. A man cannot say, 'I will compose poetry.' The greatest poet even cannot say it; for the mind in creation is as a fading coal, which some invisible influence, like an inconstant wind, awakens to transitory brightness; this power arises from within, like the colour of a flower which fades and changes as it is developed, and the conscious portions of our natures are unprophetic either of its approach or its departure. Could this influence be durable in its original purity and force, it is impossible to predict the greatness of the results; but when composition begins, inspiration is already on the decline, and the most glorious poetry that has ever been communicated to the world is probably a feeble shadow of the original conceptions of the poet." (emphasis, RB).

21 Hughes and Heinz: 54–94. Quoted by Wilson: 361: "Maybe all poetry, insofar as it moves us and connects with us, is a revealing of something that the writer doesn't actually want to say, but desperately needs to communicate, to be *delivered of*" (emphasis, RB).

22 Shelley, *op. cit.*: 54.

23 Hughes: 15–23.

24 'On Poetry and Catching Glories', and 'On Poetry and Magnanimity', RB 2013, *Imagems (1)*: 20–22 and 23–25.

25 *Note from RB*: I am indebted to Catherine Pickstock for sending me her unpublished paper 'Repetition and Things', which I had heard her deliver at the PACE Conference at Robinson College, Cambridge, on October 28, 2012, and her unpublished book *Repetition and Identity*. My idea of 'twiceness' develops from her work. See Pickstock 2013. See also notes 37, 84 and 85 below.

26 RB 2011 [3], *The Blue Butterfly*: 10.

27 RB 2015 [2].

28 *Note from RB*: Hopson, reporting on research from Paris, writes: "The fetal heartbeat will slow down when a familiar French fairy tale such as 'La Poulette' ('The Chick') or 'Le Petit Crapaud' ('The Little Toad') is read near the mother's belly. When the same reader delivers another unfamiliar story, the fetal heartbeat stays steady. ... The fetus is likely responding to the *cadence of voices and stories, not their actual words*, observes Fifer, but the conclusion is the same: the fetus can listen, learn, and remember at some level, and, as with most babies and children, *it likes the comfort and reassurance of the familiar*" (emphasis, RB). See Hopson, and RB 2015 [2].

29 RB 2011 [3], *The Blue Butterfly*: 3.

30 *Ibid.*: 4–5.

31 Eliot 1959 [1943]: 44.

32 *Ibid.*: 51.
33 RB 2011[3], *The Blue Butterfly*: 6–7.
34 Rimbaud, 'Letter to Georges Izambard', Charleville, 13 May, 1871: 304–305.
35 See Sheldrake 2009 [1981] and 2011.
36 Young: 75–123, esp. 122–123: "I understand George Eliot's moments of profoundest exchange to happen through sound. In *Daniel Deronda*, the chanting of Jewish prayer creates an aural bridge between the human and the divine. Eliot does not call upon us to listen either to evolution or the past – those, it seems, we can see. Instead, she calls us to hear what transcends human time, namely, the sounds of the Eternal." See also note 80 below.
37 Pickstock, *op. cit.* See also notes 25 above and 84 and 85 below.
38 Bohm: 225: "We proposed that a new notion of order is involved here, which we called the *implicate order* (from a Latin root means 'to enfold' or 'to fold inward'). In terms of the implicate order we may say that everything is enfolded into everything."
39 Wordsworth 1969 [1933]: 31.
40 Pound, 'Canto CXVI': 27. See also: 71 and 86 in this book.
41 Spenser: 600–604.
42 RB 2011 [1], *For the Living*: 185–195.
43 *Ibid.*: 160–161.
44 RB 2011 [5], *Under Balkan Light*, 'In the mirror': 75.
45 Stein: 187.
46 Herbert: 85.
47 Jonson, *Every Man in His Humour*, Prologue: 7.
48 Wordsworth 1956 [1933]: 152.
49 RB 1999, *Against Perfection*, 'In the room, suddenly': 41–42:

>   Not beauty, quite, if beauty is a sheen
>   holding its beholders in a steady state
>   of trance. Nor did it mean or seem to mean
>   anything words or concepts could translate.
>   Breathing just went on normally. No screen
>   or veil was drawn from eyes to shower a spate
>   of revelations through us, and no paean
>   of angel voices shook from heaven's gate.

50 RB 2011 [3], *The Blue Butterfly*: 11.
51 Celan, *op. cit.*: 396.
52 Rilke, quoted in Wood: 148.

53 See RB 2002 [1], 'Pour toi'.

54 RB 2013, *Imagems (1)*, 'A Little Further': 10: "Poetry is a challenge to mortality and a criticism of Death. Crossing deaths, poems are spacetime-travellers: they encapsulate a non-self-defeating irony, the only defeat Death might admit, if Death had words."

55 Shakespeare, Sonnet 18.

56 Villon, 'L'Épitaphe Villon' ['Villon's Epitaph'], also known as 'Ballade des Pendus' ['Ballad of the Hanged (Men)']: 159.

57 Mandelstam: 59. "Everybody has friends. Why doesn't the poet turn to his friends, to those people who are naturally close to him? The shipwrecked sailor throws a sealed bottle into the sea at a critical moment, and it has his name in it and what happened to him. Many years later, walking along the dunes, I find it in the sands, I read the letter, I learn when it happened, the testament of the deceased. I had a right to do this. I did not unseal someone else's letter. The letter sealed in the bottle was addressed to its finder. I found it. That means, then, that I am its secret addressee."

58 See Radnóti 1992, 2000 and 2010.

59 Forché: 29–47, esp. 31: "A poem that calls on us from the other side of a situation of extremity cannot be judged by simplistic notions of 'accuracy' or 'truth to life.' It will have to be judged, as Ludwig Wittgenstein said of confessions, by its consequences, not by our ability to verify its truth. In fact, the poem might be our only evidence that an event has occurred: it exists for us as the sole trace of an occurrence."

60 RB 2011 [3], *The Blue Butterfly*: 90.

61 RB 2015 [1].

62 *OED online*. Consulted July 29, 2013.

63 Chuang Tzu 2006 [1996]: 242: "A fish trap is used to catch fish, but once the fish have been taken, the trap is forgotten. The rabbit trap is used to snare rabbits, but once the rabbit is captured, the trap is ignored. Words are used to express concepts, but once you have grasped the concepts, the words are forgotten. I would like to find someone who has forgotten the words so I could debate with such a person."

64 See Gleick: esp. 230.

65 Capra: 241, 243, 265ff and 289ff.

66 Paz 1973: 69: "The Word has its roots in a silence *previous* to speech – a presentiment of language. Silence, *after* the Word, is based on a language – it is an encoded silence. The poem is the trajectory between these two silences – between the wish to speak and the silence that fuses the wishing with the speaking."

67 *Ibid.*: 67.

68. *Ibid.*: 65. "Rhythm is the original metaphor and encompasses all the others. It says: succession is repetition, time is nontime. ... [T]he poem is succession and repetition, a date on the calendar and a rite."
69. RB's translation: see RB 2011 [3], *The Blue Butterfly*: viii. For other versions, see Chuang Tsu: 48; and Chuang Tzu: 20.
70. *The Tempest*, Act IV, Scene 1, ll. 156–158.
71. See Jung 1986 [1956].
72. Evans-Wentz 1960 [1949].
73. Coleridge 1906 [1817]: 153; and on the joining of opposites: 156.
74. Carver: 329.
75. Wordsworth 1956 [1921]: 171: "I have said that poetry is the spontaneous overflow of powerful feelings: it takes its origin from emotion recollected in tranquillity: the emotion is contemplated till, by a species of reaction, the tranquillity gradually disappears, and an emotion, kindred to that which was before the subject of contemplation, is gradually produced, and does itself actually exist in the mind."
76. RB 2011 [4], *In a Time of Drought*, 'Arijana's Thread': 77.
77. Eliot 1998 [1920]: 30.
78. See also 64 in this book.
79. Herbert, 'The Forerunners': 167–168.
80. Young; and see also note 36 above.
81. Shakespeare, *The Tempest*: Act III, Scene 2, 1. 533.
82. See Barthes; also Foucault: 113–138.
83. RB 2011 [4], *In a Time of Drought*: 73–77.
84. Pickstock 1998: 24. See also notes 25 and 37 above.
85. *Ibid.*: 36.
86. Vayenas 2010 [1]: 138.
87. Jung 1969 [1] [1960]: 387–403.
88. Adorno, 'Cultural Criticism and Society'. In *Prisms*: 34.
89. Motto to the 'Svendborg Poems' ['Motto der Svendborger Gedichte']. In *Poems: Part 1, 1913–1956*: 320.
90. RB 2011 [3], *The Blue Butterfly*: 14.

The Interview as Text and Performance

Richard Berengarten and John Z. Dillon

This interview was conducted by email between South Bend, Indiana, and Cambridge, in May, June and July 2013. It was revisited and edited in November–December 2014 and March–June 2015.

JD

1

John Dillon: Conventionally the interview is not considered a stand-alone art form, but a discussion or context for situating the artist or the artwork. Do you think the interview, as a genre, could be considered an art form?

Richard Berengarten: The conventional view makes good but not complete sense. I'd argue that an interview *can* be considered as an art form, for various reasons, and that it's a 'part of the work' in a distinctive way.

JD: Could you unpack this understanding a bit?

RB: Let's start by exploring the literary interview, as text, and then branch out from there. When a published interview with a *writer* is in question, since the writer's medium is words, a statement made by that writer about his/her writing could itself be said to be integrally part of the oeuvre. Admittedly, it may be regarded as secondary, or ancillary to the main body, thrust, intention, etc. of the 'work', or as a by-product of it, or explication or commentary on it – in the same way, say, that a writer's correspondence or notebooks are, or an autobiography can be. But still, after that writer's death, an interview unquestionably becomes part of the overall work. What's more, a statement made in an interview may even be interpreted in retrospect as a key that unlocks integral themes, patterns, meanings, contexts, etc. in the rest of the work. Ted Hughes's comment about poetic intention, for example, in his famous *Paris Review* interview[1] is arguably as self-revealing and as crucial to an understanding of his own poetry as is, say,

Keats's striking comment in a letter to his brothers on 'negative capability', which illuminates his own mode of composition.² Seamus Heaney's 2008 book of interviews with Dennis O'Driscoll, a single, sympathetic and informed interlocutor, combines the candour of personal narrative with the pleasure of relaxed conversation. This big book comes across as a kind of autobiography conducted through dialogue with an ever-ready listener, and there are moments when it almost reads like an epistolary novel. The finest body of literary interviews in English is the *Paris Review* series. This has been going strong for sixty years. Its first issue in Spring 1953 contained an interview with E. M. Forster. Its first interview with a poet featured T. S. Eliot, six years later. Some of these *Paris Review* pieces are mini-classics, minor masterpieces in their own right.

Second, if you think about it structurally for a moment, in an interview with a writer, something rather interesting is going on. A condition for an interview is that the interviewer is expected to know the writer's work, i.e. to be a reader, and one who is informed, sensitive and attentive. So the interview itself is distinct from that writer's other productions in that it gets made in collaboration with this other person, who may be but is not necessarily a writer himself or herself. Not only that: in an interview the sequential order of roles between reader and writer vis-à-vis the text is reversed, since the interview starts with the reader-interviewer's question. So within the frame of the interview itself, here for once the writer (text-maker) is not the initiator. Rather, that text's first shaper and prime locutor is the reader-interviewer-interlocutor, even though of course in response to a prior text or texts by the writer. The literary interview, then, is a collaborative text motivated, prompted, encouraged – perhaps one could even say drawn out – from a writer by a reader.

Third, like a jazz duet, an interview, is improvised. One of the basic elements of conversation itself is unpredictability. Neither interviewer nor interviewee knows entirely or exactly what will emerge from their interaction. Even if either one of them has a self-rehearsed plan or model, for example a list of points or a topical or chronological ordering principle, neither participant is or can be 'in total control' in advance. The contributions of both feed into the final version, and this integral whole will be more than the simple sum of the contributions of its makers: it will have a composite character of its own. Spontaneous surprise and discovery may occur on both sides, so that a reciprocity, an intimacy, may be generated, resulting in a particular energetic quality. And chance, serendipity and synchronicity may also play their parts in composition. And what's more, by encouraging, challenging, querying and testing the writer, a sensitive and attuned interviewer may elicit the expression of *new* ideas from the writer, not to mention buried or dormant memories. This kind of probing and extension of edges, this articulation of unexpected depths and heights, itself constitutes discovery, however small or subtle. The process is necessarily heuristic. It involves the interviewee in recursive or iterative mental processes, which themselves are key components of all original composition. I remember experiencing being pleasantly and unexpectedly drawn into reflection, in the very first interview I ever gave, for a Belgian student magazine, in 1981. The theme was translation. The interviewer, Kathleen Dispa, was studying languages and translation in Ghent.

The role of the interviewer, then, is complex. There is a skill, even an art, in being an effective interviewer. The interviewer instigates and listens; prompts, guides, directs and redirects; and alternately interrupts, challenges, argues, confirms, criticises, questions, provokes, encourages, elicits, extrapolates, summarises, and, finally, is likely to signal closure. An interview is an exploration of a *field* by two participants. And in whatever way it proceeds through, across, or around its field, and whatever tracks it takes, it involves a mapping of that field. It may excavate unexplored areas and new layers, yielding unexpected findings like an archaeological dig. And it may shape the field into new patterns.

Finally, to go back to the jazz analogy, the interview, whether considered as an art form or not, and in whichever medium it occurs, first flourishes in the twentieth century. It belongs to modernity, is shaped by modernity and in turn contributes to the shaping and reshaping of modernity. And it does so alongside and entangled with other twentieth century forms, in meshes and swathes of mutual influence.

JD: I think you're spot on, especially about the last point. Could we explore the interview a bit more by looking at its basic history and structure, as we know it today, across different media? And since *anybody* can be interviewed, not just writers, could we expand outward from the literary interview?

RB: As you suggest, whether literary or otherwise, the interview has developed into an accepted modern genre which is familiar to everyone, with its own distinctive forms and expressions, varying according to whether it's printed, sound-recorded, or video-recorded. The factor common to all these is that its medium is language, and its required pattern is that of a conversation, or rather, record of a conversation, about a topic or range of topics. Primarily, it requires a minimum of two speakers or writers: an interviewer and an interviewee. The interviewer's role, by and large, is to put questions, and the interviewee's to answer them. Within this overall framework, all kinds of performative variation are possible. Questioning is also what happens or is supposed to happen, incidentally, to a witness or suspect in a law court or police interrogation, under strict rules of formal engagement with regard to what is and is not admissible as factual, truthful, relevant, and so on. An interview can be an interrogation: an interrogation is a kind of interview.

It could be an interesting project to research and document the precise history of the interview. Could we think of Plato's many dialogues, and Xenophon's *Memoirs of Socrates,* as progenitors of the interview? And Boswell's *Life of Samuel Johnson*? And Diderot's dialogues, such as *Le neveu de Rameau*?[3] I don't see why not. My guess is that the interview could even turn out to be as old as writing itself. A researcher might well come across transcriptions or records of questionings and interrogations long before the twentieth century, perhaps some of them very ancient, whether strictly legal or outside the law. Perhaps documents that were kept secret or confidential by officials? Could the first interviewees have been witnesses or suspects of crimes, and the first interviewers interrogators? Or might interviews have been recordings of legal transactions, such as contracts?

JD: So the interview was private, not public …

RB: … Or could have been. Anyway, our English word comes from French *entrevoir,* 'to have a glimpse of', *s'entrevoir* 'to see each other', from the components *voir* 'to see' and *entre* 'between'. From the past participle of *entrevoir,* you get the verbal noun *entrevue.* The *OED*'s first citation for our word, spelt *enterview,* dates from 1519, meaning "meeting of persons face to face, esp. one sought or arranged for the purpose of formal conference". The modern sense of "oral assessment or examination of a candidate", e.g. for a job or a studentship, derives from this. The other modern sense, which we're focussing on here – "meeting between a representative of the press and someone from whom he seeks to obtain statements for publication. Similarly in broadcasting" – doesn't occur until after 1850. This dating reflects that the earliest contexts of the interview as we know it today belong to journalism. The first three citations are instructive:

> 1869 *Nation (N.Y.)* 28 Jan. 67 The 'interview', as at present managed, is generally the joint product of some humbug of a hack politician and another humbug of a newspaper reporter.

1884 *Pall Mall Gaz.* 31 Dec. 3/1 Among the permanent gains of the year the acclimatization of the 'interview' in English journalism certainly should be reckoned.

1897 *Westm. Gaz.* 2 Jan. 7/1 It is claimed for him [Joseph M'Cullagh, of St. Louis] that he was the inventor of the modern newspaper interview.[4]

It's clear from these that the published interview has developed as a peculiarly *modern* genre, and the quotation marks around the word 'interview' in the first two extracts strongly suggests a neologism. The earliest so-called 'newspapers' and 'newsbooks' evolved in the early seventeenth century. First expressed in the medium of print, conversations – whether fictitious or factual – were 'reported' in *The Spectator, Tatler, Rambler*, and other eighteenth century periodicals. Those chatty, gossipy publications had large followings, and they contain plenty of conversations that were or purported to be what now we might call 'up-to-the-minute' news. The interview as we know it today began around the mid-nineteenth century. It has evolved since then through technologies that include both sound and vision: via radio, cinema and TV to Internet, YouTube, etc. The terms *broadcasting* and *publishing* both mean 'making public'.

JD: In other words, the modern interview has grown, very specifically, out of recording technologies.

RB: Yes, first from print to sound. After the invention of sound recording in France in the mid-nineteenth century, followed by Thomas Edison's invention of the phonograph in 1877, writing – including printing – no longer constituted the sole means of recording language. The power and privilege of the written word were challenged and, arguably, have waned ever since. Since then, sound recording has developed from phonograph through dictaphone, telephone, radio, gramophone, vinyl record, tape-recorder, mobile phone, digital sound-recorder, and so on. And alongside sound recording, visual recording has grown out of photograph-stills, through silent movies, sound-track movies, television, videotaping, digital movie-recording, internet videos, videophones, skyping, video-conferencing, and whatever the next wave of new inventions will bring us.

The series *Ancestors, Filmed Interviews With Leading Thinkers* is a fine example of how the interview as a genre has both been shaped by new technologies and kept up with them. Founded in Cambridge in 1982 by the anthropologist Jack Goody, this collection has been developed extensively by Alan Macfarlane, aided by his wife Sarah Harrison, both also anthropologists. Relying largely on the agglomeration of talents in and around Cambridge, this collection now contains more than two hundred interviews with thinkers, scholars and artists in many fields, and is still growing. I think I may be the first poet to have been interviewed in this series.[5] Macfarlane's procedure couldn't be simpler. The model for all his interviews is biographical: each one starts with family background ('ancestors') and continues through earliest memories to childhood and education. He sits, with a fixed camera on his lap, and asks questions as he is recording. He then sends a DVD of the session to the interviewee, along with a set of typed summary-notes, each of which is prefaced by an indication of the time of the entry measured from the beginning of the video. The interviewee checks both, and has licence to cut parts of the video and edit the notes, though not to add in anything that wasn't in the original. Finally, the interview is posted on YouTube and gathered into the archive on a dedicated website,[6] where every video is accompanied by the summary-notes in scroll-down format. In this way four separate technologies (print, sound recording, video recording and internet streaming) combine. Similarly, on our computers we can now listen to a recording of a song or a poem, and read the words of the lyric at the same time. I often do this.

What we may think of today as a single media-form, for example video-recording, is often the composite result of entirely separate inventions. Often the multimedia format itself creates innovation and goes on to combine and recombine with other technologies. Today, technologies not only co-exist alongside one another, but interpenetrate and blur, as do (most recently of all) distinctions between 'public' and 'private' communication in, for example, dialogues, discussions, arguments and commentary threads on Intranets and the Internet, especially on sites such as Facebook and Twitter. As users and consumers, we tend to take this interpenetration and blurring of communication technologies for granted, especially between vision and sound. Yet despite this fuzziness of edges, there are still distinctions to be made between spoken and written interviews.

JD: How would you characterise these distinctions?

RB: Since the ears and eyes are the two primary pairs of perceptive organs through which we receive and register language – as well as the fingers, of course, because we need to include braille – and while listening is an activity limited to the sequential absorption of speech-flow, reading is an activity that's *both* temporal *and* spatial. Because a reader's eyes can browse, scan, and backtrack, a text can be returned to as often as the reader wants, which means that repetition and recursion (iteration) are naturally built into the spatio-temporal activity of reading. These, traditionally, are the key distinctions. When reading a piece of writing, we can quickly backtrack and recheck whenever we want. But even this distinction needs modifying nowadays. Perhaps we can come back to that later…

JD: Of course.

RB: If we pause to think structurally about the development of recording technologies, the history of the English verb *to record* provides ample evidence and opens several insights. The *OED* gives thirteen definitions, the first of which is obsolete: "[t]o learn by heart, to commit to memory, to go over in one's mind; (also) to repeat or say over as a lesson or portion of memorized text, to recite". But the twin motif of *repetition* and *reiteration* present here is latent in all later instances. Another definition is: "[t]o relate, narrate, or mention in a written account; to put or set down in writing or some other permanent form; to put on record". The first cited instance of this meaning is 1340 and the most recent, 2007, even though all the examples concern writing and none relate to any "other permanent form" of registration. Another entry states: "[t]o convert (sounds, images, a broadcast, etc.) into permanent form for later reproduction or broadcast, formerly using mechanical means, now chiefly using magnetic tape or digital electronic techniques"[7] The first cited example of this later usage comes from the journal *Science* in 1888: "There is no doubt that the phonograph can accurately record all varieties of sound."[8] Yet, curiously, no citation is given in this entry for the recording of "images". For the noun *record*, the *OED* offers sixteen definitions, several of which are obsolete.

As for the 'gramophone record', Emile Berliner developed this between 1894 and 1900, and Berliner and Eldridge R. Johnson first marketed it through their 'Victor Talking Machine Company' in 1901. So at the threshold of the twentieth century, 'talking machines' led to the birth of the interview as we know it today. The common Greek etymology of the neologisms *phonograph* and *gramophone* is itself interesting: both these words were purposely constructed to suggest the idea of 'voice-writing'/'sound-writing', just as *telephone* means 'distance-voice/sound' and *telegraph* 'distance-writing'.

2

JD: It seems to me that part of Modernism is inherently linked to the idea of the autonomy of language or language 'as such'. This seems to be the critical distinction you're making and the change in thinking that occurs at the end of the nineteenth century.

RB: Linked, yes, but not bound. Connected, yes, but not exclusively. I think this early twentieth century idea of the 'autonomy of language', which has persisted through to our own day, makes sense if it means that language is distinct and separable from other 'fields', but not if language is thought of as an entirely self-sufficient system without relationship to or bearings on non-linguistic reality. Which is to say, not only syntagmatic but also paradigmatic (i.e. semantic) relationships need to be borne in mind.

On the one hand, it could well be said that linguistics as we know it today first 'arrived' in the years during and after the First World War. Daniel Jones published his groundbreaking *Outline of English Phonetics* in 1918. Ferdinand de Saussure's *Cours de Linguistique Générale* came out in 1915, based on careful notes taken by several students during his lectures at the University of Geneva between 1906 and 1914. Saussure is supposed to have said, "Une langue est un système où tout se tient," though it may have been Antoine Meillet, or someone else.[9] And, yes, Meillet launched the telling catchphrase "the autonomy of linguistics" at the first Congress of Linguists in The Hague in 1928.[10] Similar quotations can be found from many other linguists and psychologists of the period.[11] And all this was going on in the heyday of the first literary modernists, around the same time as the publication of *Ulysses* (1918-22) and *The Waste Land* (1922). I suppose it could be argued that, from *Ulysses*, right the way through the Surrealist Movement – Breton wrote the 'Surrealist Manifesto' in 1924 – and *Finnegans Wake* (1939), to Pound's last *Drafts and Fragments of Cantos* (1970), the "autonomy of language" reigned supreme over broad swathes of literary practice and theory.

On the other hand, explicit focus on language 'as such' is as old as recorded scholarship – no, even older, as old as myth.[12] There were ancient Sanskrit and Greek (Stoic) grammarians. The medieval Scholastics made key contributions to linguistic theory, as did Locke and Leibniz in the seventeenth century.[13] At that time, the Port-Royal scholars explored the idea of a universal grammar, long before Wilhelm von Humboldt in the nineteenth or Chomsky in the twentieth.[14] So it would be false to identify the *start* of scientific enquiry into language with modernity or modernism.

What's more, despite all calls or claims for autonomy, it would be equally wrong to think that throughout the modernist period language wasn't seen as indissolubly bound into other disciplines and fields of enquiry. Think of Freud writing on dream-language, puns, and slips of the tongue in *The Interpretation of Dreams*, another turn-of-the-century phenomenon, first published in German in 1900;[15] of Frazer, Freud and Jakobson, all writing from their different perspectives on language, myth and taboo;[16] of many anthropologists – from Émile Durkheim, say, through Claude Lévi-Strauss, Gregory Bateson and Mary Douglas to Victor Turner – investigating the languages of symbolism and ritual;[17] of Jung and waves of successive Jungians exploring symbolism and the archetypes;[18] of Cassirer's and Eliade's diverse enquiries into language and myth;[19] of Vygotsky on 'inner speech';[20] and of Wittgenstein on language games[21] – as just a few examples. It's clear from the writings of all these major thinkers that, right from the start, focus on language is explicit, and emphatically so, in modern psychology, cognitive studies, anthropology, philosophy, sociology, and so on. It permeates every one of these disciplines. And in evolutionary studies, the origins of human language continue to exert fascination as a topic of enquiry, as in the writings of Philip Lieberman and Derek Bickerton, with titles like *Eve Spoke* and *Adam's Tongue*[22] – even though proof of early language evolution of any kind is impossible to come by, simply because speech organs are in the soft tissue, so there are no fossil records.

For all these reasons, on the whole I'd prefer to emphasise the *connectedness* of enquiries into language with those in other fields, not its autonomy. And I'd say this of modernist artistic movements as well as of scholarship. At any rate, in the new art media and forms precipitated in the first third of the twentieth century, especially film and TV, language is one component in a bundle of many others. And incidentally, in the 1980s and 1990s, Roy Harris attacked these early twentieth century notions of language as an abstraction, calling this *the language myth* – and *segregationalist*. He proposed instead an *integrationalist* linguistics.[23] Perhaps the interview should be described as an 'integrationalist genre'.

At any rate, in thinking about the interview as a new genre, one that *arrives* with modernity – and even as one that in its own minor way characterises and its characteristic of modernity – it's the interminglings and intermeshings of influences that I find more interesting and productive for discussion. As I've suggested already, I see the interview as a genre "entangled with other twentieth century forms, in meshes and swathes of mutual influence", though I suppose it could be argued that the linguists' insistence on the 'autonomy' of language as an object of scientific study itself has acted as an attractor for other disciplines.

JD: Related to the autonomy of language, could you expand on the relation you see between 'talking machines' and the birth of the interview?

RB: I think the key point here is, so long as you know how to use the required recording equipment, that repetition and recursion become possible for a *listener* and a *viewer* as well, not just a reader. Nowadays, replay buttons for audio and video tracks are readily available. Thanks to proliferating new technologies, playback is no longer reserved just for text-readers, but functions effortlessly for listeners and watchers too. In these virtual *as-if* worlds, it's as if passing moments can be stilled and frozen, just as they can seem to be in writing, especially poetry. There is now a kind of monumentality to all these forms. A record *is* a kind of monument. (An Ozymandias, perhaps?)

At any rate, given the wave of new recording technologies that arrive with (alongside, on, beneath) the swell of modernism, an interview, to be disseminated (i.e. published), no longer needs to be a *text* in the limited sense of a *piece of writing*. All that's required is that it should be a *record* in the main sense we've met in the *OED*: something that has been "put or set down in writing or *some other permanent form*". This is to say: the nouns *text* and *record* or *recording* need to be assimilated towards each other, as do the verbs *publish* and *broadcast*. Our descriptive, analytical and critical terminologies, and with them our understanding of aesthetic and literary genres, constantly lag behind the rapidly shifting cultural realities created by new communication technologies. All new technologies spawn and proliferate new art forms, as well as innovations and expansions (or shrinkings and narrowings) in old ones; which means that we need, consciously, to keep modifying and re-modifying our understanding of what an art-form *is*, what is a literary 'work', or 'genre', what a 'performance' or 'copy', what an 'original', and so on. Aesthetic and literary theorists nearly always think retrospectively, lagging behind practitioners.

JD: What about the contemporary situation of the interview, as far as technologies are concerned?

RB: New technologies don't necessarily replace older ones. Older technologies continue alongside new ones and constantly merge with them, as I've suggested from the embedding of different technologies in Alan

Macfarlane's *Filmed Interviews*. David Edgerton's brilliant study of technologies since 1900, *The Shock of the Old*, analyses the longevity and adaptability of old technologies across many fields, including production, maintenance, war, killing and invention. Paradoxically, the picture he paints seems startlingly original to us because we don't usually notice old technologies; and the reason we don't notice them is that ever since Baudelaire's italicised injunction at the end of his poem 'Le Voyage' ("Au fond de l'inconnu pour trouver du *nouveau!*"),[24] we've been heavily programmed by the Modernist zeitgeist to be obsessed with novelty and innovation above anything else. But there's *nothing new* in new and old technologies co-existing and complementing one another. In China, there are archaeological records of ancient writing with both chisel and brush on both bone and turtle shell, and then with brush on clay, bamboo and silk; and all these technologies went on contemporaneously, even though the techniques of working with these various materials developed at different times. Add to this writing carved into stone and smelted into bronze: *many* technologies! There is actually a very interesting study by Tsuen-Hsuin Tsien entitled *Written on Bamboo and Silk: The Beginnings of Chinese Books and Inscriptions*. Similarly, in our case in point: printed media, sound-recording and video-recording all co-exist and continue to have active roles in present-day communication systems. When I write, I use pen and paper, and keypad and computer. I oscillate between the two technologies.

Evidently then, the interview today nestles comfortably among all these conditions. It's not only immensely adaptable, but blurs or shears off into other applications too, which in their turn gather and transform previous material and proliferate new techniques, content, and forms. YouTube, which now in 2015 is only ten years old, already abounds with video-recordings – not only of writers but of practitioners working in every imaginable creative field – conversing, lecturing, conferencing, taking part in seminars and workshops, and giving interviews. YouTube has spawned a fine and growing retrospective archive of modern and modernist intellectual, literary and artistic interviews. Two that I find especially rewarding are a fragment of a 1939 audio interview with Sigmund Freud and John Freeman's 1959 BBC video interview with Carl Gustav Jung.[25] There is also a polished and sometimes funny video interview with Freud by Dr. Ruth.[26] But sometimes material gets put up on YouTube and then suddenly removed because of copyright infringements. For example, a video-conversation between Henry Miller and Anaïs Nin on 'Death and Dreams', which I watched two years ago, vanished for a while, then resurfaced on a different site, while another interview with Anaïs Nin in French has appeared, as if from nowhere.[27] A huge amount of previously closeted material is constantly becoming available, almost globally.

JD: Would you say, then, that the interview has an increasingly wide role today?

RB: The interview is so common that it's entirely taken for granted. If you consider what's all around us in our contemporary media, the interview turns out to be the core of all radio journalism, as well as a good deal of radio entertainment. When it comes to television, the interview has a huge role in both news and entertainment. What we call, broadly speaking, 'The News' and 'the documentary' both extensively *depend on* interviews. Talk breeds talk. And as soon as sound and visual representation combine, the interview's tones and styles get more and more varied, ranging from the delicately explorative and the sensitively empathetic and revealing, to the explosively antagonistic and dramatically confrontational, or the purportedly objective and coolly detached. The last style applies particularly to interviews with scientists, specialists, experts.

The interview is also the core and base for all chat-shows. On the strengths of this sub-genre, chat-show hosts have assumed celebrity status, as often as not for celebrating ephemeral trivia, just as the gossipy authors of *The Spectator* did in the early eighteenth century. What's more, the interview turns out to be a perfect vehicle for comedy. Michael Parkinson, for example, has broadcast unforgettable interviews, classic performances in their own right, with actors like Peter Ustinov, David Niven, Peter Sellers, and Kenneth Williams, to name only a few.

JD: So the interview or dialogue is wide-reaching and flexible as a genre.

RB: Yes. So we need to extend our notion of an interview to its being a form available to *all* creative artists and thinkers. Here again, Alan Macfarlane's work is a model. Recently I went to the Moore-Rodin exhibition at Perry Green, once Henry Moore's home and workplace, and now centre of the Henry Moore Foundation.[28] Moore was far more than a sculptor. He worked indefatigably in many overlapping and mixed forms and media: for example making etchings, drawings, prints, photographs, books and broadcasts, and inspiring tapestries.[29] Since then, in the BBC Internet archives, I've come across an interview made with him by the poet and art critic Edward Lucie-Smith in 1981.[30] This piece, along with others like it on the same website, is unquestionably part of Moore's artistic oeuvre. And this particular one is equally part of Lucie-Smith's.

JD: So do you think interviews of this kind can help to demystify an artist or thinker?

RB: A good interview can be an equaliser in that it strips away pretensions and reveals the humanity of the interviewee. And this applies to any interviewee, not just writers, artists and thinkers. An interview can't avoid being personal and intimate. All you need to make an interview is two people: one asking and the other answering questions, plus a way of recording the exchange, followed by some editing. As the mass production of sound and video technology gets more streamlined, and as recording and playback devices get smaller, cheaper, and more easily available to billions of people, making an interview gets progressively easier. And the fact that anyone can interview *anybody* makes it a very democratic genre. You could even say that the interview is an instrument for democracy. I think the rise of journalistic reporting in the first newspapers, in Europe and North America in the seventeenth century, themselves reflected and were part of social democratisation.

JD: Can you think of any historical markers for the interview being keyed with democracy or democratisation?

RB: A significant twentieth century marker is the *Mass Observation* movement that began in England in 1937, founded by the poet Charles Madge, filmmaker Humphrey Jennings, and ecologist and polymath Tom Harrisson. Their work was entirely modelled on real-life interviews.[31] As the first widespread information-gathering experiment of its kind, it was grounded in socialist beliefs. *Mass Observation* was a hugely innovative movement. It aimed to give voice to 'ordinary people', not via interpretations overlaid by the ideologies of the ruling élites, but through their own statements, their own words. The interviewers were volunteers.

Mass Observation also showed that interviews record not just 'facts' but beliefs, ideas, opinions, and that these, organised statistically, could clarify patterns, trends, movements in and among subjectivities in a relatively 'objective' way – relatively, because the notion of any wholly detached, impartial observer had been exploded. Statistical analysis of interviews, then, reveals *intersubjective* patterns at least as relatively objective and probabilistic tendencies, if not exactly as 'facts' in their own right. The movement later gave rise not only to opinion polls and the established role of questionnaires and interviews in sociological research, but also to market research as we know it today. Today, carefully structured interviews have become a basic and required instrument for qualitative research.

Similarly, an interview with an expert or skilled person of any kind – whether theoretician or practitioner – is capable of offering insights into the interviewee's underlying beliefs, premises and motivations, regardless of that person's fields of interest and activity. So the specialist, who was perhaps once forbidding or awesome – in fact, anyone 'on a pedestal' – can be humanised, simply because what dialogue of any kind most clearly characterises and reveals *is* the human. In a video-interview, even if the interviewee aims to disguise facets of personality, these are likely to be picked up by visual clues. A good video-interview, then, can break down mystiques. It can reveal and it can debunk. When there's a human story to tell, understanding becomes easier, and perhaps empathy ensues – or its opposite. The video-interviews I've mentioned with Freud and Jung, for example, give direct insights into their personalities that couldn't have been achieved in any other way. As every politician knows, the relative effectiveness of a candidate's performance in televised interviews has a strong influence on voters.

As for 'revealing', there is a further way in which the video-interview functions as an immensely powerful and direct communicative medium: that is, in historical witnessing. The video-interview has played a vital role in uncovering, narrating and documenting unpleasant or shocking truths that might otherwise have remained hidden or at least not easily have become accessible. Here, I'm thinking in particular of the work of the Yad Vashem Holocaust History Museum, Jerusalem and of the Shoah Foundation, Los Angeles, in documenting atrocities. The Yad Vashem International School for Holocaust Studies has an extensive online Video Resource Center containing video interviews with survivors, and these are a key part of the presentations in the museum itself.[32] The Shoah Foundation in LA was founded in 1994 by Steven Spielberg after his experience in directing *Schindler's List*. Situated at the University of Southern California (USC), the Foundation's original purpose was "to gather video testimonies from survivors and other witnesses of the Holocaust". I was taken on a tour of their Centre, with my son Gully Burns, a research scientist at USC, during Holocaust Memorial Week in 2012, when I was giving a poetry reading there from my book *The Blue Butterfly*. So far, the Shoah Foundation has conducted testimonies in more than sixty countries and thirty-nine languages. The Visual History Archive includes "more than 52,000 testimonies of Holocaust survivors and other witnesses", and has recently also incorporated documentation from the 1994 Rwandan Tutsi Genocide, the 1937 Nanjing Massacre in China, and the First World War Armenian Genocide.[33] The entire structure of the USC Archive has been based on the video-interview and built up around it, with meticulously chosen questions and scrupulously standardised procedures. State-of-the-art digital technology underlies complex operations in indexing and cross-referencing, enabling researchers to access information increasingly quickly. Clearly, the educational and research work of both these Institutes would function considerably less effectively without the video-interview, whose immediacy strongly, simply and swiftly authenticates testimony.

Today, the vast potential of the interview to document facts and to express thoughts and ideas is taken so much as a matter of course that it hardly even seems to be innovative. I don't think the potential of the interview as a form or genre is ever likely to be exhausted. The interview is always directly human, and richly and often poignantly personal. What I'm interested in doing with it vis-à-vis the art of poetry is taking it in new directions, and as far as one can go, particularly in the depth and detail offered by collaborative editing, so as to weave those many loose strands back into its fabric that, in conversation, invariably fly off and get lost. Just as we are doing here.

3

JD: I'd like to ask some further questions that tie in with the development of the interview as a genre. I know that Lévinas and his work on the face are important to your thinking.[34] Do you think that it's necessary for the interview to be done in person? Does the potency of the interview depend on sitting in the flesh so to speak, next to the person?

RB: Physical facing grants the dramatic immediacies of contact. In a radio interview made by two people together, proximity can be intuited and inferred by a listener, even though the voices are disembodied. For performative qualities of sheer liquid speed and fluent spontaneity, as well as wit, verve, humour, elegance, and a certain kind of intimacy, nothing beats a sound or video interview in which participants face each other, especially if the interviewee is alert and quick-witted. These effects derive directly from physical proximity, whether supposed or directly perceived. With video, the viewer's ability to register evident human interaction increases to include eye contact, facial expression and body gesture.[35] Incidentally, all these factors work brilliantly for comedy. Think, for example, of classic sketches like 'The Frog and Peach' and 'Teaching Ravens to Fly under Water' by the English comedians Peter Cook and Dudley

Moore, featuring interviews with the hilarious fictional character Sir Arthur Streeb-Greebling, or the more recent sketches in the same tradition by John Bird and John Fortune, such as their brilliant skits on investment banking and the financial crisis.

What's more, for the contemporary audio-visual interview, once again technology comes into play. Via telephone, which has been around for a hundred and fifty years, and now via Skype, which was founded twelve years ago (2003), long-distance interviews and conferences have become the norm for both radio and TV, for example in conflict coverage. Radio and TV broadcasts both *assume* distance between speakers as well as from listeners and/or viewers. From the listener's or viewer's perspective, even if receiving broadcaster's voices and/or faces from different locations isn't quite as immediate as registering speakers' physical proximity to each other, it can still transmit communication in an authentic way. That's one side of the coin: direct sound, direct vision: immediacy. But interviews that are meant to be read rather than listened to or watched get made and need thinking about in a quite different way.

JD: Right. Some of the interviews and sections of interviews in this book were conducted via email and over long stretches of time ...

RB: Two of the interviews began as recorded conversations: Ruth Halkon's, at my house in Cambridge, and Sean Rys's, in front of a live audience in Santa Barbara. The others, including this one, have been conducted entirely via email, and in some cases with many interruptions, over a period lasting months. Whether the interviews began as spoken or email exchanges, their development has been a fascinating process. Each interviewer and I have together extensively expanded, developed and co-edited the transcripts via ensuing emails. In each case, we've found ourselves working on the texts not only by progressive extension, but also by recursive and iterative procedures, that is, deletions and accretions. We've found these reworkings occurring *at any point*, just as in the making of any text. So these procedures treat the text spatially, as a 'field'. And by saying that, I don't intend only the basic spatial metaphor. I mean as if we were *digging* it, and *cultivating* it.

JD: Emailing is becoming a common way of doing literary interviews. What are its specific features? And how do you think it changes the genre?

RB: First, it involves writing. It's epistolary. By comparison with oral delivery, written exchanges of any kind automatically lengthen the time gap between correspondents reading and responding to each other's messages. Email is obviously much faster and more immediate than snailmail. But it's still mail, still 'correspondence'. Time gaps between communications inevitably lengthen. As for space, far from requiring proximity, email simply relinquishes it. Like a letter, postcard or telegram, it *assumes* the fact of physical distance, both between interviewer and interviewee and between writer and reader.

But I think email does something else, too, something quite curious, that snailmail doesn't achieve. First because its transmission is almost instantaneous, second because it's global, and third because it's virtual (paperless), the combined psychological effects of its speed, universality and lack of materiality are to 'shrink' or 'shatter' – or 'demolish' or 'abolish', or, if you like, 'float on' or 'flatten' *both time and space* – I mean, it combines space and time into a relativity that's *genuinely felt*, personalised, rather than just being apprehended mentally, theoretically, abstractly. I'm suggesting, then, that email brings relativity into my *immediate* mental and physical being and environment – into my head and body, via my laptop, iPad or smartphone, wherever I happen to be. So relativity is no longer apprehended only as an idea that belongs to the remote academic domains of maths and physics, like a cloud in Einstein's hair, as it were,[36] but as a living and thoroughly lived actuality. The email interview *simultaneously* dematerialises communication and locates it increasingly firmly in a relativistic, intersubjective zone: an interesting combination.

JD: Could you unpack this idea a bit more? What are the effects on correspondence, on the interview, because of this dematerialisation?

RB: In practical terms, in an email exchange, for one thing, it doesn't matter *where* the correspondents are. Place is incidental and more or less irrelevant. The 'zone' where the act of communication takes place is *in the text*. Today, for example, I've been exchanging emails with friends in Belgrade, Buenos Aires, Cambridge, Gaeta (Italy), London, Marseillan (France) and South Bend (USA). All this without batting an eyelid. Now, the *text* (a word that's cognate with *texture* and *tissue*) exists on a screen. It doesn't need to exist anywhere else. It's been dematerialised. So the *material* of the text no longer needs to be material at all: it's no longer inscribed on bone, shell, stone, clay, bronze, bamboo, silk, or even paper. What we call its *virtuality*, that is, its *as-ifness*, itself creates a new *actuality*: a relativistic reality.

JD: Yes, and this is all part of an entirely new set of phenomena that's affecting us all right now. The Internet, Google, email, Skype, iPads, eBooks, Kindles, blogs, and so on, all mean fundamental changes in the ways we think, use language, and write.

RB: Yes. Or, rather, *perhaps*. For *how* 'fundamentally' I'm not sure. Distinctions between what is public and what is private change all the time and from one culture to another. In a single culture, patterns often seem to oscillate cyclically: closed, open, closed, and so on. The interview itself, as used in statistical research, has often broken into zones previously regarded as private. Think of the Kinsey Reports of 1948 and 1953 in the USA, the first on male and the second on female sexuality. The 1948 study involved around 5,400 interviews and the 1953 study around 6,000. Incidentally, the findings on sexuality by members of the *Mass Observation* team in the UK were repressed at the time.

JD: Could we go back to the more fundamental and traditional distinctions between audio-visual interviews and written interviews?

RB: Isn't it astonishing how quickly and seamlessly we adapt and keep adapting to this spate of new technologies, and forget methods that have fallen by the wayside? Who remembers audio cassettes these days? Actually, *I* do! I still have my old collection, and recently I bought a second-hand ghetto-blaster, so I often play my old audiotapes. So here again, I'm using an older technology as well as new ones. ... Even so, I think all these increasingly interconnecting and faster developing technologies do posit – and are crucially part of – interesting times not only for technology but perhaps for human consciousness too. They have far-reaching implications, not just in communications but in the ways we now inhabit and relate to our own identities and those of others, and how we'll do so in future. And also to how we inhabit and relate to time, and space. This is a vast subject. In its small way, I think our exploration here of the growth and patterning of the interview as an integrative and intersubjective art form, and across various media, may be an expression of these wider issues and may serve as a route into them.

As for the question of the similarities and distinctions between working in speech and in writing, it applies, obviously, not only to the interview, but to the art of poetry itself.

4

JD: Shall we take this opportunity of exploring, then, how the performative aspects of the interview inform other forms of composition? And basing our discussion in the interview, as an instance, broaden out from that to include poetry too?

RB: I think you can look at this issue in various ways, most of which ultimately come down to how a piece of work is processed, configured, edited, transmitted and received in time and space. Again, let's take the interview as our starting point.

Conversation is like a river, deep and fast-flowing. It gathers up whatever's thrown into it. If you're in it, it rushes you on. In a spoken interview, there's little or no chance of going back to previous points or positions which, responding to on the spur of the moment, you may not have covered adequately or satisfactorily. But while multiple and complex thoughts often arrive synchronously or pile up one behind one another, sometimes with unexpected force, so long as your aim is comprehension by another person, any delivery of words, in any language – and by the nature of all languages – absolutely demands sequential delivery. So in an oral interview, as in any conversation, sometimes you have the sense that you 'can't get it all out'. What's more, you may have so much to say simultaneously in answer to a single question that the most immediately dominant, obvious, or available thought simply blocks out others which might well be – or have been – deeper, finer, more interesting, and more subtle. And if or by the time you remember what had been blocked or locked out, the dialogue is likely to 'have moved on', so that your previous point seems irrelevant. And anyway, by then you and your interlocutor may both have interrupted each other, or you may have interrupted yourself, or both. A conversation, then, is a skein consisting of multiple strands, all interwoven, but many of which get frayed or suddenly terminated: cut. A conversation *consists of* a sequence of interruptions – of interruptions of interruptions of interruptions.

So you 'forget what you wanted to say'. And whatever that point or idea might have been may vanish forever without trace. Or, as Osip Mandelstam put it: "I have forgotten what I wanted to say, / and a bodiless thought returns to the world of shadows."[37] What is more, in a conversation, even if there are implicit guidelines, codes or restrictions with respect to relevance that have been imposed by exterior games-rules (as in a court of law or police interrogation) and/or by participators' consent (as in any co-operative verbal interchange), any utterance can follow any other. This is a cardinal rule in what linguists call *pragmatics*, which is a kind of huge conceptual bin into which performative aspects of language get thrown if they can't be explained structurally, i.e. grammatically. In this respect, the unexpectedness of a riposte or following question may be a virtue, a relief, a shock, or a pleasure, but in any dialogue, including the interview, the non sequitur – far from breaking *open*, i.e. exploring and revealing an idea from a new and original angle – may have the effect of breaking *apart* a nascent or partly formed thought, and so, effectively, fragmenting it, smashing it to smithereens.

JD: So in the spoken interview, from the interviewee's perspective, how would you say this affects composition?

RB: In the unedited spoken interview, performance *is* composition and composition *is* performance. There's no distinction between them. They are identified, so delivery consists of *both*. Instantiation, which *is* dual performance and composition, is as unique as it's unrepeatable. And (to expand discussion outwards from the interview, as you suggested we might do here), this is also the case in art forms such as oral poetry, whether in the traditional stories and epics of analphabetic societies – one thinks of Lord's classic study of oral bards in former Yugoslavia, *The Singer of Tales* – or in contemporary rap, slam, and sound poetry. An oral performance-composition's delivery is particular, an event, a happening. There's only one authentic version of it. It is its own original. Its totality can't be copied, repeated, recorded, duplicated, published, broadcast, etc. To register, receive and respond to its total, totalising effect, you have to *be there*, as and when it's being delivered, at and in the instant of its unique time-space …

JD: … and this is because the gap between art and life blurs …

RB: In a manner of speaking, yes. Not the totality of being, of course, but part of what constitutes 'being', if we construe this word, as a present participle, to mean 'being-in-the-present'. … And isn't this true too of rock music and jazz, of any improvised performance? How many times have we heard someone say, "Were you actually *at* that amazing Rolling Stones concert?" (Or Jimi Hendrix concert, or Janis Joplin or Otis Redding concert…?) Events of this kind are perceived as belonging to mythical time, to what Mircea Eliade calls *illud tempus*, i.e. '*that* (other) time', as distinct from '*this* (quotidian, humdrum) time': *there* as opposed to *here*, *then* as opposed to *now*.[38]

JD: So do you think watching or listening to a recording can really take us into '*that* time'?

RB: We're so dependent on our recording technologies, we inhabit them so fully, that it's hard now even to imagine that there was a time before they existed. Or that Confucius and Aristotle and Aquinas, and Dante and Milton and Blake, and Bacon and Leibniz and Nietzsche – all lived in a world before them, without them. For us, thanks to these technologies, sound and visual recordings *can* be enjoyed, possibly even for perpetuity, and these can re-enact and retain at least some of the flavours of immediacy, freshness and speed of the original and, with every innovation and improvement, do so with increasing effectiveness. A recording defies time and mortality, or at least appears to do so. We all die, but if we leave archives, records, recordings behind us, they live on after us, preserving us, freezing us in our very ephemerality, enabling us, potentially – or ghosts of us – to be 'taken out of storage' at any time after.

Even so, I can't help wondering if in some respects watching or listening to even the finest recording isn't *always* a reminiscence, a replay, of an irrecoverable original event. And every recording is processed and filtered in some way: that is to say, it is *edited* – just as we've been collaboratively editing this interview through a series of further emails.

JD: I agree entirely. But I don't think we're so dependent on our recording technologies, and so intertwined with them, that we don't still feel the nostalgia or longing for the 'real'.

RB: In a sense, recordings, whose function is precisely to *enable repetition*, are the next best thing to 'having been there'. They take us at least part of the way (*back*, always further back) into myth-time. Even so, on screen, I wonder if we can ever *quite* re-enter the sacramental, ritual power of that original. If through a video-recording we do manage to get a glimpse, scent, taste, residual after-image of it, the experience is never quite full enough, never quite actualised completely, but always remains on an *as-if* basis, nostalgically. If we only could convince ourselves that we *could* enter fully, without and outwith the inviolable resistance of the past to being opened in its entirety and plenitude, might we somehow almost arrest or cancel the running down of historic time, the inevitability of entropy?

But even if we may make a conscious decision to ignore the fact that, *surreptitiously*, the editing process has created an entirely new artefact, I do think we can get slightly closer to a sense of original – or, rather, originary – experience through a sound-recording than through a video.

JD: How is that?

RB: Perhaps it's because emphasis on hearing to the exclusion of sight fosters more scope for opening ourselves to the *thisness* of the recording, even bearing in our awareness all its *thatness*. If you close your eyes and just listen, you can exclude and cancel input from the limits of the world that actually surrounds you and enter the otherness of the virtual world you've chosen. Many people do this when listening to music. Hearing seems more 'intimate' and 'older' than sight. I suspect this is partly to do with the fact that our hearing abilities develop at the foetal stage. The human foetus starts hearing between sixteen and twenty-four weeks after gestation.[39] Sight doesn't happen until the newborn opens eyes on the world. I've written a piece on this, and its implications for poetry.[40]

JD: Turning to another aspect of performance, you've mentioned improvisation? What is its role?

RB: It's a commonplace in all performing arts to talk about improvisation, and the need for speed, and appropriateness of impromptu responses to unexpected eventualities. In practice, both of these mean that the composer-performer needs to fully follow, and run with – and within – the flow of time. Hesitation, recapitulation, cutting, pasting, redrafting, thinking again, and so on, simply aren't options. You forget your lines, you miss a note, you hit a wrong one, you sneeze or stumble, then the sole injunction and restriction then is *forward, onward* – or *out* – because while it's being made, the show, the performance, must go on. Although repetition belongs both to preliminary rehearsal and to recording, it can't be indulged in by the maker-performers during the actual creation (performance) of the work. In this situation, there's no bi-directional symmetry between forward and back, no two-way hinge on time's arrow.[41]

But what's more interesting here, I think, is that improvisation itself needs to be based in and derived from a readily available fund, a large pool of possibilities, all of which are stored in memory. The keys to proficiency in delivery of all these art forms, then, are the intertwined and more-or-less simultaneous skills of quick access and immediate recuperation *out of* the memory fund, and their activation *into* performance. Speed of timing, pertinence and accuracy of response are all crucial. All performing arts involve the finely selected and fluently tuned presentation of material from memory. The most proficient performers of oral epic poems tend to be older practitioners who, by years of sustained practice, have developed long and capacious memories.[42] I characterise the mode of creative thinking of these art forms as *memory-based, performative, improvisational* and *recuperative* – all at once. And this description fits the oral interview.

JD: Isn't this explanation a bit too neat? Could you say a bit more about the talent of improvisation?

RB: I've had – and have – several friends who are wonderful conversationalists. These are rare people. It's a pleasure to be in their company because whatever the conversation is about, they lift it. I think of my old friend Peter Mansfield. He could make any topic interesting, take it into wholly unexpected directions. Or Laurence Phillips, the travel-writer,[43] who has a stunning gift for lateral thinking in the midst of conversation, which can send you into fits of laughter – not to mention diagonal, spiral, zigzag and vertical thinking. How do such gifted people do it? For one thing, sometimes their intuitive minds move their responses so quickly into their mouths that their own analytical minds catch up later. Second, they listen carefully, they give you full attention, they interact so totally that they're always several thoughts ahead. And third, they perform and know they are performing because, when they improvise, they listen to themselves. So they're fully in the now and have a curious way of knowing they are in the now. They think fast, their minds move multi-dimensionally, you never know quite what they're going to say next. They seem to have a vast reservoir of reference. Sometimes it's almost as if their own speed of response surprises them too, so they laugh at and with themselves. Conversation itself is a kind of jazz. They lift you too in response and participation.

JD: How does this connect with the heuristic nature of the interview?

RB: Improvisation is heuristic by default. It means you give surprises and get them by giving them. You don't know what's going to happen next. Your uncertainty meshes with the puzzle of *nowness* that is the now, and whatever comes in the next moment after now, and the moment after that, and so on. You find out – you can *only* find out – by doing, and there's always more to do, so you never stop finding out. But while you're doing it, *you can't edit it.*

JD: So how does this model differ from the written or printed composition?

RB: As we've agreed, in genres based in writing, the process of making occurs in space as well as time, as does its reception in reading. The making of any piece of writing is itself a formation that can be interrupted and returned to. Like the products of many other plastic arts, a piece of writing can – and sometimes must – be made in stages. It doesn't simply flow or grow continuously along the current of linear time. All of which is to say: you *can and do* edit.

What's more, the resulting made 'thing' – the 'work' – becomes an object inhabiting a space, a *locus*, and hence it itself becomes a space, a *locus*, in its own right. It isn't just an irrevocable and transitory movement. So, far from simply happening in a unique time-space, like the oral performance-composition, a piece of writing *takes place*. That is to say, it places itself and, in doing so, takes into itself place itself and placement itself. And the place it takes is preservable and, so long as it's preserved, is available for endless non-identical repetition(s) and variation(s), for example in an *edition* – i.e. in many copies, which *take places* (plural). Unless of course the artist deliberately builds ephemerality (collapse, disintegration, decay) into the process, as in an ice sculpture, sand sculpture, or sand mandala.

JD: And recursive/iterative procedures? Can you explore these processes that go into composing in more detail?

RB: Within the physical limitations of the materials and technologies needed to make it, the mutating object that is the art-work, in the process of being made, is likely to require processes of re-vision, re-consideration, deliberation, deletion, alteration, re-drafting, re-casting, re-modelling, and so on. Eventually, you hope, the resultant completed work will have benefited, and have been enriched and deepened, by all these integrally and carefully connected, constructive processes of patterning and re-patterning. And all of which, you also hope, will embed the multi-layered, cumulative and accretive processes that will have gone into its slow making, as a corresponding multifaceted, *polysemic* quality.

Because this is so, this kind of work – for example, a piece of writing – will never be absolutely identifiable with any single performance or reading of it. So it will always be incomplete, even when completed (written). That is to say: even though it will constantly demand a reading or performance in order to complete itself, any such reading or performance will inevitably be no more than a version, interpretation, derivation, deviation, or misinterpretation; it will always be open, unfinished.

What's more, by defying total encapsulation by any single instantiation or rendering of it, the work itself will exist both *in* and *out of* the flow that linear time pours unstoppably through the ever-porous instant, the *now*. That is to say, while it will obtain some degree of permanence or at least longevity, even if only to exist unread on a library shelf or in a box in an archive, or buried for centuries like the Dead Sea Scrolls or the Mawangdui texts, there will always be something more or else to be got out of it in further renderings, reading, performances, future instantiations. It will still always have *potential*. And insofar as it will accrete *pastness*, so it will also invoke (call out, imply, assume and possess) *futurity*. And it will itself become both a fund of meanings and a source and breeder for other works: that is, so long as its language is decipherable, and "so long as men" – *and women* – "can breathe or eyes can see."

Here, then, perhaps, is a version of the myth of eternal return.

JD: So the written text incorporates both sequential and spatial absorption?

RB: That's right. All writing and reading systems need to *reiterate* (re-enact, mime, copy) diachronic sequencing. They do so, universally, by transmuting diachronic sequence into spatial sequence: i.e. into *lines*. Linear sequencing is common to all writing systems in the world, whether alphabetic, hieroglyphic or ideogrammatic, whether set out vertically like traditional Chinese or Japanese or horizontally, and if the latter, whether directionally right to left, like Arabic, Hebrew, Persian and Urdu, or left to right, like West European languages – or *boustrophedon*. Training to write and read always involves learning to repeat *lines*.

But that isn't all there is to it. As I we've seen, in the process of writing, so long as you're working in a malleable material, you can alter things as you go along. You can pause, delay, leave off, come back later, approach your partly formed text in a new mood, look at it in another light, and do all these things again and again. You can erase, delete, cut and paste, edit, tinker, change your mind, think of something better, revise, oscillate between alternatives, hold different possibilities in your mind, and manipulate. This is what the iterative or recursive process involves. Return and repetition inhere in all writing and in all reading.

JD: So how, finally, would you sum up the differences between the two modes, the oral-visual and the written?

RB: If conversation is like a river (line, thread), flowing sequentially in one unstoppable direction, a text (or a recording, in the sense in which I've been using the word) is more like a lake, a reservoir. That is to say, it can be imaged, pictured, approached and re-approached, as a *space* in, though, around and over which – even while you're actively doing things in it and to it, and shaping and bounding it – you have the freedom both of overview of the whole and of insights into its parts. It could also be said that the process of writing is like the making or walking of a path through a field. Two steps forward, one step back. *Reculer pour mieux sauter*. And one can exit the field and come back to it, any time. So, whereas performative speaking and listening (the reciprocal work of voice delivering language-sounds via mouth and receiving language-sounds via ears) are bound irreducibly into linear time, in writing and reading (the corresponding work of delivery-and-reception of visual-language-signs via hands to eyes), *space* gets added to the mix in a dynamic way.

And now, thanks to interactive oral and visual techniques, much of this also applies to watching and listening to recordings too. As I've suggested, the meanings and associations of the word *record* have expanded: for many years, our 'records' have included not only written texts but soundtracks (78s, 45s, LPs, CDs, digital) and they now extend to videos: all these, arguably, have become 'readable texts'.[44]

Finally, to return to the traditional field of written literature, in practice what the spatial dimension of the text means for both writer and reader is the reality of *homing*, of *return*, of breaking the arrow of time – or, rather, turning it into a boomerang. These, in turn, also mean that for arts based in writing, composition actively enables, invites and integrates procedures that are *both accretive and iterative*, as distinct from those these are *performative, improvisational* and *recuperative*. In writing, beginnings are everywhere. And all ends take you back to beginnings.

South Bend and Cambridge
May–July 2013,
November–December 2014
and March–June 2015

Notes

1. See Hughes and Heinz: "Maybe all poetry, insofar as it moves us and connects with us, is a revealing of something that the writer doesn't actually want to say, but desperately needs to communicate, to be delivered of."
2. Keats 1970: 41. 'Letter to George and Thomas Keats', December 21, 27 (?), 1817.
3. *Note from RB*: Thanks to Anthony Rudolf for this addition.
4. *OED online*. Consulted July 15, 2015.
5. See Macfarlane and Berengarten.
6. See Macfarlane *et al.*
7. *OED online*. Consulted June 15, 2015.
8. Issue of 25 May, 247 [2], as quoted in the *OED*.
9. "A language is a system where everything holds together" or "where everything coheres." Hurford, referring to Koerner, says that this sentence "is such a hoary truism that its origins are lost in the mists of linguistic historiography."
10. Jakobson 1973: 25.
11. For example, Alexander Luria, an associate of Vygotsky, described language as "a system of codes signifying objects and actions" and as "a system sufficient in itself for the expression of any abstract relationship or thought". Quoted by Jones 2009: 167.
12. See Cassirer.
13. See Locke 253–294; and Leibniz (online; consulted June 15, 2015).
14. Jakobson, *op. cit.*: 13–14.
15. See, for example, Freud 1961.
16. See Frazer: 244–262, Freud, *op. cit.*; and Jakobson 1985 [1] and [2].
17. See Durkheim, Bateson, Lévi-Strauss, Douglas, and Turner.
18. See, for example, Jung, *Collected Works*, Vol. 9, 1. 1968 [1959].
19. Jakobson 1985 [1] and [2]; Cassirer, *op. cit.*; and Eliade.
20. Vygotsky: 306 (index).
21. See Wittgenstein.
22. See Lieberman 1998 and Bickerton 2009, as well as their other writings in the References.
23. Harris 1981 and 1996. See also Jones 2009.
24. "In the depths of the Unknown, to find the new!"

25 See Freud 1938 and Freeman.

26 See Freud and Ruth.

27 See Miller and Nin; and Nin and Seguin.

28 See Feldman.

29 See Sanesi, and Garrould and Power.

30 See Moore and Lucie-Smith.

31 See *Mass Observation Archive*.

32 See *Yad Vashem Video Testimony Resource Center*.

33 See *USC Shoah Foundation Visual History Archive*.

34 Lévinas 2000, 2003 [1] and 2003 [2].

35 *Note from RB*: Alan Macfarlane writes, "I have come to the conclusion that the recorded sound interview is generally very inferior to the filmed interview. Most human communication is a mixture of the face and voice – half at least is lost without the film." Private email, June 19, 2015.

36 A reference to a sonnet by Nasos Vayenas, translated by RB and Paschalis Nikolaou: "Where are you going in that cloud of hair?" Vayenas 2010 [1]: 114.

37 *Note from RB*: From the fifth verse of a much-translated poem, number 113 in *Tristia*, written in November 1920 and usually referred to as 'The Swallow'. See for example Mandelstam 1973: 52, and 1987: 90–91. These lines are bravely quoted by Lev Vygotsky as the epigraph to the final chapter of his *Thought and Language* (1934), as a telling indicator of his theory of 'inner speech' – bravely, because Mandelstam was already under Stalin's suspicion. See Alex Kozulin's 2012 translation: 223. Variant translations for Russian 'bezplotnaya' include *voiceless, unvoiced, unbodied, unembodied* and *intangible*, as well as *bodiless*.

38 See Eliade, 51–92, esp. 73, 85.

39 See Hopson.

40 See RB 2015 [2].

41 See Price.

42 Lord, *op. cit.*

43 See, for example, his *Lille*.

44 In the final stages of editing this piece in June 2015, we came across an interesting academic study of the literary interview, published in 2014, some of whose key ideas dovetail with those presented here. The main argument, the hybridity of the genre, is explicit in the title: 'The Literary Interview: Toward a Poetics of a Hybrid Genre'. See Masschelein *et al.*

Acknowledgements

Three of these interviews have been published online in slightly different form. 'UNDER GREEK LIGHT' and 'I MUST TRY THIS TELLING' appeared in *The International Literary Quarterly* 21, 2014: http://interlitq.org/issue21/index.php. 'THE INTERVIEW AS TEXT AND PERFORMANCE' appeared in *The Fortnightly Review*, February 2016: http://fortnightlyreview.co.uk/2016/02/interview-text-performance/.

The editors wish to thank all the interviewers for their attentiveness and patience in making revisions to successive drafts. Additional thanks to Kim Landers, Danai Tachtara and Nasos Vayenas for checking and adding to factual information in 'Under Greek Light'; to Anastasia Parianou for advice on transliterations; to Catherine Byfield for advice on referencing; to Richard Pine for help with indexing; and to Anthony Rudolf for valuable comments on a draft of 'The Interview as Text and Performance'.

Richard Berengarten also wishes to thank his wife, Melanie Rein, for her constant support and, above all, for continual illuminating conversations about the theories of Carl Gustav Jung.

References

WRITINGS BY RB

RB indicates the name Richard Berengarten for publications after 2007, and Richard Burns for publications before then. For a fuller bibliography, see Jope *et al.* 2016: 404–419.

1968 [1]   'The Easter Rising 1967'. Poster poem attached to *The London Magazine* 7(10), January. (Pseudonym: Agnostos Nomolos)
1968 [2]   'The Exile'. *Hellenic Review* 1(1), June: 6. (Pseudonym: Agnostos Nomolos)
1969 [1]   *The Easter Rising 1967*. Brighton: Restif Press. (Pseudonym: Agnostos Nomolos)
1969 [2]   'With Face to the Wall'. (Review of Miltos Sahtouris's book of the same title, trans. Kimon Friar). *The Southern Review*, Spring: 605–610.
1969 [3]   'Arrenopi morfi paizontas diplo avlo'. ('Male Figure Playing a Double Flute', trans. into Greek, Agni Sotirakopoulou-Schina). *Nea Estia* 85(999), February 21, 1969: 242.
1970 [1]   'Euripides never slept here'. *Greek Report* 12, January: 26.
1970 [2]   'First-hand experience'. *Cambridge Evening News*, July 7: 10.
1971   *The Return of Lazarus*. Cambridge: Bragora Press.

1972 [1]   *Double Flute*. London: Enitharmon Press.
1972 [2]   *Avebury*. London: Anvil Press Poetry with Routledge and Kegan Paul.
1975   'Ston kipo ton progonon tou' ('In His Ancestral Garden', trans. into Greek, Nasos Vayenas). *Nea Estia* 97(1148), May 1: 598–599.
1980 [1]   *Learning to Talk*. London: Enitharmon Press.
1980 [2]   'Extracts from *The Manager*'. *Poetry South East* 5: 11–13.
1981   *Keys to Transformation: Ceri Richards and Dylan Thomas*. London: Enitharmon Press.
1983 [1]   *Black Light. Poems in memory of George Seferis* (first edition). Cambridge: Los Poetry Press.
1983 [2]   'Thirty Extracts from *The Manager*'. *boundary 2: A Journal of Postmodern Literature* XII(1), Fall: 15–31.
1985   *Black Light. Poems in memory of George Seferis* (second edition). Cambridge: Los Poetry Press.
1988   'Three Extracts from *The Manager*'. In Elaine Feinstein (ed.), *New Poetry II*. London: Quartet Books, 21–25.
1989   'A Grove of Trees and a Grove of Stones'. Online at: http://www.berengarten.com/site/Grove-of-trees.html. Consulted December 26, 2015.
1990   *Menadžer* (*The Manager*, trans. into Serbian, Vladimir Sekulić and Jasna B. Mišić). Titograd: Udruženje književnika Crne Gore [Writers' Association of Montenegro].
1995   *Black Light. Poems in Memory of George Seferis* (third edition). Norwich: The King of Hearts.
1996   'With Peter Russell in Venice 1965–1966'. In James Hogg (ed.), *The Road to Parnassus: Homage to Peter Russell on his Seventy-Fifth Birthday*. Salzburg: University of Salzburg. Reprinted 1997, *Notre Dame Review* 4, Summer: 117–132.
1999   *Against Perfection*. Norwich: The King of Hearts.
2001   *The Manager* (first edition). London and Bath: Elliott and Thompson.
2002 [1]   'Pour toi'. Address to the Conference, *Une poétique mondiale de la poésie?* La Bibliothèque nationale de France, Paris, May 13, 2002. Online at: http://www.berengarten.com/site/Pour-toi.html. Consulted December 26, 2015.
2002 [2]   'Codas pour *Le Manager*' ('Codas to *The Manager*', trans into French, Robert Davreu). In *Po&sie* 98: 52–58.
2003   *Book With No Back Cover*. London: David Paul.
2004   '"My" Anne Frank' (unpublished).
2005   *For the Living: Selected Longer Poems 1965–2000* (first edition). Cambridge: Salt Publishing.
2006 [1]   *The Manager* (second edition). Cambridge: Salt Publishing.
2006 [2]   *Mavro fos. Poiimata eis mnimin Yorgou Seferi* (*Black Light. Poems in Memory of George Seferis*, bilingual Greek-English edition, trans. Nasos Vayenas and Ilias Layios). Athens: Typothito.

2006 [3] *Manual, the first 20*. Paekakiriki, New Zealand: Earl of Seacliff Art Workshop.
2007 *Holding the Darkness (Manual, the second 20)*. Paekakiriki, New Zealand: Earl of Seacliff Art Workshop.
2008 [1–5] *Selected Writings* [1–5]: [1] *For the Living* (second edition); [2] *The Manager* (second edition); [3] *The Blue Butterfly* (second edition); [4] *In a Time of Drought* (second edition); and [5] *Under Balkan Light* (first edition). Cambridge: Salt Publishing.
2008 [6] *Holding the Sea (Manual, the third 20)*. Paekakiriki, New Zealand: Earl of Seacliff Art Workshop.
2009 [1] 'Borderlines: An Introduction to the "Volta" Project'. *The International Literary Quarterly* 9. Online at: http://interlitRH:org/issue9/berengarten/job.php. Consulted December 26, 2015.
2009 [2] 'The "Volta" Project'. *The International Literary Quarterly* 9. Online at: http://interlitq.org/issue9/volta/job.php. Consulted December 26, 2015.
2009 [3] 'Volta' (trans. into Greek, Ilias Layios). *The International Literary Quarterly* 9. Online at: http://interlitq.org/issue9/volta/greek/volta.pdf. Consulted December 26, 2015.
2009 [4] *Manual, the fourth 20*. Paekakiriki, New Zealand: Earl of Seacliff Art Workshop.
2011 [1–5] *Selected Writings* [1–5]: [1] *For the Living* (third edition); [2] *The Manager* (third edition); [3] *The Blue Butterfly* (third edition); [4] *In a Time of Drought* (third edition); and [5] *Under Balkan Light* (second edition). Exeter: Shearsman Books.
2011 [6] 'The Cambridge Poetry Festival: 35 years after'. *Cambridge Literary Review* 1: 148–160; and online at: http://www.cambridgeliteraryreview.org/vol1/issue1/. Consulted December 26, 2015.
2012 [1] *Black Light / Luz negra* (bilingual Spanish-English edition, trans. Miguel Teruel Pozas and Paul S. Derrick). Valencia: JPM Ediciones.
2012 [2] 'A Nimble Footing on the Coals – Tin Ujević, Lyricist: Some English Perspectives'. *sic* 2. Online at: http://www.sic-journal.org/ArticleView.aspx?aid=117. Consulted January 1, 2016.
2012 [3] *Do vidjenja Danice / Goodbye Balkan Belle*, (bilingual Serbian-English edition, trans. Vera V. Radojević). Belgrade: Srpska književna zadruga.
2013 *Imagems (1): six statements on poetics*. Bristol: Shearsman Books.
2014 *Manual, the first hundred*. Bristol: Shearsman Books.
2015 [1] *Notness, metaphysical sonnets*. Bristol: Shearsman Books.
2015 [2] 'On Poetry and Sound (1): The Ontogenesis of Poetry'. Online at: http://www.interlitq.org/englishwriters2/richard-berengarten-1/job.php. Consulted December 26, 2015.
2016 *Changing*. Bristol: Shearsman Books.

Some Critical Texts on RB, and Previous Interviews

Calder, Angus. 2004. 'A Spectacular Variety of Registers'. *The London Magazine*, December/January: 88–95. Reprinted in Jope *et al.* 233–239.

Derrick, Paul Scott and Rys, Sean (eds.). *Managing the Manager. Essays.* (Forthcoming 2017–18).

Dispa, Kathleen and Burns, Richard. 'The Translator is a Dancer in Chains: Interview with Richard Burns, poet'. *Janus* 5(3), no pagination.

Filippakopoulou, Maria. 2011 [2009]. 'Foreign in Our Own Country'. In Jope *et al.* 193–210; and *The International Literary Quarterly* 9. Online at: http://interlitq.org/issue9/filippakopoulou/job.php. Consulted December 26, 2015.

Gelashvili, Manana and Kobakhidze, Temur. 2011. '*The Manager*: Tradition and the Individual Talent'. In Jope *et al.* 240–250.

Gery, John. 2011. 'Explicit and Implicit: Ezra Pound's Influence on Richard Berengarten's "Angels"'. In Jope *et al.* 144–174.

Hamilton-Emery, Chris. 2008 and 2011. 'Preface'. In *The Manager*. Cambridge: Salt Publishing; and Exeter: Shearsman Books, xi–xvii.

Hooker, Jeremy. 2011. 'Richard Berengarten's Art of Transformation'. In Jope *et al.* 68–80.

Jope, Norman. 2010. 'Introduction: *Everywhere Centre*'. In Jope *et al.* 1–8.

Jope, Norman; Derrick, Paul Scott; and Byfield, Catherine E. (eds.). 2010. *The Salt Companion to Richard Berengarten* (first edition). Cambridge: Salt Publishing. Also 2016. *The Companion to Richard Berengarten* (second edition). Bristol: Shearsman Books.

kuhn, philip. 2011. '"'Tis Death is dead, not he" or Reading Richard Reading Richard Reading'. In Jope *et al.* 92–116.

Limburg, Joanne. 2002. 'Human Above All'. *The Jewish Quarterly* 185, Spring: 17–23.

Macfarlane, Alan and Berengarten, Richard. 'Interview with the poet Richard Berengarten (Burns) March 2015'. Online at: https://www.youtube.com/watch?v=j6Xsq4pVk5s; and http://www.sms.cam.ac.uk/media/2010297. Consulted September 20, 2015.

Moody, Neli. 2011. 'A Syntax of Stones: Pre-Text, Edifice, and the Sacred Space in Richard Berengarten's "Avebury"'. In Jope *et al.* 118–134.

Moses, Antoinette and Burns, Richard. 2003. 'Straddling Two Genres: An Interview with Richard Burns'. *Spiked* 13: 26–27.

Nicolao, Mario. 2011. 'The Ghost of the Mediterranean'. In Jope *et al.* 43–47; and in *Margutte* 2014. Online at: http://www.margutte.com/?p=8197andlang=en. Consulted December 14, 2015.

Nikolaou, Paschalis. 2015. 'The *Dictio* Interview: Richard Berengarten'. *Dictio, 2014 Yearbook of the Ionian University's Department of Foreign Languages, Translation and Interpreting* 7: 75–103.

Query, Patrick. 2011. 'Form and Redemption in *The Manager*'. In Jope *et al.* 251–258.

Rudolf, Anthony. 1990. 'Predgovor' [Preface]. In *Menadžer* (trans. into Serbian, Vladimir Sekulić and Jasna B. Mišić). Titograd: Udruženje književnika Crne Gore [Writers' Association of Montenegro]: 7–9.

Vayenas, Nasos. 2011. 'The Black Light of the Poets'. In Jope *et al.* 175–180.

Wilson, Stephen. 2011. 'Hath Not a Jew Hands?' In Jope *et al.* 361–373; and *The International Literary Quarterly* 8, 2009. Online at: http://interlitq.org/issue8/stephen_wilson/job.php. Consulted December 14, 2015.

Woelfel, Craig. 2011. 'The Descent through Croft Woods'. In Jope *et al.* 221–232.

References: General

Abrams, M. H. *et al.* (eds.). 1979 [1962]. *The Norton Anthology of English Literature*. New York, NY: W. W. Norton (two vols).

Adorno, Theodor W. 1967. *Prisms* (trans. Samuel and Shierry Weber). London: Spearman.

Arnaudov, Mikhail. 1971 [1924]. *Studii vurhu bulgariskite obredi i legendi* [*Studies of Bulgarian Rituals and Legends*]. Sofia: Bulgarian Academy of Sciences.

Barthes, Roland. 1977. 'The Death of the Author' (trans. Stephen Heath). *Image-Music-Text*. London: Fontana Press, 142-148.

Bateson, Gregory. 1973. *Steps to an Ecology of Mind*. St Albans: Paladin.

Baudelaire, Charles. 1968 [1857]. *Fleurs du mal* (eds. Jacques Crépet and Georges Blin). Paris: Librairie José Corti.

———. 'Au lecteur'. Online at: http://fleursdumal.org/poem/099 and http://fleursdumal.org/poem/231. Consulted October 19, 2015.

Bauman Zygmunt. 1989. *Modernity and the Holocaust*. Cambridge: Polity Press.

———. 1991. *Modernity and Ambivalence*. Cambridge: Polity Press.

———. 1993. *Postmodern Ethics*. Oxford: Blackwell.

———. 1997. *Postmodernity and its Discontents*. Cambridge: Polity Press.

Beaton, Roderick. 2003. *George Seferis. Waiting for the Angel: a Biography*. New Haven, CT and London: Yale University Press.

Beckett, Samuel. 1956. *Waiting for Godot*. London: Faber and Faber.

Berliner, Emile. 'Emile Berliner and the Birth of the Recording Industry'. Library of Congress document collection. Online at: http://memory.loc.gov/ammem/berlhtml/berlhome.html. Consulted December 17, 2015.

Bernstein, Basil. 1971. *Class, Codes and Control*. London: Routledge and Kegan Paul.

Bevan, William Ham. 2010. 'The Varsity Protest that Shaped a Generation'. *The Independent,* November 23. Online at http://www.independent.co.uk/news/education/education-news/the-varsity-protest-that-shaped-a-generation-2141131.html. Consulted January 1, 2016.

Bickerton, Derek. 1990. *Language and Species*. Chicago, IL and London: University of Chicago Press.

———. 2009. *Adam's Tongue: How Humans Made Language, How Language Made Humans*. New York, NY: Hill and Wang.

Bird, John and Fortune, John. 'Silly Money'. Online at: http://www.youtube.com/watch?v=9z70BKwfSUA; and the repeat, 'Subprime Crisis', http://www.youtube.com/watch?v=mzJmTCYmo9g. Consulted December 6, 2015.

Blake, William. 1956 [1804–1820]. *Poetry and Prose of William Blake* (ed. Geoffrey Keynes). London: The Nonesuch Library.

Bloom, Harold. 1997 [1973]. *The Anxiety of Influence: A Theory of Poetry*. Oxford: Oxford University Press.

Bohm, David. 1980. *Wholeness and the Implicate Order*. London and New York, NY: Routledge.

Boswell, James. 1986 [1791]. *Life of Samuel Johnson* (ed. Harold Bloom). New York, NY: Chelsea House.

Brecht, Bertolt. 1976. *Poems: Part 1, 1913–1956* (eds. John Willett and Ralph Manheim). London: Eyre Methuen.

Breton, André. 1972 [1924]. *Manifestoes of Surrealism* (trans. Richard Seaver and Helen R. Lane). Ann Arbor, MI: University of Michigan Press.

Brown, Norman O. 1959. *Life Against Death: The Psychoanalytical Meaning of History*. London: Routledge and Kegan Paul.

Cambray, Joseph. 2009. *Synchronicity: Nature and Psyche in an Interconnected Universe*. Austin, TX: Texas University Press.

Cambridge Evening News. 1970. 'It's all-quiet as 1,000 march to Greek rally'. May 11.

Camus, Albert. 2012. *The Outsider* (trans. Matthew Ward). New York, NY: Random House.

Camus, Marcel (dir.). 1959. Film, *Orfeu Negro* (*Black Orpheus*).

Capra, Fritjof. 1986 [1973]. *The Tao of Physics*. London: Fontana.

Carver, P. L. 1928–9. 'The Evolution of the Term "Esemplastic"'. *Modern Language Review*, 24(3), July: 329.

Cassirer, Ernst. 1946. *Language and Myth* (trans. Susanne K. Langer). New York, NY: Harper.

Cavell, Stanley. 1982 [1979]. 'What a Thing is (Called)'. In *The Claim of Reason*. New York, NY, and Oxford: Oxford University Press, 65–85.

Celan, Paul. 1980. *Poems* (trans. Michael Hamburger). Manchester: Carcanet New Press.

———. 2001. *Selected Poems and Prose* (trans. John Felstiner). New York, NY: W.W. Norton.

Chuang Tsu. 1974. *Inner Chapters* (trans. Gia-Fu Feng and Jane English). London: Wildwood House.

Chuang Tzu. 2006 [1996]. *The Book of Chuang Tzu* (trans. Martin Palmer *et al.*). London: Penguin Books.

Coe, Richard N. Undated. 'Beckett's English'. Online at: https://ohiostatepress.org/Books/Complete%20PDFs/Beja%20Samuel/05.pdf. Consulted October 31, 2015.

Coleridge, Samuel Taylor. 1816. *Christabel, Kubla Khan, and the Pains of Sleep*. London: John Murray.

———. 1906 [1817]. *Biographia Literaria*. London: J. M. Dent and Co., Everyman edition.

Cook, Peter and Moore, Dudley. 'The Frog and Peach' and 'Teaching Ravens to Fly Under Water'. Online at: http://www.youtube.com/watch?v=JhS35f015SQ and https://www.youtube.com/watch?v=7fY-M41FGzI. Consulted October 5, 2015.

Cookson, William. 2001 [1985]. *A Guide to the Cantos of Ezra Pound*. London: Anvil Press Poetry.

Cornford, F. M. 1923. *Greek Religious Thought: from Homer to the Age of Alexander*. London: J. M. Dent.

Cowley, A. C. (ed.). 2004 [1956]. *Everyman and Medieval Miracle Plays*. London: J. M. Dent, Everyman Books.

Damon, S. Foster. 1979 [1973]. *A Blake Dictionary*. London: Thames and Hudson.

Daskalopoulos, Dimitris. (ed.). 2003. *Ellinika Kavafoyeni Poiemata (1909–2001)* [Greek Cavafy-inspired Poems (1909–2001)]. Patras: Patras University Press.

Dante Alighieri. 1902. *The Divine Comedy of Dante Alighieri* (vol. 1): *Hell* (trans. Charles Eliot Norton). Boston and New York, NY: Houghton, Mifflin and Company.

Derrida, Jacques and Defourtmentelle, Anne. 2000. *Of Hospitality: Anne Defourtmentelle Invites Jacques Derrida to Respond* (trans. Rachel Bowlby). Stanford, CA: Stanford University Press.

Diderot, Denis. 1891. *Le neveu de Rameau*. Online at: http://www.gutenberg.org/ebooks/13862. Consulted June 20, 2015.

Donne, John. 1959. *Devotions*. Ann Arbor, MI: University of Michigan Press.

Douglas, Mary. 1966. *Purity and Danger: An Analysis of the Concepts of Pollution and Taboo*. London: Routledge and Kegan Paul.

Duffy, Carol Ann. 1998. 'Poetry'. Review of *PEN New Poetry II*. *The Guardian*, July 29.

Durkheim, Émile. 1963. *Selections* (ed. George Simpson). New York, NY: Crowell.

Edgerton, David. 2006. *The Shock of the Old: Technology and Global History since 1900*. London: Profile.

Eliade, Mircea. 2005 [1954]. *The Myth of the Eternal Return: Cosmos and History* (trans. Willard R. Trask; Bollingen Series XLVI). Princeton, NJ: Princeton University Press.

Eliot, George. 1876. *Daniel Deronda*. London and Edinburgh: William Blackwood and Sons.

Eliot, T. S. 1961 [1917]. 'Tradition and the Individual Talent'. In *Selected Essays*. London: Faber and Faber, 13–22.

———. 1961 [1934]. 'The Metaphysical Poets' [1921]. In *Selected Essays*. London: Faber and Faber, 281–291.

———. 1959 [1943] *Four Quartets*. London: Faber and Faber.
———. 1972 [1922]. *The Waste Land and Other Poems*. London: Faber and Faber.
———. 1998 [1920]. *The Sacred Wood and Major Early Essays*. New York, NY: Dover Publications.
Eliot, T. S. and Hall, Donald. 1959. 'The Art of Poetry, No. 1'. *Paris Review* 29, Spring-Summer. Online at: http://www.theparisreview.org/interviews/4738/the-art-of-poetry-no-1-t-s-eliot. Consulted June 19, 2015.
Elytis, Odysseus. 1980. *The Axion Esti* (trans. Edmund Keeley and George Savidis). London: Anvil Press Poetry in association with Rex Collings.
Evans-Wentz, W. Y. 1960 [1949]. *The Tibetan Book of the Dead*. London, Oxford and New York, NY: Oxford University Press.
Feinstein, Elaine (ed.) *P.E.N. New Poetry II*. London: Quartet Books.
Feldman, Anita *et al*. 2013. *Moore Rodin*. Perry Green: The Henry Moore Foundation.
Forché, Carolyn. 1993. *Against Forgetting*. New York, NY: W. W. Norton.
Forster, E. M., Furbank, P. N., and Haskell, F. J. H. 1953. 'The Art of Fiction, No. 1'. *Paris Review* 1, Spring. Online at: http://www.theparisreview.org/interviews/5219/the-art-of-fiction-no-1-e-m-forster. Consulted December 4, 2015.
Fostieris, Antonis and Niarchos, Thanasis (eds.). 2012. *Poiitikes Synomilies. Ellinika Poiimata yia Ksenous Poiites* [Poetic Conversations: Greek Poems about Foreign Poets]. Athens: Odos Panos.
Foucault, Michel. 1977. 'What is an Author?' (trans. Donald Bouchard and Sherry Simon). In Donald F. Bouchard (ed.), *Language, Counter-Memory, Practice: Selected Essays and Interviews*. Ithaca, NY: Cornell University Press, 113-138.
Franz, Marie-Louise von. 1974. *Number and Time: Reflections Leading Towards a Unification of Psychology and Physics* (trans. Andrea Dykes). London: Rider and Co.
———.1979 [1964]. 'The Process of Individuation'. In *Man and His Symbols* (eds. Carl Gustav Jung and M.-L. von Franz). London: Aldus Books, 158–229.
Frazer, Sir James. 1959 [1922]. *The Golden Bough,* abridged version. London: Macmillan.
Freud, Sigmund. 1938. 'Sigmund Freud Speaks: The Only Known Recording of His Voice'. BBC radio recording: Open Culture. Online at: http://www.openculture.com/2012/05/sigmund_freud_speaks_the_only_known_recording_of_his_voice_1938.html. Consulted July 13, 2013.
———. 1961 [1954]. *The Interpretation of Dreams* (trans. James Strachey). London: George Allen and Unwin.
Freud, Sigmund and Dr. Ruth. Undated. 'Dr. Ruth and Sigmund Freud: The Full Interview'. Online at: https://www.youtube.com/watch?v=0GCUfwirTjA/. Consulted January 23, 2016.
Frye, Northrop. 1969 [1947]. *Fearful Symmetry: A Study of William Blake*. Princeton, NJ: Princeton University Press.

'Garden House riot'. Online at: https://en.wikipedia.org/wiki/Garden_House_riot. Consulted January 1, 2016.

Garrould, Ann and Power, Valerie. 1998. *Henry Moore Tapestries*. Perry Green: The Henry Moore Foundation.

Gatsos, Nikos. 1966. 'Amorgos'. In *Four Greek Poets* (trans. Edmund Keeley and Philip Sherrard). London: Penguin Books, 93–101.

Gimbutas, Marija. 1996 [1974]. *The Goddesses and Gods of Old Europe, 6500–3500 BC, Myths and Cult Images*. London: Thames and Hudson.

———. 2001 [1999]. *The Living Goddesses*. Berkeley, CA., Los Angeles, CA and London: University of California Press.

———. 2001 [1989]. *The Language of the Goddess*. London: Thames and Hudson.

Gleick, James. 1992. *Genius: Richard Feynman and Modern Physics*. London: Little, Brown and Company.

Graham, W. S. 1970. *Malcolm Mooney's Land*. London: Faber and Faber.

———. 1977. *Implements in Their Places*. London: Faber and Faber.

Grimm, Jakob. 1835. *Deutsche Mythologie* (1). Göttingen: Dieterichsche Buchhandlung.

Grosvenor Myer, Valerie. 1977. *Jane Austen: Obstinate Heart: A Biography*. New York, NY: Arcade Publishing.

Harris, Roy. 1981. *The Language Myth*. London: Duckworth.

———. 1996. *Signs, Language and Communication*. London: Routledge.

———. 2002 [1986]. *The Origin of Writing*. London: Duckworth.

Harrison, Jane. 1922 [1903, 1908]. *Prolegomena to the Study of Greek Religion*. Cambridge: Cambridge University Press.

Heidegger, Martin. 1962. *Being and Time* (trans. John Macquarrie and Edward Robinson). Oxford: Blackwell Publishing.

Heaney, Seamus and O' Driscoll, Dennis. 2008. *Stepping Stones: Interviews with Seamus Heaney*. London: Faber and Faber.

Herbert, George. 1961. *The Poems of George Herbert* (ed. Helen Gardner). London: Oxford University Press.

Herodotus. *The History of Herodotus* (chapter 1) (trans. George Rawlinson). http://classics.mit.edu/Herodotus/history.html. Consulted March 2, 2013.

Hill, Geoffrey and Phillips, Carl. 2000. 'The Art of Poetry, No. 80'. *Paris Review* 154, Spring. Online at: http://www.theparisreview.org/interviews/730/the-art-of-poetry-no-80-geoffrey-hill. Consulted November 3, 2015.

Hobsbawm, Eric. 1959. *Primitive Rebels*. New York, NY: Norton.

———. 2000. *Bandits*. New York, NY: The New York Press.

Hogg, James (ed.). 1996. *The Road to Parnassus: Homage to Peter Russell on his Seventy-Fifth Birthday*. Salzburg: University of Salzburg.

Hopson, Janet L. 1998. 'Fetal Psychology'. *Psychology Today*, October. Online at: https://www.psychologytoday.com/articles/199809/fetal-psychology. Consulted January 1, 2016.

Hughes, Ted. 1970 [1967]. *Poetry in the Making*. London: Faber and Faber.

Hughes, Ted and Heinz, Due. 1995. 'The Art of Poetry, No. 71'. *Paris Review* 134, Spring. Online at: http://www.theparisreview.org/interviews/1669/the-art-of-poetry-no-71-ted-hughes. Consulted October 28, 2012.

Hurford, James R. Undated. 'Random Boolean Nets and Features of Language'. Online at: http://www.lel.ed.ac.uk/~jim/ozpaper.html#fn1. Consulted July 9, 2015.

Ivanov, V. V. and Toporov, V. I. 1974. *Issledovanya v oblasti slavyanskih drevnotstei* [Researches in the Field of Slavonic Antiquities/Folklore]. Moscow: Nauka.

Jakobson, Roman. 1973. *Main Trends in the Science of Language*. London: George Allen and Unwin.

———. 1985 [1]. 'Slavic Gods and Demons'. In *Selected Writings: Contributions to Comparative Mythology. Studies in Linguistics and Phonology, 1972–1982* (vol. VII). Berlin, New York, NY, and Amsterdam: Mouton Publishers, 3–11.

———. 1985 [2] 'Linguistic Evidence in Comparative Mythology'. In *Selected Writings: Contributions to Comparative Mythology. Studies in Linguistics and Phonology, 1972–1982* (vol. VII): Berlin, New York, NY, and Amsterdam, Mouton Publishers: 12–32.

Jakobson, Roman and Waugh, Linda. R. 1987 [1979]. *The Sound Shape of Language*. Berlin and New York, NY: Mouton De Gruyter.

Johnson, B. S. 2008 [1969]. *The Unfortunates*. New York, NY: New Directions.

Jones, Daniel. 1972 [1918]. *An Outline of English Phonetics*. Cambridge: Cambridge University Press.

Jones, Peter E. 2009. 'From "External Speech" to "Inner Speech" in Vygotsky: A Critical Appraisal and Fresh Perspectives'. *Language and Communication* 29: 166–181. Online at: http://lchc.ucsd.edu/mca/Mail/xmcamail.2009_07.dir/pdf9Un00JYIk5.pdf. Consulted July 13, 2015.

Jonson, Ben. 1959. *Five Plays*. London: Oxford University Press.

Joyce, James. 1922. *Ulysses*. Paris: Shakespeare & Co.

———. 1939. *Finnegans Wake*. London: Faber and Faber.

Julius, Anthony. 2003 [1995]. *T. S. Eliot, Anti-Semitism, and Literary Form*. London: Thames and Hudson.

Jung, C. G. 1968 [1951]. 'Foreword' to *I Ching: the Richard Wilhelm Translation* (trans. from German, Cary F. Baynes). London: Routledge and Kegan Paul.

———. 1986 [1956]. *Symbols of Transformation: Collected Works* (vol. 5) (trans. R. F. C. Hull). London: Routledge and Kegan Paul.

———. 1968 [1959]. *The Archetypes and the Collective Unconscious: Collected Works* (vol. 9, part 1) (trans. R. F. C. Hull). London: Routledge and Kegan Paul.

———. 1969 [1] [1960]. 'The Stages of Life'. In *The Structure and Dynamics of the Psyche: Collected Works* (vol. 8) (trans. R. F. C. Hull). London: Routledge and Kegan Paul, 387–403.

———. 1969 [2] [1960]. 'Synchronicity: An Acausal Connecting Principle'. In *The Structure and Dynamics of the Psyche: Collected Works* (vol. 8) (trans. R. F. C. Hull). London: Routledge and Kegan Paul, 417–532.

———. 1979 [1964]. 'Approaching the Unconscious' In *Man and His Symbols* (eds. Carl Gustav Jung and M. L. von Franz). London: Aldus Books, 18–103.
Jung, C. G. and Freeman, John. 1959. 'Face to Face with Carl Jung'. BBC interview. Online at: https://www.youtube.com/watch?v=eTBs-2cloEI. Consulted January 23, 1916.
Jung, C. G. and Pauli, W. 1955. *The Interpretation of Nature and the Psyche* (trans. R. F. C. Hull). London: Routledge and Kegan Paul.
Kampanellis, Iakovos. 1965. *Maouthaousen* [The Mauthausen Chronicle]. Athens: Themelio.
Karadžić, Vuk Stefanović. 1852 [1818]. *Srpski Rječnik* [Serbian Dictionary]. Vienna: Typis Congretationis Mechitaristicae / Jermenskoga Namastira.
———. 1957 [1867]. *Život i običaji naroda srpskoga* [Life and Customs of the Serbian People]. Belgrade: Srpska književna zadruga.
Kazantzakis, Nikos. 1967. *The Odyssey. A Modern Sequel* (trans. Kimon Friar). New York, NY: Simon and Schuster.
Keats, John. 1885. *The Poetical Works of John Keats* (ed. Harry Buxton Forman). London: Reeves and Turner.
———. 1970. *Letters of John Keats, A Selection* (ed. Robert Gittings). Oxford: Oxford University Press.
Keeley, Edmund. 1982. *A Conversation with George Seferis*. Athens: Agra.
Keeley, Edmund and Sherrard, Philip (eds.). 1966. *Four Greek Poets*. London: Penguin Books.
Kermode, Frank. 1966. *The Sense of an Ending: Studies in the Theory of Fiction*. Oxford: Oxford University Press.
Kinsey, Alfred C. *et al.* 1948. *Sexual Behavior in the Human Male*. Philadelphia, PA: W. B. Saunders.
———. 1953. *Sexual Behavior in the Human Female*. Philadelphia, PA: W. B. Saunders.
Knight, Gareth. 1965. *A Practical Guide to Qabalistic Symbolism*. Toddington: Helios Books (two vols.).
Koerner, E. F. K. 1999. *Linguistic Historiography: Projects and Prospects* (Studies in the History of the Language Sciences, vol. 92). Amsterdam: John Benjamins.
Koestler, Arthur. 1969. 'Books of the Year, a Personal Choice'. *Observer Review*: 21 December.
Laing, R. D. 1965 [1960]. *The Divided Self*. London: Pelican Books.
Laing, R. D. and Esterton, A. 1970 [1964]. *Sanity, Madness and the Family*. London: Pelican Books.
Leavis, F. R. 1975. *The Living Principle: 'English' as a Discipline of Thought*. London: Chatto and Windus.
Leibniz, Gottfried. 1765. *Nouveaux essais sur l'entendement humain*. In *Oeuvres philosophiques*. Amsterdam and Leipzig: Rud.
———. *New Essays on Human Understanding*. In *Some Texts from Early Modern Philosophy* (Book 3, ed. Jonathan Bennett). Online at: http://www.earlymoderntexts.com/authors/leibniz. Consulted January 6, 2016.

Leontis, Artemis. 1995. *Topographies of Hellenism: Mapping the Homeland*. Ithaca, NY: Cornell University Press.
Lessing, Doris. 1979 [1973]. *The Golden Notebook*. London: Panther.
Lévinas, Emmanuel. 2000. *God, Death and Time* (trans. Bettina Bergo). Stanford, CA: Stanford University Press.
———. 2003 [1]. *Time and the Other* (trans. Richard A. Cohen). Pittsburgh, PA: Duquesne University Press.
———. 2003 [2]. *Totality and Infinity* (trans. Alphonso Lingis). Pittsburgh, PA: Duquesne University Press.
Lévi-Strauss, Claude. 1962. *La Pensée Sauvage*: Paris: Librairie Plon.
Lieberman, Philip. 1967. *Intonation, Perception and Language* (Research Monograph No. 38.) Cambridge, MA: MIT Press.
———. 1975. *On the Origins of Language*. New York, NY: Macmillan.
———. 1977. *Speech Physiology and Acoustic Phonetics*. New York, NY: Macmillan.
———. 1998. *Eve Spoke*. New York, NY: W. W. Norton.
———. 2006. *Toward an Evolutionary Biology of Language*. Cambridge, MA: The Belknap Press of Harvard University Press.
Locke, John. 1998 [1689–90]. *An Essay Concerning Human Understanding* (Book 3). Ware: Wordsworth Editions; online at Project Gutenberg: http://www.gutenberg.org/cache/epub/10616/pg10616-images.html. Consulted June 15, 2015.
Lord, A. B. 1960. *The Singer of Tales*. Cambridge, MA: Harvard University Press.
Lowry, Malcolm. 1967. *Selected Letters of Malcolm Lowry* (eds. Harvey Breit and Margerie Bonner Lowry). London: Jonathan Cape.
Luria, Alexander Romanovich. 1982. *Language and Cognition*. Washington, DC: Winston and Sons.
Lykiard, Alexis and Trist, Alan. 1967. *Paros Poems*. Athens: Difros.
MacDiarmid. Hugh. 1978. *Complete Poems 1920–1976* (vol. 1). London: Martin Brian and O'Keeffe.
Macfarlane, Alan *et al. Filmed Interviews with Leading Thinkers*. Online at: http://www.alanmacfarlane.com/ancestors/. For index, see: http://www.alanmacfarlane.com/ancestors/audiovisual.html]. Consulted June 8, 2015.
Magee, Brian. Date unknown. 'Jung – Sea of Faith – BBC documentary'. Online at: http://www.youtube.com/watch?v=RWB8Gx2j0R0. Consulted July 12, 2015.
Main, Roderick. 2007. *Revelations of Chance: Synchronicity as Spiritual Experience*. New York, NY: State University of New York Press.
Mamangakis, Nikos. 1964. *O Erotokritos tou Vitzentzou Kornarou* [*The Erotokritos by Vitzentzos Kornaros*]. With Manos Katrakis, Vera Zavitsianou and Kostas Karras. Lyra 3501. LP.
Mandelstam, Osip. 1973. *Selected Poems* (trans. Clarence Brown and W. S. Merwin). Harmondsworth: Penguin Books.

———. 1977. 'About an Interlocutor'. In *Selected Essays* (trans. Sydney Monas). Austin, TX: University of Texas Press, 58–64.

———. 1987. *Tristia* (trans. Bruce McClelland). Barrytown, NY: Station Hill Press.

Manning, Olivia. 1998 [1987]. *The Balkan Trilogy*. London: Arrow Books.

Marvell, Andrew. 1962. *Some Poems* (ed. James Winny). London: Hutchinson.

Mass Observation Archive, 'History of Mass Observation', Online at: http://www.massobs.org.uk/about/history-of-mo. Consulted December 8, 2015.

Masschelein, Anneleen *et al.* 2014. 'The Literary Interview: Toward a Poetics of a Hybrid Genre'. *Poetics Today* 35(1–2). Durham, NC: Duke University Press. Online at: http://poeticstoday.dukejournals.org/content/35/1-2/1.full.pdf+html. Consulted June 18, 2015.

Memmi, Albert. 1968. 'Negritude and Judeity'. *European Judaism* 3(2), 4–12.

Miller, Arthur. 2000 [1949]. *Death of a Salesman*. London: Penguin Modern Classics.

Miller, Henry and Nin, Anaïs. 'Henry Miller & Anaïs Nin sur la mort et les rêves' ('Henry Miller and Anaïs Nin on Death and Dreams'). Online at: http://www.tagtele.com/videos/voir/77719/. Consulted, January 1, 2017.

Moore, Henry and Lucie-Smith, Edward. 1981. 'Henry Moore', in *Conversations with Artists*. BBC Archive Radio 3 broadcast, December 6. Online at: http://www.bbc.co.uk/archive/henrymoore/8816.shtml. Consulted June 16, 2015.

Mosley, Nicholas. 1990. *Hopeful Monsters*. London: Secker and Warburg.

Musgrave, Rosie. 2016. *Rosie Musgrave: Stone Carver, Sculptor*. Online at: http://www.rosiemusgrave.com/. Consulted February 3, 2016.

Neumann, Erich. 1972 [1963].*The Great Mother: Analysis of the Archetype* (trans. Ralph Mannheim; Bollingen Series XLVII). Princeton, NJ: Princeton University Press.

Nikolaou, Paschalis (ed.). 2015. *12 Greek Poems after Cavafy* (trans. Paschalis Nikolaou and Richard Berengarten). Bristol: Shearsman Books.

Nin, Anaïs and Seguin, Fernand. Undated. 'Entrevista legendada'. Online at: https://www.youtube.com/watch?v=7SXVzJGA4mk. Consulted January 23, 2016.

Olson, Charles. 1970 [1960]. *The Maximus Poems*. London: Cape Goliard Press.

Onions, C. T. 1966. *The Oxford Dictionary of English Etymology*. Oxford: Oxford University Press.

Oxford English Dictionary [*OED*]. 2013. Online edition at: http://www.oed.com/. Consulted February 10, 2016.

Paris Review, the Interviews. 1953–2013. Online at: http://www.theparisreview.org/interviews. Consulted June 14, 2015.

Parkinson, Michael. BBC Interviews, with: Peter Sellers, http://www.youtube.com/watch?v=9qyGX6z7cpg; David Niven, http://www.youtube.com/watch?v=HvtrWuLXuzQ; Peter Ustinov, https://www.youtube.com/watch?v=SfxxEfdmn_Y; and Kenneth Williams, http://www.youtube.com/watch?v=ufpO0r3TYS0. Consulted July 11, 2015.

Pavlou, Savvas. 2005. *Seferis ke Kypros* [Seferis and Cyprus]. Nicosia: Author.
Paz, Octavio. 1967. *The Labyrinth of Solitude* (trans. Lysander Kemp). London: The Penguin Press.
———. 1973. *Alternating Current* (trans. Helen Lane). New York, NY: The Viking Press.
———. 1975 [1974]. *Conjunctions and Disjunctions* (trans. Helen Lane). London: Wildwood House.
Petropoulos, Ilias. 1968. *Rebetika Tragoudia* [Rebetika Songs]. Athens: privately published by author at 32 Dimokritou Street.
Phillips, Laurence, 2015. *Lille*. Bradt Travel Guides.
Pickstock, Catherine. 1998. *After Writing: On the Liturgical Consummation of Philosophy*. Oxford: Blackwell.
———. 2012. 'Repetition and Things'. (Unpublished.)
———. 2013. *Repetition and Identity*. Oxford: Oxford University Press.
Pinter, Harold. 1960. *The Caretaker*. London: Methuen.
Plato, Index to *Works* (Project Gutenberg). Online at: http://www.gutenberg.org/ebooks/29441/ Consulted: January 23, 2016.
Plotnikova, Ana. 1999. 'Dodola'. In I. Tolstoy *et al.* (eds.), *Slavyanskie Drevnosti: etnolingvitichenski slovari* [Slavonic Folk-Customs: an Ethnolinguistic Dictionary] (vol. 2). Moscow: Meždunarodnije otnošenja, 100–103.
Popper, Karl. 1959 [1939]. *The Logic of Scientific Discovery*. London: Routledge and Kegan Paul.
Pound, Ezra. 1970. *Drafts and Fragments of Cantos CX–CXVII*. London: Faber and Faber.
Price, Huw. 1997. *Time's Arrow and Archimedes' Point*. Oxford: Oxford University Press.
Pring, J. T. 1982 [1965]. *The Oxford Dictionary of Modern Greek*. Oxford: Oxford University Press.
Radnóti, Miklós. 1992. *Foamy Sky* (trans. Zsuzsanna Ozsvath and Frederick Turner). Princeton, NJ: Princeton University Press.
———. 2000. *Camp Notebook* (trans. Francis Jones; Visible Poets 2). Todmorden: Arc Publications.
———. 2010 [2003]. *Forced March* (trans. George Gömöri and Clive Wilmer). London: Enitharmon Press.
Rechy, John. 1963. *City of Night*. New York, NY: Grove Press.
Rilke, Rainer Maria. 1957 [1946]. *Sonnets to Orpheus* (bilingual German-English edition, trans. J. B. Leishman). London: Hogarth Press.
Rimbaud, Arthur. 1970 [1966]. *Complete Works, Selected Letters* (bilingual French-English edition, trans. Wallace Fowlie). Chicago, IL: University of Chicago Press.
Ritsos, Yannis. 1971. *Gestures and Other Poems, 1968–1970* (trans. Nikos Stangos). London: Cape Goliard.
Roethke, Theodore. 1975 [1937]. *Collected Poems*. New York, NY: Anchor Books.

Russell Peter (ed.). 1973 [1950]. *An Examination of Ezra Pound*. New York, NY: Gordian Press.
Sahtouris, Miltos. 1968. *With Face to the Wall* (trans. Kimon Friar). Washington, DC: The Charioteer Press.
Samarakis, Antonis. 1969. *The Flaw* (trans. Peter Mansfield and Richard Burns). London: Hutchinson; New York, NY: Weybright and Talley.
Sanesi. Roberto. 1977. *Sul linguaggio organico di Henry Moore / On the Organic Language of Henry Moore* (bilingual Italian-English edition, trans. Richard Burns). Macerata: La Nuova Foglio.
Sartre, Jean-Paul. 1987 [1944]. *Huis Clos. Twentieth Century French Texts* (ed. Keith Gore). London: Methuen.
Saussure, Ferdinand de. 1971 [1918]. *Cours de Linguistique Générale* (eds. Charles Ballyn and Albert Sechehaye with Albert Riedlinger). Paris: Payot.
Seferis, George. 1960. *Poems* (trans. Rex Warner). London: The Bodley Head.
———. 1969. *Collected Poems, 1924–1955* (trans. Edmund Keeley and Philip Sherrard). London: Jonathan Cape.
———. 1974. *A Poet's Journal: Days of 1945–1951* (trans. Athan Anagnostopoulos). Cambridge, MA: The Belknap Press of Harvard University Press.
———. 1977. *Meres, E: 1 Genari – 19 Aprili* [Days V: January 1–April 19, 1951]. Athens: Ikaros 1977.
———. 2007. *A Levant Journal* (trans. Roderick Beaton). Jerusalem: Ibis Editions.
Sewell, Elizabeth. 1960. *The Orphic Voice*. London: Routledge and Kegan Paul.
Shakespeare, William 1954 [1905]. *The Complete Works of William* Shakespeare (ed. W. J. Craig). London: Oxford University Press.
Sheldrake, Rupert. 2009 [1981]. *A New Science of Life: The Hypothesis of Formative Causation*. London: Icon Books.
———. 2011 [1] [1999]. *Dogs That Know When Their Owners Are Coming Home*. London: Arrow Books.
———. 2011 [2] [2003]. *The Presence of the Past: Morphic Resonance and the Habits of Nature*. London: Icon Books.
Sheldrake, Rupert, McKenna, Terence and Abraham, Ralph. 1992. *Chaos, Creativity, and Cosmic Consciousness*. Rochester, VT: Park Street Press.
Shelley, Percy Bysshe. 1919. *The Complete Poetical Works of Percy Bysshe Shelley* (ed. Thomas Hutchinson). Oxford: Oxford University Press.
———. 1923 [1840]. 'A Defence of Poetry'. In *The Four Ages of Poetry* (ed. H. F. B. Brett-Smith). Oxford: Basil Blackwell, 23–59.
Sherrard, Philip. 1956. *The Marble Threshing Floor: Studies in Modern Greek Poetry*. London: Vallentine, Mitchell.
Sillitoe, Alan. 1962. 'The Rats'. In *Loneliness of the Long-Distance Runner*. London: Pan Books, 181.
Simpson, D. P. 1963 [1927]. *Cassell's New Compact Latin Dictionary*. London: Cassell.

Skeat, Rev. Walter. 1888. *An Etymological Dictionary of the English Language*. Oxford: Clarendon Press.
Spenser, Edmund. 1912. *The Poetical Work of Edmund Spenser* (eds. J. C. Smith and E. de Selincourt). Oxford: Oxford University Press.
Spencer Brown, G. 1969. *Laws of Form*. London: George Allen and Unwin.
Stavropoulos, D. N. 2008 [1998]. *Oxford Greek-English Learner's Dictionary*. Oxford: Oxford University Press.
Stein, Gertrude. 1922. 'Sacred Emily'. In *Geography and Plays*. Boston, MA: The Four Seas Company, 187.
Stevens, Wallace. 1997. *Collected Poetry and Prose*. New York, NY: Library of America.
Svevo, Italo. 1925. *La coscienza di Zeno*. Milan: Giuseppe Morreale.
Swiderski, Richard M. 1980–1981. 'Bouvet and Leibniz: A Scholarly Correspondence'. *Eighteenth Century Studies* 14(2), Winter: 135–150.
Theodorakis, Mikis. 1966. *Maouthaouzen / Eksi Tragoudia*. [The Ballad of Mauthausen / Six Songs]. Columbia 70204. LP.
Thomas, Dylan. 1952. *Collected Poems 1934–1952*. London: J. M. Dent and Sons.
———. 1957 [1954]. *Under Milk Wood*. London: J. M. Dent and Sons.
Tsien, Tsuen-Hsuin. 2013 [1962]. *Written on Bamboo and Silk: The Beginnings of Chinese Books and Inscriptions*. Chicago and London: University of Chicago Press.
Turner, Victor. 1969. *The Ritual Process: Structure and Anti-Structure*. Chicago, IL: Aldine Publishing Company.
Tutu, Archbishop Desmond. 1998. 'Foreword'. In *Exploring Forgiveness* (eds. Robert D. Enright and Joanna North). Madison, WI: University of Wisconsin Press, xiii–xiv.
Tylor, Edward. 1871. *Primitive Culture: Researches into the Development of Mythology, Philosophy, Religion, Art and Culture*. London: John Murray (two vols.).
USC Shoah Foundation Visual History Archive. Online at: https://sfi.usc.edu/vha. Consulted August 22, 2015.
Vayenas, Nasos. 1978. *Biography* (trans. Richard Burns). Cambridge: Lobby Press.
———. 1979. 'Eden' and 'Empty' (trans. Richard Burns). London: Menard Press, Mencard series.
———. 1989. *I Ptosi tou Iptamenou* [Flyer's Fall]. Athens: Stigmi.
———. 2000. *Synomilontas me ton Kavafi: Anthologia Ksenon Kavafoyenon Poiimaton* [Conversing with Cavafy: An Anthology of Foreign Cavafy-inspired Poems]. Thessaloniki: Kentro Ellinikis Glossas.
———. 2010 [1]. *The Perfect Order: Selected Poems 1974–2010* (eds. Richard Berengarten and Paschalis Nikolaou). London: Anvil Press Poetry.
———. 2010 [2]. *Sti Niso ton Makaron* [On the Isle of the Blest]. Athens: Kedros.
Villon, François. 2005. *Oeuvres Complètes*. Paris: Arléa.
Vygotsky, Lev Semyonovich. 2012 [1934]. *Thought and Language* (trans. Eugenia Hanfmann *et al.*) Cambridge, MA: MIT Press.

Wace, A. J. B. and Thompson, M. S. 1972 [1914]. *The Nomads of the Balkans: An Account of Life and Customs Among the Vlachs of Northern Pindus*. London: Methuen, and New York, NY: Biblo and Tannen.
Waldmann, Anne. 1978 [1975]. *Fast Speaking Woman*. San Francisco, CA: City Lights Books.
Weir, Ruth Hirsch. 1962. *Language in the Crib*. The Hague: Mouton.
Whitman, Walt. 1975. *The Complete Poems* (ed. Frances Murphy). Harmondsworth: Penguin Books.
Whitwell, Giselle. E. 'The Importance of Prenatal Sound and Music'. Online at: http://www.birthpsychology.com/lifebefore/sound1.html Consulted February 28, 2015.
Williams, William Carlos. 1963 [1946]. *Paterson*. New York, NY: New Directions.
———. 2004 [1925]. *In The American Grain*. New York, NY: New Directions.
Wittgenstein, Ludwig. 1972 [1953]. *Philosophical Investigations* (trans. G. E. M. Anscombe). Oxford: Basil Blackwell.
Wood, Frank. 1958. *The Ring of Forms*. Minneapolis, MN: University of Minnesota Press.
Wordsworth, William. 1969 [1933]. *The Prelude*, 1805 text (ed. Ernest de Selincourt). London: Oxford University Press.
———. 1956 [1921]. 'Preface to Lyrical Ballads'. In *Poetry and Prose* (ed. David Nichol Smith). Oxford: Clarendon Press, 150–176.
Xenophon. 1970. *Memoirs of Socrates & The Symposium* (trans. Hugh Tredennick). Harmondsworth: Penguin Books.
Yad Vashem Video Testimony Resource Center. Online at: http://www.yadvashem.org/yv/en/remembrance/multimedia.asp. Consulted August 22, 2015.
Yeats, W. B. 1961 [1933]. *The Collected Poems of W. B. Yeats*. London: Macmillan and Co Ltd.
Young, Kay. 2010. *Imagining Minds: The Neuro-Aesthetics of Austen, Eliot, and Hardy*. Columbus, OH: Ohio State University Press.
Zhuangzi. See variant spellings above, Chuang Tsu, Chuang Tzu.

Index

Acropolis, 26, 43n.15
ADC Theatre, 33, 44n.36
Adorno, Theodor, 140–141, 146n.88
ancestors, 88–90, 92–93
Ancestors, 151–152, 156–157
Anghelaki-Rooke, Katerina, 28, 36
Anglo-Jewish, 16, 83, 112; *see also* Jewish
anti-Semitism, 69, 105–106; *see also* Jewish
Antonio 'Makaronas', 18–19
archetype, archetypal, 73, 97, 98, 102, 113, 115, 135, 155
Arnaudov, Mikhail, 114, 142n.15
art for art's sake, 50
Arts Council of Great Britain, 31
Arvanitika, 17
Athens, 16, 17, 18, 19, 20, 22, 23, 24, 25, 26–30, 32, 36, 42n.2, 43n.15, 70, 93
aurality, 117
Auschwitz, 140–141
autobiography, autobiographical, 9, 11, 47–48, 50–51, 53, 102, 147–148
autre, see other

Babis-the-Vlach, 20, 27
Barba Stavrou's (Athens), 27
Barthes, Roland, 137, 139, 146n.82
Bauman, Zygmunt, 54, 58, 77nn.12 & 13, 78n.25
Beaton, Roderick, 35
Bellew, Ib, 64
Bellou, Sotiria, 27, 29–30, 34, 43n.27
Berengarten, Richard:
  and 'Agnostos Nomolos', 30; and 'Bruno, Jordan Charles', 11, 12, 50, 53
Poetry books:
Against Perfection, 12, 63, 82, 124, 144n.49; *Avebury*, 12, 25, 26, 36, 40, 43nn.22 & 23, 57, 92ff, 108nn.31 & 33, 109nn.36 & 38; *Balkan Trilogy, The*, 12, 110–113, 122, 129, 132, 140, 142n.1; *Black Light*, 9, 11, 32, 34, 36, 37, 38, 40, 41, 43n.13, 47, 57, 61, 63, 87, 100, 109n.50; translation into Greek, 87–88; *Blue Butterfly, The*, 9, 13, 32, 90, 34, 44n.38, 84–85, 88, 90, 98–99, 107n.6, 108n.22, 109n.52, 110–113, 118–120, 122, 125, 127, 130–131, 134, 140, 142nn.1 & 3, 143nn.26, 29 & 30, 144nn.33 & 50, 145n.60, 146nn.69 & 90; *Book With No Back Cover*, 12, 62, 109nn.43, 45 & 46; *Changing*, 43n.20, 108n.19; *Double Flute*, 25, 26, 36, 37, 44nn.44, 45 & 48, 78n.22; *For the Living*, 42n.3, 43nn.13, 23 & 24, 44nn.44 & 47, 45n.50, 78nn.23 & 24, 107n.8, 108nn.31 & 33, 109nn.36, 38, 40, 50 & 53, 142n.6, 144nn.42 & 43; *Imagems (1)*, 78n.18, 108n.28, 116, 126, 142n.18, 143n.24, 145n.54; *In a Time of Drought*, 43n.13, 79n.43, 113, 134–135, 138, 142nn.1, 9, 10 & 11, 146n.83; 146nn.76 & 83; *Learning to Talk*, 36, 44n.46, 45n.54, 56, 77nn.2, 5 & 6, 108n.30; *Manager, The*, 9, 11, 12, 37, 39, 46–76, 77nn.3, 5, 6, 10 & 11, 78nn.25, 26, 27, 32 & 33, 79nn.45, 47, 48, 51 & 57, 80nn.59, 62, 63, 64, 66, 68, 73, 74 & 75, 88, 98, 101, 108n.20, 109n.51, 119, 126; *Manual*, 85, 94, 107n.7, 109n.34; *Mavro Fos*, 45n.50; *Notness*, 77n.4, 128; *Return of Lazarus, The*, 33, 43n.24; *Under Balkan Light*, 42n.6, 77n.4, 108n.24, 124, 134, 142n.1, 144n.44
Poems and sequences:
'Against the Day', 57, 124; 'Angels', 57, 112; 'Arthur Rimbaud', 45n.57; 'Conversation between a blue butterfly and a murdered man...', 127,

130–131; 'Croft Woods', 57, 88, 95, 109n.40; 'Day Estate', 57; 'Don't send bread tomorrow', 109n.52, 119; 'Easter Rising 1967, The', 11, 15ff, 21, 23, 30–31, 32, 57; 'Euripides never slept here', 44n.33; 'Exile, The', 44n.33; 'Following', 96–97; 'For the New Year 1976', 38, 48, 108n.30; 'Guest, The', 36; 'Household Gods, The', 57; 'In his Ancestral Garden', 44n.48; 'In the room suddenly', 125, 144n.49; 'John Keats', 45n.57; 'Male figure, playing a double flute', 25–26, 36; 'May', 101, 102, 109n.53; 'Nine Codas', 62, 109nn.45 & 46; 'Noon', 36, 44n.46; 'Ode on the End of the Second Exile', 57; 'Ode on the End of the Third Exile', 37, 44n.47; 'Offence of Poetry, The', 57; 'Only the Common Miracle', 45n.50, 124; 'Orphead, The', 57; 'Orpheus Singing', 36, 44, 46, 78n.22; 'Salt', 38; 'Sappho', 39, 45n.57; 'Sketches With Voice-Overs', 62, 77n.4; 'Song, for Petro', 43n.13; 'Telling, The', 116–117, 125, 141; 'Tree', 12, 57, 85; 'Voice in the Garden, The', 88, 108n.24; 'Zeimbekiko', 27
Essays:
'A Little Further', 145n.54; 'Arijana's Thread', 10, 79n.43; 'Cambridge Poetry Festival: 35 years after, The', 44n.43; 'Grove of Trees and a Grove of Stones, A', 88; '"My" Anne Frank', 88–89; 'On Poetry and Sound: the Ontogenesis of Poetry', 'Pour toi', 45n.62, 108n.29, 142n.8, 145n.53, 117–118; 'Ten Drachmas for a Pound', 29; 'With Face to the Wall', 44n.33; 'With Peter Russell in Venice 1965–1966', 103
Translation:
'Volta' project, 88, 108n.21
see also Burns, Richard
Beckett, Samuel, 64, 71, 79n.42, 123, 134

Berliner, Emile, 153
Bernstein, Basil, 64
Bible, biblical, 37, 47, 83, 86; *Song of Songs, The*, 74
Bickerton, Derek, 155, 173n.22
biography, biographical, 35, 39, 40, 51, 70, 152
Bird, John, 162
Bithikotsis, Grigoris, 34
Blake, William, 47, 51, 68, 77n.8, 84, 85, 86, 107n.9, 114, 166; minute particulars, 52, 77n.8, 84, 86, 108n.20
Bohm, David, 71, 80n.65, 86, 96, 107n.12, 123, 144n.38; implicate order, 60, 71, 86, 96, 123, 144n.38
Böhme, Franz, 118
boundary 2, 62
Brassens, George, 111
Brecht, Bertolt, 140, 146n.89
Breton, André, 154
British Council, 24, 26, 29
British Institute (Athens, Thebes), 16
Britton, Jasper, 75
Brown, Norman O., 53, 77n.10
Bruno, Giordano, 11, 50, 53
Burns, Alexander (*aka* Berengarten, RB's father), 103
Burns, Gully (Alexander, RB's son), 33, 160
Burns, Lara Sophia (RB's first daughter), 31
Burns, Richard (RB), 63, 107n.1, 175, 178, 189, 190
Burns, Rosalind (RB's mother), 29–30, 32, 88, 103
Burns, Sarah (RB's first sister), 101
Burns, Seymour (RB's uncle), 103
butterfly, 12, 84, 110, 116, 117, 122, 124, 131, 140, 141; as messenger, 111ff, 132; and soul, 111ff, 131–132; as symbol of transformation, 132; *see also* Berengarten, *The Blue Butterfly*
Byron, George Gordon, Lord, 33, 40

California, 12, 20, 110, 160

call, calling, 111ff
Cambray, Joseph, 90
Cambridge, 9, 15, 16, 19, 20, 22, 24, 25, 32, 33, 35, 36, 41, 43n.14, 46, 55, 59, 76, 77n.14, 81, 89, 97, 102, 103, 104, 105, 106, 141, 147, 151–152, 162, 163, 172; reading English at Cambridge, 89; Cambridge School (of poetry), 137
Cambridge Poetry Festival, 31, 35–36, 44.n.43
Cambridgeshire College of Arts and Technology (CCAT), 32, 44n.29, 52
Carcanet, 43n.14, 61, 78n.31
Caretaker, The (Pinter), 71, 123
Cassirer, Ernst, 155, 173nn.12 & 19
Cavafy, Constantine P., 34, 40–41
Cavaliero, Glen, 55, 77n.14
Cavell, Stanley, 111, 142n.4
Celan, Paul, 13, 113, 114, 125, 126, 142n.8, 144n.51
chance, 107n.5, 110, 148; *see also* synchronicity
change, 50, 55, 56, 57, 65, 74, 88, 91, 107n.5, 110, 111, 132, 143n.20, 163, 164; changeability, 53
Charioteer (sculpture), 25
China, Chinese, 88, 98, 115, 132, 157, 160
Christian, Christianity, 85, 92, 134, 135
Chuang Tsu, Chuang Tzu, *see* Zhuangzi
class, 19, 48, 49, 59, 69, 198
cliché, 22, 49, 67, 123
Clodd, Alan, 29, 43n.25
code, codes, 64, 78n.44, 165, 173n.11
coherence, cohering, 10, 60, 71, 86, 97, 123, 173n.9
coincidentia oppositorum, 133
Coleridge, Samuel Taylor, 60, 78n.3, 133, 146n.73
collaboration, 37, 61–62, 81, 148ff, 161, 167
collage, 52, 119
comedy, comic, 65, 74
communication, 66, 85, 152, 162, 163, 164, 174n.35; communication modes, systems, technologies, 9, 152, 156, 157, 160
Companion to Richard Berengarten, The, 10, 12, 38, 81, 87, 93, 105; *see also* Jope
confession, confessional poetry, 102–103, 145n.59
connectedness, connectivity, connectors, 13, 36, 60, 86, 88, 90, 92, 97, 98, 102, 112, 114, 116, 121, 122ff, 127, 142nn.2 & 5, 143n.21, 154–155, 170, 173n.1; interconnectedness, 81, 84, 90
contextuality, 69, 116, 118–120, 122–123, 140
contradiction, 12, 23, 48, 49, 105, 116, 124, 130, 136, 141
conversation, 9, 12, 13, 26, 35, 37, 40, 72, 81, 104, 110, 113, 114, 120–121, 127, 130–131, 132, 134, 141, 148ff, 157, 161, 162, 165ff, 171
Cook, Peter, 161–162
coup, coup d'état (Greece), 15, 20, 23, 36, 42n.1
craft, crafting, craftwork, 10, 63, 116, 120, 131, 134
Croat, Croatia, Croatian, 56, 59, 87, 121
Cyclades, Cycladic, 25–26, 93, 95

Daniel Deronda (George Eliot), 89, 121, 135, 143n.36
Dante Alighieri, 68, 78n.21, 79nn.53 & 54, 125, 166; *Divina Commedia, La*, 57, 68, 77n.21, 79nn.53 & 54
Dao, Daoism, Daoist, 85, 86, 124, 127ff
Davis, Richard (Dick), 19
de Castro, Rosalía, 39
death, the dead, 21, 38, 50, 58, 60, 68, 79n.57, 88, 93, 103, 121, 123, 124, 126–127
Defourtmentalle, Anne, 99
Delos, 26, 95
Delphi, 25

democracy, democratisation, 32, 91, 159
Dempsey, Michael, 31
depersonalisation, 138
Derrick, Paul Scott, 7
Derrida, Jacques, 99, 137ff
development: of hearing in the foetus, 117–118, 168; of the interview, 149ff, 161ff; in *The Manager*, 52–55; of memory, 168; of recording technologies, 153ff; of a style, 64
dialogue, dialogues, 13, 47, 71, 121, 127, 131, 148, 150, 152, 158, 160, 165
Diary of Anne Frank, The, 88
Dillon, John Z., 6, 9–13, 147–172
dimotika (Greek music), 19, 42n.11
dimotiki (Greek language), 42n.2
disjunction, disjunctive, 12, 49, 55, 65, 68, 71
Dispa, Kathleen, 149
documentary, documentation, 101, 118–120, 132–133, 160–161; documentary as news, 158
Dolní Věstonice, Venus of, 93–94
double helix, 97–98
drama, dramatic, 47, 70–71, 75, 123, 137, 158, 161
dream, dreams, 52, 65, 67, 85, 100, 101, 102, 131, 155, 157
Duffett, Michael, 20, 23, 24, 43n.14, 61
Duffy, Carol Ann, 63
Durkheim, Émile, 155, 173n.17

Earl of Seacliff (publisher), 85
East London College, 31, 32, 63, 70, 106, 112, 163
Edgerton, David, 157
editing, 9, 58, 61ff, 152, 159, 165, 167, 169, 171
  co-editing, 37, 39, 43n.14, 81, 110, 147, 161–162, 167, 174n.44
ego, *see* 'I'
Eliade, Mircea, 155, 166, 173n.19, 174n.38
Eliot, George, 89, 121, 126, 144n.36

Eliot, T. S., 39, 67ff, 79nn.52 & 55, 80nn.58 & 60, 89, 99, 104–106, 119, 134, 143n.31, 144n.30, 146n.77, 148; *Murder in the Cathedral*, 101, 134; 'Tradition and the Individual Talent', 89; *Waste Land, The*, 66ff, 154
Elliott, David, 57, 64, 68
Elytis, Odysseus, 34
email, 9, 15, 46, 65, 73, 81, 135, 147, 162–163, 167
empathy, 121, 137, 160
Engle, Ed, 51, 75
Englishness, 83
ennui, 50
epiphany, 22, 113
eros, erotic, 70, 72, 73–74, 94, 138; *see also* sexuality
Erotokritos, *see* Kornaros
Erythrai (Kriekouki), 17, 21
'Establishment' (the British), 82
eternal return, myth of, 171
Europe, European, 82–83, 91–92, 131, 159, 171; European identity, 12, 83, 107n.1
Everyman, 49

fantasy, fantasies, 11, 15, 53, 65, 72, 74
fascism, fascist, 29, 54, 91, 105, 118, 124
Feinstein, Elaine, 63, 75
field, 9, 124, 133, 149, 154, 162, 171; morphic field, 121; semantic field, 66, 86
film, filmic, 26, 52, 62, 151–152, 155, 157, 174n.35
foetal hearing, 117–118, 168
'following', 12, 96, 116
Forché, Carolyn, 127, 145n.59
Fortune, John, 162
Fostieris, Antonis, 40
Foucault, Michel, 137, 139, 146n.82
found poems, 119–120
Frank, Anne, 88–89
Franz, Marie-Louise von, 72, 80n.68, 90, 98

195

Frazer, Sir James, 91, 114, 142n.14
Freeman, John, 157, 174n.25
Freud, Sigmund, 71, 155, 157, 160, 173nn.15 & 16, 174nn.25 & 26
Friar, Kimon, 28, 31, 33ff
frontistirio (Greece), 16, 19, 24
Frye, Northrop, 11, 51, 77n.7, 114, 115, 142n.19

Gate of Horn, The (Levy), 93
Gatsos, Nikos, 26, 34, 43n.22
Georgakas, Dan, 33
Gery, John, 105, 109n.56
Gilbreath, Alexandra, 75
Gilgamesh, The Epic of, 86, 127
Gimbutas, Marija, 94, 109n.35
Ginsberg, Alan, 47, 57, 72–73, 105
goddess, 93, 94–95; *see also* Dolní Věstonice; Willendorf
Goodman, Henry, 75
Goody, Jack, 151
Gordon, Giles, 63
Gordon, James, 34, 44n.39
Gotto, Aude, 63, 79n.40
Graham, W. S., 66, 79n.46
Greece, Greek, 11, 15–45, 46, 47, 57, 61, 82, 87, 107n.1, 108n.17, 111, 131, 153, 154; Easter in Greece, 21–22; Greek dance, 19, 42n.12; Greek language, 15; Greek music, 11, 19, 22, 27, 33ff, 42nn.10, 11, 12 & 13, 43nn.15 & 19, 107n.1, 108n.17, 131; Greek rhythm, 11; Greek sculpture, 98; military dictatorship (1967–74), 15ff, 32ff
Greek Report, 33
Grimm, Brothers, 90, 113, 142n.13
Grosvenor-Myer, Valerie and Michael, 31, 43n.28

Halkon, Ruth, 6, 9, 12, 81–109
hand, hands, 12, 84–85, 94, 97, 99, 172; hand and butterfly, 110, 111, 116, 140, 141
Hardwick, Graham, 24
Harris, Roy, 98, 109n.49, 155, 173n.23

Harrison, Sarah, 151–152
Harrisson, Tom, 159
hasapiko (Greek dance), 19, 42n.12
Heaney, Seamus, 99, 148
Hellenic Review, 33
Herbert, George, 98, 125, 135, 144n.46, 146n.79
heuristic experience, moment, process, 13, 54, 112, 116, 125, 133, 149, 169
hierarchy, 59, 83, 105
history, histories, historical, 11, 40, 53, 68, 70, 86, 89, 90, 91, 92, 93, 95, 108n.20, 119, 124, 127, 130, 132, 138, 160, 167
Hobsbaum, Eric, 91
Holocaust, 88, 91, 112, 160 –161
homoerotism, 40–41; *see also* sexuality
Hooker, Jeremy, 67, 73–74, 75, 79n.38; and Mieke Hooker, 63
Hopkins, Gerard Manley, 39, 84, 107n.5, 117; inscape, instress, 84, 107n.5
Hughes, Ted, 114, 116, 143nn.21 & 23, 147, 173n.1

I Ching, see *Yijing*
I, ego, 53, 101–102, 113, 120, 125, 129, 133–140; dropping the 'I', 136; ego of child, 137; ego-trip, 129; denial or elimination of 'I', 79n.43, 113, 120, 125, 134–138, 139–140; 'I' and depersonalisation, 138; 'I' and 'Thou', 138
identity, identities, 12, 49, 82–83, 84, 86, 88–89, 101, 122, 139, 140, 143n.25, 164
idiolect, 65
imagem, 56, 78n.18, 99, 108, 114, 116, 123, 126, 130, 140, 142n.28
imagination, 11, 53, 55, 123, 133
improvisation, 148, 168–169, 172
inspiration, 40, 56, 84, 86, 113, 115, 117, 120, 122, 139, 143n.20
interlocutor, 9, 10, 92, 126, 148, 165
intention, 47, 55, 65–66, 76, 114–115, 120, 135, 137, 139, 147; *see also* will

international, internationalism, 36, 82ff, 86, 107n.1, 108nn.20 & 21, 160
Internet, 151, 152, 158, 163
interruption, 9, 12, 58ff, 65, 71, 78n.26, 99–101, 120, 149, 162, 165, 19, 69
intersubjective, intersubjectivity, 48, 102–103, 159, 163, 164
intertextuality, 38
interview, 9–13, 147–174; etymology of, 150; history of, 13, 149ff, 159
irony, ironies, 16, 20–21, 33, 40, 42n.4, 47, 50, 59, 67, 69, 70, 84, 101, 119, 145n.54
Italy, Italian, 17, 18, 19, 31, 36, 56, 82, 88, 103–106, 107n.1, 108n.17, 163
iteration, iterative, *see* recursion
Ivanov, V. V., 114, 142n.17

Jakobson, Roman, 113, 142n.12, 155, 173nn.10, 14, 16 & 19
jargon, *see* language
jazz, 65, 103, 148, 149, 166, 169
Jelena (RB's stepdaughter), see Vojvodić
Jennings, Humphrey, 158
Jewish, Jews, 22, 29, 46, 70, 88, 89, 105, 106, 111, 126, 144n.36; Anglo-Jewish identity, 16, 83, 112; Judaism, 70
Jewish Quarterly, 46
Johnson, B. S., 55
Jones, Daniel, 154
Jope, Norman, 10, 87, 107n.14; *see also Companion to Richard Berengarten, The*
Journal of the Hellenic Diaspora, 33
journalism, journalist, 101, 150–151, 158, 159
Joyce, James, 52, 67, 71–72; *Ulysses*, 154; *Finnegans Wake*, 71, 154
Julius, Anthony, 69, 106
Jung, Carl Gustav, Jungian, 55, 71, 72, 80n.68, 90, 97, 98, 110ff, 115, 135, 140, 142nn.2, 5 & 7, 146nn.71 & 87, 155, 157, 160, 173n.18, 175
Junta (Greece), *see* Greece, military dictatorship

juxtaposition, 61, 65, 70–71, 119–120, 122, 124

Kabbalah, 23, 85
Kadmon, Adam, 85
kalambouri (Greece), 15
Kampanellis, Iakovos, 44n.37; *Mauthausen*, 34
Karadžić, Vuk, 90–91, 113
katharevousa (Greek language), 15
Keats, John, 40, 45nn.57 & 58, 78n.20, 148, 178n.2
Keeley, Edmund, 28, 35, 43n.22
Kerr, Jim, 24
King of Hearts, The (publisher), 63, 79n.40
King's College, Cambridge, 35, 46; chapel, 97
Kinsey Reports, 164
Knight, Gareth, 23
Kodzias, Alexandros, 35–36, 44n.41
Koestler, Arthur, 31
Kornaros, Vitsentzos, 34, 44n.40; *Erotokritos*, 34, 37, 44n.40, 47
Kragujevac, 12, 84, 101, 110
Kriekouki, *see* Erythrai

laika (Greek music), 19, 27, 42n.11
Laing, R. D., 72; and Esterton, A., 79n.67
Landers, Kim (RB's first wife), 16ff, 32ff, 57, 104, 105, 109n.55, 175
Language Poets, 137, 138
language, languages, 64–65, 66, 67–68, 86, 87, 123, 128–129, 138–139, 145n.64, 149, 154; banal language, 123; jargon, 42n.2, 47, 54, 66–67; language games: 155; language of officialdom, 119; language register, variety, 64–65, 67–68; limitations of language, 128–129; materiality of language, 138
Larkin, Philip, 82, 83, 99
Layios, Ilias, 38, 45n.51
Leavis F. R., 102, 109n.54

Leibniz, Gottfried Wilhelm, 154, 166, 173n.13
Leontis, Artemis, 42n.10
Lessing, Doris, 72–73. 80n.70
Lévinas, Emmanuel, 94, 109n.37, 126, 161, 174n.34
Lévi-Strauss, Claude, 91, 155, 173n.17
Levy, Rachel, 93
Liadis family (Thebes), 17ff
Lieberman, Philip, 118, 155, 173n.22
Limburg, Joanne, 6, 11, 12, 46–76
linear time, *see* time
linguist, linguistic, linguistics, 10, 11, 13, 20, 43n.16, 54, 61, 154–155, 156, 165, 173n.9
Loizou, Renos, 32, 44n.32
London, 16, 19, 25, 28ff, 35; London Bridge, 68
London Magazine, The, 31, 38
long poem, 36, 48, 55ff, 67, 87, 98ff, 112, 127, 131
Lord, A. B., 166, 174n.42
Lowry, Malcolm, 23, 52, 64, 79n.41; Margerie, 23
Lucie-Smith, Edward, 158, 174n.30
Lykiard, Alexis, 22, 24, 31, 32
lyric, lyrical, lyricism, 56–57, 67, 73, 74, 84, 85, 99, 118, 119, 121, 125, 127, 138, 152

MacDiarmid, Hugh, 87, 107n.13
Macfarlane, Alan, 151, 157, 158, 173nn.5 & 6, 174n.35
MacSweeney, Barry, 62, 78n.33
Madge, Charles, 159
mageiritsa (soup), 21–22
Main, Roderick, 90
Mamangakis, Nikos, 34, 44n.40
Mandelstam, Osip, 126, 145n.57, 165, 174n.37
mangas, 2, 20, 23, 43nn.15 & 19
Mansfield, Peter, 16, 20, 23–24, 27, 28, 31, 33–34, 43nn.13 & 14, 59, 61–62, 64, 78n.28, 113, 135, 169; Dimitra (née Proestopoulou, later King), Francesca and Angela, 33–34

Marble Threshing Floor, The (Sherrard), 28
Mass Observation, 159, 164, 174n.31
Mauthausen (Kampanellis, Theodorakis), 34, 44n.37
Mawangdui texts, 127, 170
McConville, Alan, 52
Mediterranean, 29, 37, 88, 108n.17
Meillet, Antoine, 154
mental breakdown, 71–72, 73
Mercouri, Melina, 32
Merrill, James, 28
metaphor, metaphorical, 10, 11, 66, 86, 96, 117, 123, 130, 135, 146n.68, 162
Michelangelo Buonarotti, 92
Miller, Arthur, 49, 73, 128; Willy Loman, 49
Miller, Henry, 72, 128, 157, 174n.27
Mišić, Jasna (RB's second wife), 63
Mitso-the-Hook, 19–20
modern, modernism, modernity, 6, 29, 34, 49, 50, 54, 67–68, 71, 74, 103, 106, 108n.20, 149, 150, 151, 154ff; *see also* postmodern
Monastiraki (Athens), 20, 23, 27, 28, 43n.15
Montenegro, 66; Writers' Association, 63
Moody, Neli, 93, 108n.15
Moore, David, 24
Moore, Dudley, 161–162
Moore, Henry, 158–159, 174n.30
Mosley, Nicholas, 55, 77n.15
Moses, Antoinette, 63, 79n.39
mother (RB's), *see* Burns, Rosalind
Murder in the Cathedral (Eliot), 101, 134
music, musicality, 11, 19, 22, 27, 29, 33ff, 42nn.10, 11 & 12, 43nn.15 & 19, 71, 85, 93, 97, 98, 101, 103, 117, 120ff, 127, 134ff, 166, 168; music and Caliban, 136; music and empathy, 121; *see also dimotika*, Greek music, jazz, *laika*, *rebetika*
Musgrave, Rosie, 97, 109n.44
Mykonos, 23

myth, mythology, 13, 16, 36, 57, 78n.18, 98, 113–114, 142n.18, 154, 155, 171; mythical time, 166–167
narrative, 37, 44n.40, 47, 52, 54ff, 108n.20, 117, 122; narrator, 11, 49, 17
nationalism, nationality, 10, 83, 86, 87, 91–92
Nazi, Nazis, 12, 87, 88, 91, 111, 112
Nea Estia, 37
Neumann, Erich, 94, 209n.35
Niarchos, Thanasis, 40
Nike of Samothrace, 92, 93–94
Nikolaou, Paschalis, 6–7, 9–13, 15–41, 45n.61
Nin, Anaïs, 157–158, 174n.27
non sequitur, 59, 60, 71, 120ff, 165
notness (non-being), 127–129; *see also* Berengarten, *Notness*
Novi Sad, 17
number, 98, 109n.49, 116; numerology, 12

O'Driscoll, Dennis, 148
Olson, Charles, 94, 127
Oppen, George, 63, 104, 106
Orfeu negro (Marcel Camus), 56
Orlando, Vito, 28
'other', otherness, 61, 72, 99, 101–102, 111, 116, 120–122, 125–127, 129, 136, 166; *see also* Rimbaud
Oxford English Dictionary, 150, 153, 156

Padua, 104
panygiri (Greece), 19
Papastavrou, Stavros, 33
parataxis, 119
Paris Review interviews, 147–148
Parker, Sir Peter, 55
Parkinson, Michael, 158
Paros, 23–24
Paz, Octavio, 40, 54, 74, 77n.13, 90, 94, 108nn.20, 26 & 27, 130, 145nn. 66, 67 & 68; *Double Flame, The*, 74; *Labyrinth of Solitude, The*, 90

performance, performative, 13, 65, 75, 134, 147, 150, 156, 158, 160, 161, 164ff
Persephone myth, 114
persona, personae, 11, 47–48, 49, 53, 61, 72, 83, 138
Pesmazoglou, Stefanos, 32
Petropoulos, Ilias, 34
Phillips, Laurence, 169
Pickstock, Catherine, 122, 139, 143n.25, 144n.37, 146nn.84 & 85
Pinter, Harold, 71, 123
Piraeus, 23, 24, 25
Plaka (Athens), 26–27, 43n.15
Plato, Platonic, 96, 97, 150
Plotnikova, Ana, 114, 142n.16
poetic, 124, 125; non-poetic, 127; poetic canons, 10; poetic communication, 89, 92, 129, 143nn.20 & 21, 173n.1; poetic composition, 115; poetic discourse, 139; poetic form, 11, 12; poetic 'Establishment', 83; poetic experience, 57; poetic heritage, 26; poetic intention, 147; poetic language, 125, 139; poetic modes, models, 71, 134; poetic space, 11; poetic temperament, 39; poetic voices, 101;
poetics, 12, 29, 41, 97, 108n.21, 116, 118, 132, 137, 142n.18, 174n.44
Poetry South East, 62
polysemy, 78n.18, 123, 133, 142n.19, 171
postmodern, postmodernism, postmodernity, 49, 54, 62, 72, 78n.25, 88
Pound, Ezra, 28–29, 71, 80n.64, 86, 94, 103–106, 107n.10, 123–124, 144n.40, 154
Price, Huw, 90
Pringle, Roger, 75
Printzos, Dimitrios, 20
pronouns, 48, 56, 77n.4, 135, 138
prosody, 117, 118; breath pause, 119; caesura, 37, 60; *dekapendasyllavos*, 37, 47; fourteener, 37, 47, 131; iambic pentameter, 117, 131; lineation, 119–

120; long-line forms, 37, 47, 131; *vers libre*, 47; verse-paragraph, 47; *verset*, 37; *see also* rhythm
Prynne, J. H., 137
psychology, 54, 66, 70–71, 90–91, 115, 155

quantum physics, 9, 138

radio, 15, 20, 34, 65, 151, 158, 161, 162
Radnóti, Miklós, 126–127, 145n.58
rain maiden, 113–114
Raine, Kathleen, 28
Rakosi, Carl, 106
Ramp, Philip and Sarah, 30
rebetika (Greek music), 23, 27, 34, 42n.12, 43nn.15 & 19
record, recording, 148–153, 156ff, 162, 166–172; *see also* sound recording, video recording
recursion, recursive, 9, 13, 39, 121, 149, 153, 156, 162, 170, 171
Rein, Melanie (RB's wife), 75, 80n.76, 175
religion, religious, 22, 69, 83, 85–88, 87, 91
repetition, repeating, 61, 121–123, 130, 143n.25, 146n.68, 153, 156, 157, 166, 168, 170, 171
resonance, resonate, 10, 40, 103, 112, 116, 117, 123, 130, 134, 135, 136 *see also* 'morphic resonance'
responsibility, 12, 61, 111, 115–116, 120, 139
return, 10, 59, 61, 121, 122, 123, 153, 165, 169, 171, 172
Reznikoff, Charles, 106
rhythm, rhythms, 11, 47, 56, 62, 64, 65, 71, 98, 117, 121–122, 130ff, 135, 146n.68
Rilke, Rainer Maria, 36, 125–126, 144n.52
Rimbaud, Arthur, 39, 45, 120, 144n.34; *autre*, 120, 136

Ritsos, Yannis, 32, 34
Roethke, Theodore, 53, 77n.9
Romania, 17, 43n.16
Rondanini Pietà, 95
Ross, Alan, 31
Rousseas, Dimitrios and Roula, 24
Rowan-Robinson, Michael, 36
Rudge, Olga, 104–105
Rudolf, Anthony, 37, 53, 61, 63, 64, 66, 68, 108n.27, 173n.3, 175
Russell, Peter, 28–29, 103–105
Ruth, Dr., 157
Rys, Sean, 7, 9, 13, 110–146

Sahtouris, Miltos, 33–34, 175
Samarakis, Antonis, 30–31, 61; *The Flaw*, 30, 61
satire, satirical, 23, 47, 64, 119–120
Saussure, Ferdinand de, 128, 154; *signifiant, signifié*, 128
Schelling, Friedrich, 133
sculptor, sculpture, 25, 92–97, 158, 170; *see also* Charioteer, Cycladic, Dolní Věstonice, Moore, Michelangelo, Nike, Rondanini, Willendorf
Seferis, George, 9, 28, 33ff, 40, 41, 44n.42, 46, 47, 74, 75, 80nn.72 & 74, 87, 89, 104, 108n.25; *Collected Poems*, 34–35; conference on (Cambridge), 36
Sekulić, Vladimir, 63
semantic, semantics, 117, 118, 154; semantic field, 66, 86
Serb, Serbia, Serbian, 12, 17, 53, 56, 59, 63, 66, 82, 87–88, 91, 111, 113, 119, 120, 121, 126
Serbo-Croat, 63, 67, 87
sex, sexuality, 70, 72, 73–74, 83
Shakespeare, William, 75, 90, 126, 145n.55; Caliban, 136; Desdemona, 102; Hamlet, 83; *Hamlet*, 98; Othello, 102; Prospero, 131; *Tempest, The*, 131, 146nn.70 & 81
Shekhinah, 75
Sheldrake, Rupert, 121, 144n.35
Shelley, Percy Bysshe, 114, 115, 120, 136, 143nn.20 & 22

Sherrard, Philip, 28, 35, 43n.22
Shoah Foundation, 160–161, 174n.33
Shock of the Old, The (Edgerton), 157
Sicherheit, 122
Sillitoe, Alan, 69, 79nn.56 & 57
Singer of Tales, The (Lord), 166
Sinopoulos, Takis, 36
Skype, 65, 151, 162, 163
sonnet, sonnets: 36, 39, 56, 78n.20, 93–95, 109n.5, 126, 128, 145n.55, 174n.56
soul, souls, 12, 50, 111, 131–132; *see also* butterfly
sound, sounds, 56, 96, 117–118, 121, 136, 144n.36; sound poetry, 166; sound recording and technologies, 149–153, 157ff, 167, 172, 174n.35; *see also* speech-sounds
South Bend, Indiana, 51, 147, 163
Southern Review, The, 33
space, 54, 99, 122, 127, 163ff, 169ff; lyric space, 118; poetic space, 18; space-time, 23, 71, 126, 145n.54; *see also* time
Spanos, William G, 62
speech, 65, 71, 118, 123, 145n.66, 152; child-speech, 118; speech-acts, 71, 123; speech and silence, 145n.66; speech and writing, 42n.2; speech-rhythms, 47, 71, speech-sounds, 65, 118, 171
Spencer-Brown, G., 98, 109n.47
Stangos, Nikos, 30, 32, 36
Stevens, Wallace, 78n.29, 96, 109n.42, 117
Stone, Bernard, 23
Stratford-upon-Avon, 33; Poetry Festival, 75
style, styles, 23, 64, 79n.42, 134–135, 158
Surrealist Manifesto, 154
symbol, symbolic, symbolism, 13, 70, 85, 95, 122–123, 132, 155
synaesthesia, synaesthetic, 117, 133
synchronicity, 13, 59, 90, 98, 110ff, 140, 142nn.2 & 5, 148
Synge, J.M., 87, 125

taiji, 85
Teacher, The, 31
telephone, 20, 29, 39, 66, 68, 151, 153, 162; mobile phone, 65, 66, 151; smartphone, 65, 163
Taylor, Brian (RB's cousin), 29
television, TV, 20, 65, 151, 155, 158, 160, 162
Tennyson, Alfred Lord, 99
Thebes, 16ff
Theodorakis, Mikis, 27, 34, 44n.37
Theodoros (Hotel *Ideal*, Athens), 26
thisness, 122, 129, 167ff
Thomas, Dylan, 55, 127, 128, 129
Thomas, Elizabeth, 31
Thompson, Brad, 57, 62, 64
Tibetan Book of the Dead, The, 132
time, 60, 97, 121, 122, 123, 127, 129, 130, 139, 164ff; control over time, 54; effects of time, 70; flattened time, 58, 60, 62, 78n.25, 132, 163; historic time, 167; linear (diachronic, sequential) time, 59, 89, 124, 130, 132, 169ff; moments out of time, 57, 119, 121; mythical time, 166–167; physics of time, 98; suspending time, 123; tearing time, 59; time's arrow and time reversal, 89–90, 168, 172; time-gaps, 162–163; timescales, 60; transcending time, 121, 144n.36; *see also* space
Times Educational Supplement, The, 31
Tomlinson, Charles, 74
Toporov, V. I., 114, 142n.17
translating, translation, 6–7, 11, 13, 26, 28, 30, 31ff, 37ff, 43n.15, 45nn.57 & 61, 46, 53, 61, 63, 68, 72, 74, 87, 101, 120, 128, 134, 139, 144, 149, 174nn.36 & 37
transpersonal, 113, 136, 137, 138
Tribune, 31, 33
Trist, Alan, 24, 32

Trist, Christie, 18
Tsien, Tsuen-Hsuin, 157
Tsitsanis, Vassilis, 34
Tsoumali's (Athens), 23–24, 27, 28, 29
Turner, Victor, 155, 173n.17
Tutu, Desmond, 92

Universal Declaration of Human Rights, The, 91
universalism, universality, 12, 40, 41, 83, 84, 86, 88, 91–92, 93–94, 108nn.20 & 21, 139, 163, 171; universal grammar, 154
University of California, Santa Barbara, 7, 9, 12, 110, 162

Valeri, Diego, 103–104
Valtinos, Themistocles, 18
Vamvakaris, Markos, 34
Vayenas, Nasos, 7, 11, 35, 36, 37ff, 45nn.49, 50, 52, 53, 54, 56, 57, 59, 60 & 61, 46–47, 61, 139, 146n.86, 174n.36, 175; *Biography*, 11, 38–39, 46–47; *Conversing with Cavafy*, 40; *Flyer's Fall*, 38; 'Identity and Poetic Language', 139; *Perfect Order, The*, 37, 39
Venice, 29, 33, 85
vers libre, 47
video, video-recording, 52, 65, 149ff, 156, 157–158, 161–162, 167, 168
Vlach, *Vlachika*, Vlachs' Wedding, 20, 21, 27, 43n.15
Vlachos, Helen, 33
voice, voices: authorial voice, 61; vocal chords, 118; elimination of personal voice, 79n.43, 113, 120, 134ff; poem's voices, 64–65, 67, 75, 83, 101–102, 116 –117, 120, 124, 130, 139; poet's voice, 11, 12, 139; voices of the dead, 88–89, 117, 126
Vojvodić, Jelena, 82
von Frantz, Marie, 72, 90, 98
Vygotsky, Lev, 155, 173nn.11 & 20, 174n.37

Waiting for Godot (Beckett), 71, 123
Waldman, Anne, 72, 80n.69
war, wars, 66, 70, 87, 157; First World War, 154, 160; Second World War, 18, 19, 33, 91, 119, 126; Six Day War, 23; war museum, 84
Warner, Rex, 35
Warsaw Ghetto, 112
Waste Land, The (Eliot), 66ff, 154
Whitman, Walt, 47, 84, 86, 117, 125
Wide Sargasso Sea (Rhys), 72
will, 48–49; 85, 109n.49, 114–115, 120, 136–137, 139–140, 141n.20
Willendorf Venus, 92–93
Williams, Kenneth, 65, 158
Williams, Raymond, 33
Williams, William Carlos, 86–87, 97, 125, 127; *In the American Grain*, 87
Wilson, Stephen, 108n.18, 143n.21
Wittgenstein, Ludwig, 145n.59, 155, 173n.23
Woelfel, Craig, 95, 109n.41
Wordsworth, William, 86, 107n.11, 123, 125, 133, 144nn.39 & 48, 146n.75
Written on Bamboo and Silk, 157

Xarhakos, Stavros, 27
Xylouris, Nikos, 34

Yad Vashem, 160–161, 174n.32
Yeats, William Butler, 6, 87, 98, 109n.48
Yijing, 43n.20, 84, 88, 98, 124, 127
Young, Kay, 110, 121, 135, 144n.36, 146n.80
YouTube, 52, 152, 157
Yugoslav, Yugoslavia, 63, 68, 82, 87–88, 107n.1, 108n.17, 110–111, 166

Zampetas, Yorgos, 34
zeibekiko (Greek dance), 19, 42n.12
Zhuangzi, 86, 128ff; Chuang Tzu, 145n.63, 146n.69
Zukofsky, Louis, 106

www.ingramcontent.com/pod-product-compliance
Lightning Source LLC
Chambersburg PA
CBHW022009160426
43197CB00007B/341